BOW VALLEY ROCK

*A Guide to Rock Climbs
East of Banff*

Chris Perry, John Martin
& Sean Dougherty

ROCKY MOUNTAIN BOOKS - CALGARY

ACKNOWLEDGMENTS

The preparation of this guidebook has been very much a group effort with many members of the Calgary Mountain Club and the Banff and Canmore climbing communities making important contributions. The Authors would particularly like to thank Jon Jones for his assistance with the Heart Creek section. Other contributors worthy of special mention are Peter Charkiw, Steve DeMaio, Andy Genereux, Urs Kallen, Gordon Smith, Steve Stahl and Colin Zacharias. Special thanks also go to publishers Tony and Gillean Daffern who provided continuing encouragement. The photographs of Yamnuska on pages 157 and 173 and of Ripple Wall are courtesy of Urs Kallen.

Front cover: Mark DeLeeuw on Mighty Mite (5.12a) in Grotto Canyon, photo Tom Fayle
Back cover: Pitch 3 of Astro Yam - Brian Wallace and Jeff Powter, photo Karl Nagy

Copyright © 1988 Chris Perry & John Martin
All rights reserved. No part of this book may be reproduced in any form without permission in writing from the publisher, except by a reviewer who may quote brief passages in a review.

Published by Rocky Mountain Books
106 Wimbledon Crescent,
Calgary, Alberta T3C 3J1
Printed and bound in Canada by
Imprimerie Gagné Ltée

ISBN 0-9690038-6-2

TABLE OF CONTENTS

Introduction 1
Heart Creek 7
McConnell Ridge 34
McGillivray Slabs 35
Pigeon Mountain 40
Wind Valley 41
The Three Sisters Area 46
Chinaman's Peak 49
Mount Rundle 57
Grotto Mountain 75
Grotto Canyon 81
Steve Canyon 113
Exshaw Slab 115
Goat Mountain 117
Yamnuska 155
CMC Valley 187
Mount Doom 185
Index 218

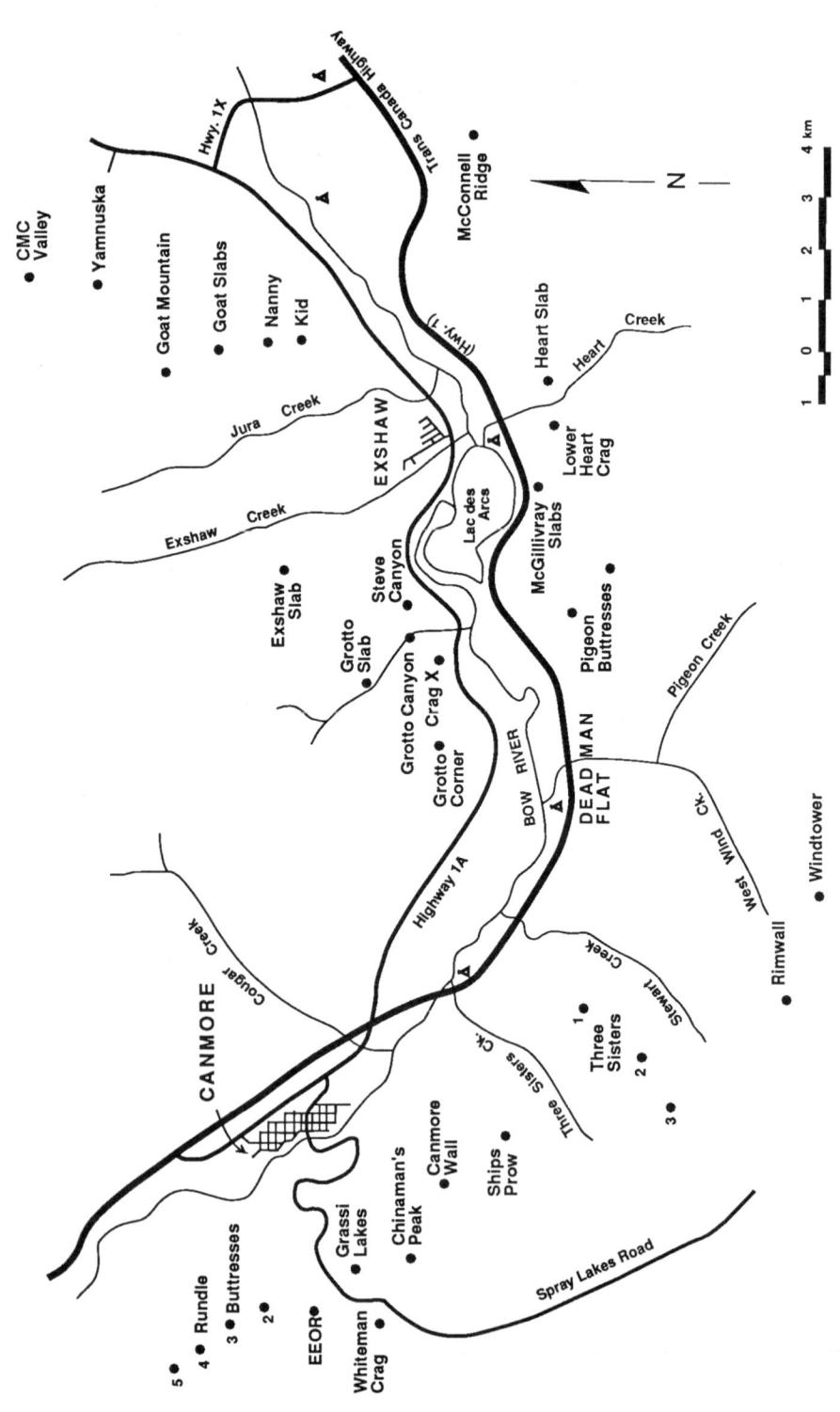

INTRODUCTION

This guidebook covers rock climbing areas in the Bow River valley from Yamnuska in the east to the Banff Park boundary in the west, enlarging upon and updating earlier guidebooks to the Canmore area (G. Spohr, 1976) and to Yamnuska (U. Kallen, 1977). The locations of the main climbing areas are shown opposite, Heart and Grotto Canyons are depicted on pages 6 & 80 respectively and the Goat and Yamnuska areas and CMC Valley are shown in more detail on page 116. Topographic mapping of the entire area is provided at a scale of 1:50,000 by National Topographic System sheet 82-O/3 (Canmore).

Access to the climbs is generally from Highway 1 (the Trans-Canada Highway) or Highway 1A. The Smith-Dorrien—Spray Trail (Spray Lakes Road), which heads south from Canmore, provides access to climbs on EEOR, Chinaman's Peak, and the Windtower area. Gas and food are available at Exshaw, Canmore, and Dead Man Flat (near Pigeon Mountain). Provincial campgrounds are located at Kananaskis River, Bow Valley Park, Lac des Arcs, Dead Man Flat, and Bow River Crossing, but most climbers camp in the vicinity of the Yamnuska parking lot.

CLIMATE

Generally, the weather in the Bow Corridor is good compared to other areas of the Canadian Rockies, but not as good as in most climbing areas in the western United States. The climbing season normally extends from April through October, although in bad years, April, October and even September may be write-offs. In good years February and March offer climbable conditions on south and west-facing crags. It is unusual to find climbable days in November, December, or January. Wind is often a major factor in the weather equation, particularly during spring and fall.

THE CLIMBING

All of the routes in the Bow Valley are on limestone, but there is nevertheless a great diversity in the climbing. Routes vary from 10-m boulder problems to serious 500-m walls, from low angle friction slabs to overhanging walls, and from straightforward beginner's routes to strenuous, highly technical test-pieces.

Nearly all the climbs lie on two great cliff-forming rock formations: the Eldon (Yamnuska, CMC Valley, Goat Mountain) and the Palliser (Grotto, Rundle, Chinaman's, Three Sisters, Heart). A few climbs have also been developed on Livingstone Formation exposures (Upper Heart Creek, Pigeon). There is little to choose among the three - at its best each offers superb climbing on impeccable rock while at its worst each is terrible.

Most of the existing routes, particularly the shorter, harder ones, exploit areas of sound rock. Ledges are nearly always scree-covered and it is, therefore, advisable to wear a helmet on multi-pitch routes and to keep close track of parties above or below you. In fact, climbing behind another party is not recommended. Most of the newer, shorter routes have been extensively cleaned and are commonly climbed without helmets.

The local rock tends to be very compact with few or no cracks as well as brittle. These features should always be kept in mind when attempting new routes, both in terms of equipment taken and the length of runouts contemplated. The brittleness is also a factor to be considered when soloing.

EQUIPMENT

Nearly all of the short, new routes in the Bow Valley can be climbed with a standard rack of nuts and Friends; however, it is strongly recommended that a hammer and a small selection of pitons, particularly blades and small angles, be carried on all other routes. Indeed, a hammer is absolutely essential on most of these routes as even well-known climbs usually lack fixed rappel stations and often cannot be adequately protected without pitons. Fixed pitons may loosen quickly in the local climate and should be tested. Pitons in vertical and especially downsloping cracks are particularly suspect.

Bolts are in place on many of the routes, especially the shorter ones. Virtually all the bolts are 5/16" self-drill concrete anchors which can be laded to about 2000 kg. None of these anchors have been known to fail. Various other types of bolts may be found on some older routes, mainly on Yamnusks. These anchors are suspect and should be treated with caution. A few bolts, particularly at Heart Slab and Grotto Slab, have aluminum hangers with small (1/2") holes that will not accept certain carabiners; so it's a good idea to carry a few carabiners that will fit the the smaller size hole when climbing in these areas.

STYLE

Locals consider that how you climb in the Bow Valley is pretty much your own affair, provided that you follow a couple of basic rules: no addition or subtraction of fixed protection on established routes, and no manufacturing of climbs by creating or altering holds. Exceptions: bad fixed pitons should be removed and replaced if possible, and placement of good bolts at belay stations is encouraged, particularly on popular routes.

All the long routes in the area have been established from the ground up, while most of the harder short climbs have been established from the top and are primarily bolt protected.

RATINGS

The climbs in the Bow Valley are graded using the standard Yosemite Decimal System. For the most part the gradings are consistent with those in other areas. However, some of the older climbs in the 5.6 - 5.8 range may seem undergraded, particularly if you are new to limestone climbing.
A star system is used to indicate route quality. The best half, approximately, of the climbs have been given either one, two or three stars, with three stars being reserved only for the best routes. Lack of a star does not imply that a route is of low quality, and in fact many of the routes which lack stars are well worth climbing.
The symbol "†" in front of a route name indicates that the route has not been repeated, or the route information has not been checked. Grades and quality ratings assigned to these climbs are tentative.

HISTORY

The first known rock climb in the guidebook area was guide Lawrence Grassi's 1925 first ascent of the First Sister by what is now the normal route. Perhaps more famous as a master trail builder, Grassi was also an excellent climber who pioneered a number of routes in the Rockies, the best known of which is the normal route on Eisenhower Tower northwest of Banff. Grassi also made the first ascents of Mts Inglismaldie and Peechee.
No further routes were pioneered until 1952, when two Austrian guides, Hans Gmoser and Leo Grillmair climbed Grillmair Chimney route on Yamnuska with Isabel Spreat. Later the same year, Gmoser returned with another Austrian, Franz Dopf, to climb Calgary Route. Gmoser and Grillmair were fascinated by the line of corners leading directly to the summit of Yamnuska and in 1957, after several attempts, completed Direttissima with Heinz Kahl. Later the same year, Brian Greenwood and Ron Thompson climbed Belfry, also on Yamnuska. They used only natural runners! While these routes (mild 5.8) may seem moderate by today's standards, they were major achievements given the equipment availble at the time.
A significant event for Bow Valley rockclimbing occurred in 1962 with the formation of the Calgary Mountain Club (CMC). The CMC in those days consisted of a few keen skiers, mountaineers and rockclimbers who were not satisfied with what the Alpine Club of Canada had to offer. From that time on, CMC members have been responsible for virtually all the new routes in the guidebook area. Foremost among them during the 60's were Heinz Kahl, the Britons Brian Greenwood and Dick Lofthouse and Canadians Lloyd MacKay and Don Vockeroth. Yamnuska continued to be the main focus of activity, although new routes were established on Chinaman's Peak and Goat Mountain as early as 1961. The early 60's were years of consolidation; standards did not rise although some new routes were established, notably Red Shirt and Chockstone Corner.

The first definite advance in standards since the milestone climbs of 1957 occurred in 1964, with the establishment of Missionary's Crack and Forbidden Corner (or Verboten Corner as it was known then). Later in the decade came many other Yamnuska classics: The Bowl, Pangolin, Bottleneck, Corkscrew, Mum's Tears and finally Balrog. However, not all of these were established as free routes.

Major changes occurred during the 1970's. Numerous new climbs, evenly divided between Brits and young Canadians, provided the impetus for exploration throughout the Bow Valley. Major walls such as Goat Mountain, Windtower Northeast Face, Rimwall and Chinaman's North Face were climbed, but at the same time there was a move toward shorter "cragging" routes, mainly in the CMC Valley. There was even a brief flirtation with "big-wall" climbing engineered by the now-legendary Billy Davidson. CMC Wall, The Yellow Edge and Iron Suspender are the legacies of this short-lived experiment. The main advances in free climbing standards occurred in CMC Valley, with such climbs as Dirty Dago, False Modesty, Hurricane Holocaust, Isengard and Groundfall Wall culminating in 1977 with Bruce Keller and John Lauchlan's The Maker, the hardest free route of the decade and the quintessential expression of 70's climbing style - bold and runout. Despite its boldness, however, The Maker introduced the use of bolt runners, a major ethical step at the time but one quickly accepted as essential for the development of the best climbing that local limestone had to offer - on the steep and open faces.

With the 80's came more changes. Dave Morgan showed the way ahead in 1981 by establishing some short but very hard climbs in Grotto Canyon, including the area's first 5.11, Stormy Weather. It was becoming clear, however, that few hard climbs would be possible using traditional methods and the first rappel-bolted route appeared the next year. In 1984 Morgan advanced the standard again with Across the River and Into the Trees (5.11b), and in 1985, among a flood of rappel-bolted climbs, Sean Dougherty bumped the state-of-the-art to 5.11c with the amazing Tower of Pisa. Dougherty continued to lead the way in 1986 with The Importance of Being Ernest (5.12a), the first limestone 5.12 in the Rockies. In 1987 yet another technical advance occurred with Bruce Howatt's Tropicana (5.12c)

While these developments were occurring in Grotto Canyon, short routes of up to 5.11b were blossoming on other crags throughout the Bow Valley and progress was also being made on the bigger cliffs. Interest in freeing the long classics on Yamnuska and other cliffs was strong, and in 1984 it resulted in the area's first long 5.11a as B.J. Wallace and Bill Stark eliminated the last aid from CMC Wall. Strong efforts to free Yellow Edge were also made, but the prize eventually fell to visiting climbers Peter Croft and Colin Zacharias at 5.11b in 1986. 1986 also marked the establishment of the first long, hard free routes from the ground up - Astro Yam and Above and Beyond (both 5.11c), by Jeff Marshall, Brian Gross and Steve DeMaio. Bold and runout, these routes have yet to see attempted repeat ascents.

RESCUE AND REGISTRATION

Rescue in the guidebook area is the responsibility of the R.C.M.P. and emergency calls should be directed to the Canmore office (678-5516). Alternatively, the Kananaskis Country emergency centre may be contacted at 591-7767 on a 24 hour bases.

Although there is no requirement to register for climbs, Bow Valley Provincial Park (on Highway 1X near the Trans-Canada Highway) offers a voluntary registration service. As well, there is a registration book at the quarry gate below Yamnuska but it is not checked on a regular basis. When signing in here include destination and a contact telephone number.

HOW TO USE THIS GUIDE

The climbing areas are described in a clockwise sequence starting at Heart Creek that runs from east to west along the south side of the Bow Valley and then from west to east along the north side finishing at CMC Valley. Climbs on each cliff are described in a left-to-right sequence, and all directions given assume that the climber is facing the rock. Metric units are used throughout the guide.

1 m	=	3.28'	5'	=	1.5 m
5 m	=	16'	10'	=	3 m
10 m	=	33'	25'	=	8 m
20 m	=	66'	50'	=	15 m
30 m	=	98'	75'	=	23 m
40 m	=	131'	100'	=	30 m
50 m	=	164'	150'	=	46 m

NEW ROUTE INFORMATION

New route information, corrections and additions should be sent to the authors care of Rocky Mountain Books, 106 Wimbledon Cresc. S.W., Calgary, Alberta T3C 3J1 for inclusion in future editions of the guidebook.

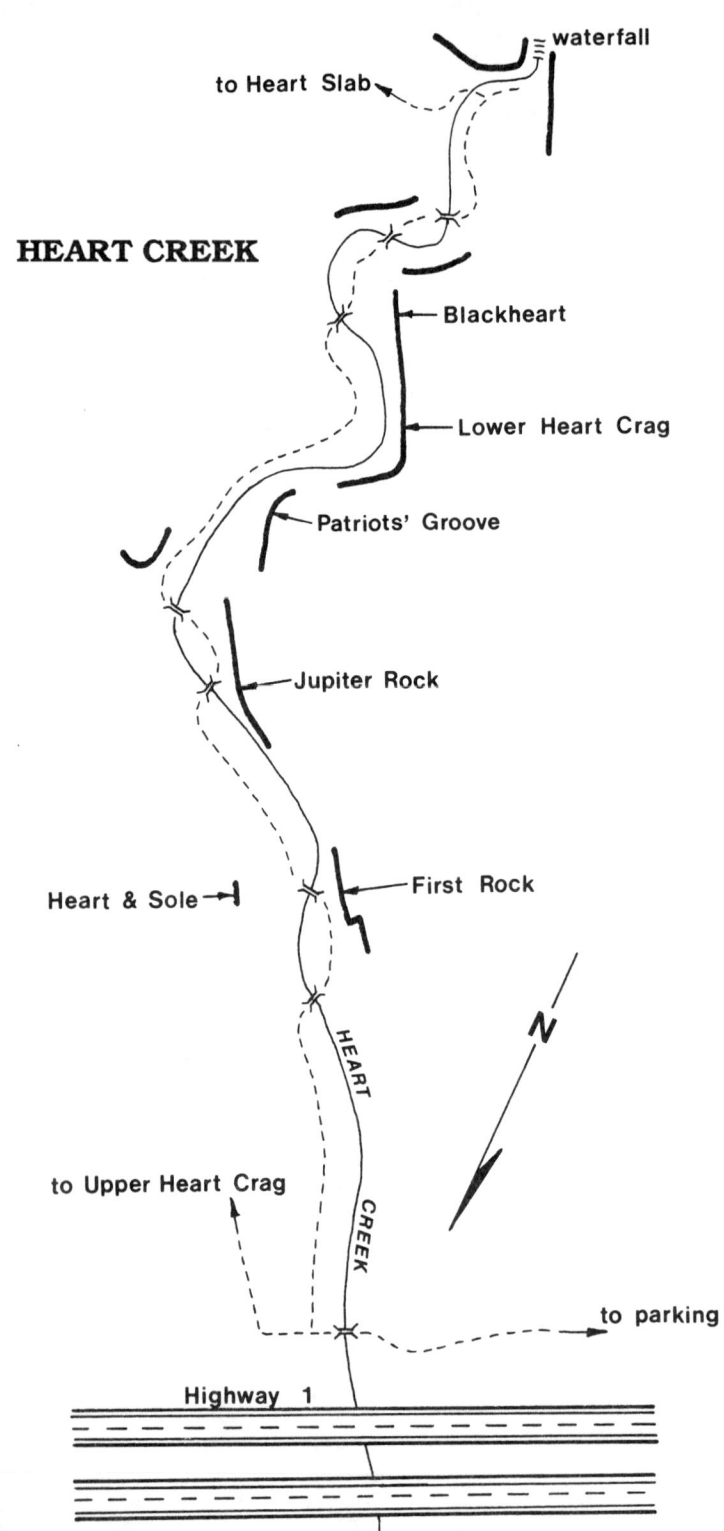

HEART CREEK

Heart Creek crosses the Trans-Canada Highway just east of the Lac des Arcs interchange and drains a narrow valley between Heart Mountain and Mount McGillivray. The valley has long been popular with hikers and recently several small climbing areas have been developed. Ease of access, pleasant surroundings, and the shortness of the climbs makes this area ideal for afternoon or evening climbing.
Approach: It is no longer possible to park where the creek crosses the Trans-Canada Highway. A new trail starts at a parking are located in the southwest quadrant of the Lac des Arcs interchange. The trail parallels the highway for about 700 m and then continues up the creek.

FIRST ROCK

First Rock is a small buttress located on the west side of the creek and is the first obvious climbing rock one sees when walking up the valley.

POTENTILLA PILLAR   45 m, 5.8
J.Martin, C.Perry, A.C.Gurholt and L.Howard, June 1984

The climb follows an indistinct rib near the left end of the rock. Start on a grassy ledge at the left side of the rock.
From the end of the ledge, climb up trending right on easy rock. Move left to a faint rib and climb up to a round pocket with a bolt runner. Step up left and then go back right into a shallow groove. Climb this to a shrub (the potentilla),then move up left to a dead tree. Continue up the edge of the buttress to the top.
Descend to the left (south).

HEARTLINE   45 m, 5.8
J.Martin and L.Howard, May 1986

Starting near the left end of the rock, climb up and right to a short left-leaning corner and continue up this to a ledge. Climb easy rock to a bolt at a small roof. Step right, pull over the roof, and then continue to the top, staying left of a chossy groove.

CHOC-A-BLOC   50 m, 5.4 - 5.6
First ascent unknown

The route follows the prominent slanting groove line in the left central portion of the face. Start as for Potentilla Pillar or Heartline.
Move right and climb up to the base of the groove. Surmount a short steep section or detour it to the right and continue easily to the top.

LESS THAN ZERO   20 m, 5.8
J.Martin, L.Howard and S.Stahl, June 1987

This short climb follows a line slightly left of Back to Zero using all natural protection.

FIRST ROCK - LEFT

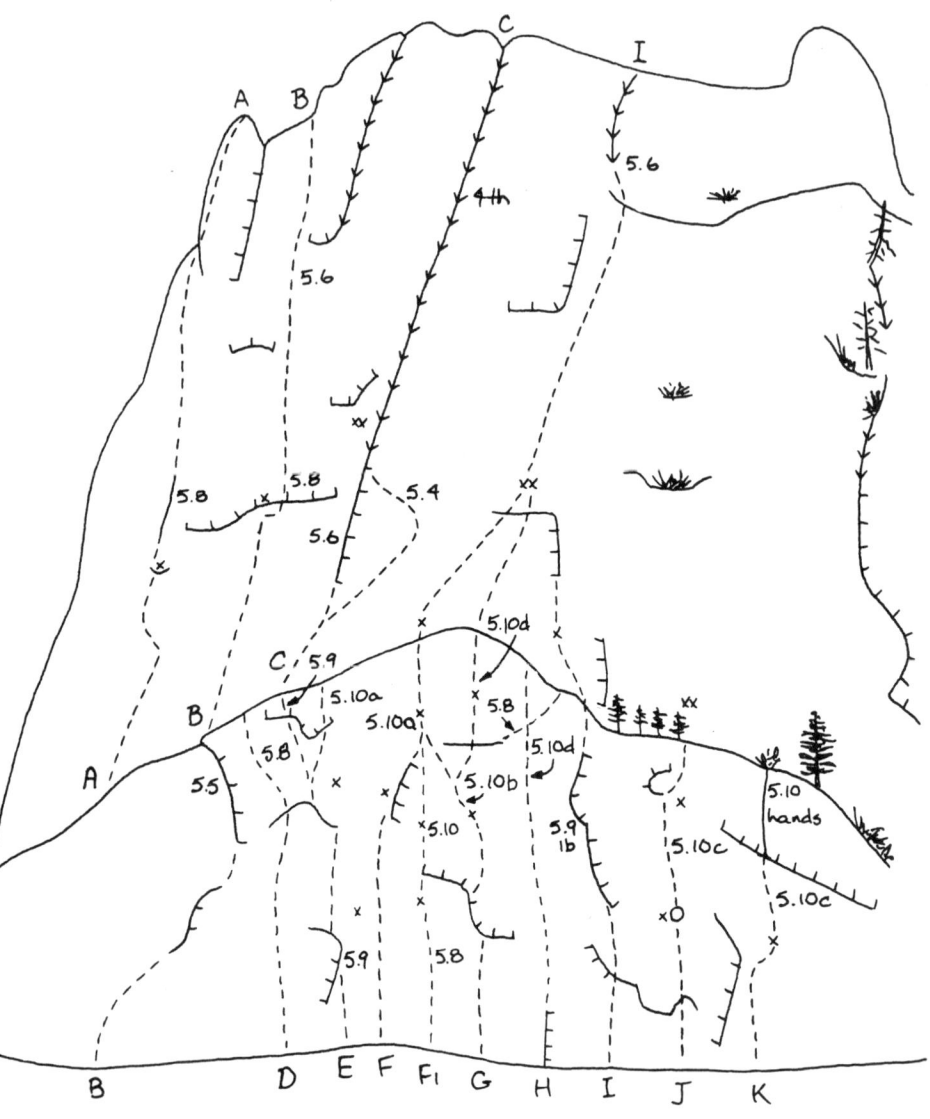

A) Potentilla Pillar
B) Heartline
C) Choc-a-Bloc
D) Less Than Zero
E) Back to Zero
F) Feel on Baby
F_1) Feel on Baby Direct
G) Dynamic Dumpling
H) Caveling
I) Cavebird
J) Midnight Rambler
K) Honkey Tonk Woman

BACK TO ZERO 25 m, 5.9
J.Jones and A.Genereux, 1986

Climb to the top of a right-facing flake. Clip a bolt to the right and then continue up a steep wall, passing to the left of a bolt. Continue partway up Choc-a-bloc to a two bolt belay.

FEEL ON BABY ** 20 m, 5.10a
A.Genereux and J.Jones, 1986
Direct: A.Genereux and J.Jones, May 1987

This mini-classic starts just right of Back To Zero. Climb a steep wall, reaching left to clip a bolt, to a left-facing flake. Climb to the top of the flake and make tricky moves up a steep wall to a ledge with a bolt. Trend right up a short wall to a two bolt belay at another ledge. The direct start climbs slightly further right past two bolts to the top of the flake.

DYNAMIC DUMPLING ** 20 m, 5.10b or 5.10d
A.Genereux and W.Rennie, 1986

Climb past a left-facing flake to a bolt. Difficult moves lead up and left, then back right to a small ledge with another bolt. Climb the short difficult wall above (or take an easier alternative to the right) to a ledge and then continue up an easier wall to the belay of Feel On Baby. It is also possible to move left above the first bolt and finish on Feel On Baby.

CAVELING * 20 m, 5.10d (toprope)
J.Martin and L.Ostrander, June 1987

This pumpy, eliminate toprope problem climbs the steep wall between Dynamic Dumpling and Cavebird

CAVEBIRD 50 m, 5.9
W. Lee and J. Martin, July 1983

This climb starts below a steep, left-facing, left-leaning corner capped by a small overhang.
1) 28 m, 5.9. Angle up right to the base of the corner and climb it to the overhang. Step up right over the overhang and gain a ledge with a small tree. Move up left a short distance to a bolt, and then climb a short steep wall to a grassy ledge with two bolts.
2) 22 m, 5.6. Climb moderate slabs above, trending right to avoid a small loose overhang, and gain a round grassy ledge below a steep section. Step left and up into an unusual solution groove to reach the top.

MIDNIGHT RAMBLER * 13 m, 5.10c
A.Genereux and F.Sutherland, 1986

Climb the steep wall right of Cavebird past two bolts to a ledge with a double bolt belay.

HONKY TONK WOMAN * 13 m, 5.10c
A.Genereux and F.Sutherland, 1986

This route takes a short overhanging handcrack right of Midnight Rambler. Starting near a short right-facing corner, make awkward moves to a bolt. Gain the crack after some tricky face climbing and jam this to the ledge near the Midnight Rambler belay.

FIRST ROCK - RIGHT

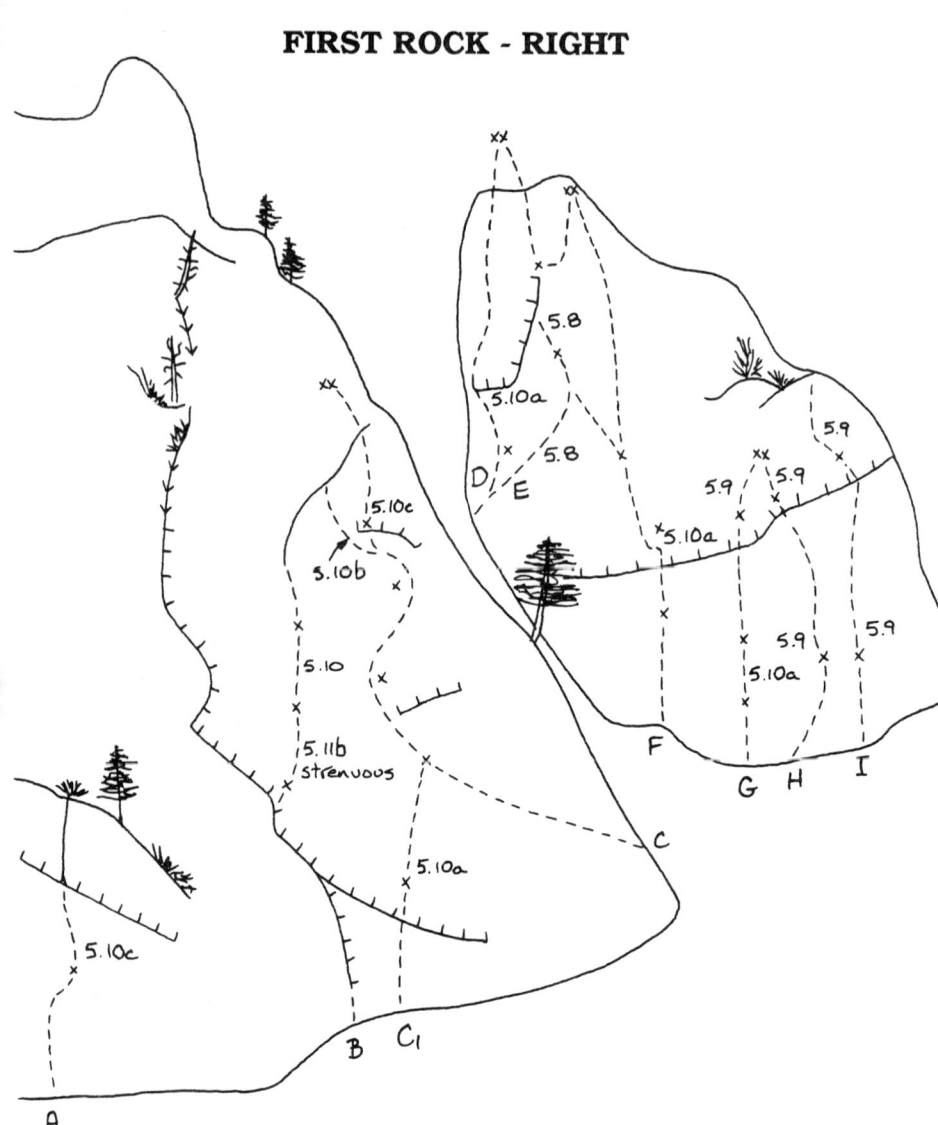

A) Honky Tonk Woman
B) Bitch
C) Sticky Fingers
C₁) Sticky Fingers Direct
D) Dirty Work
E) Dandelions
F) Dead Flowers
G) Brown Sugar
H) Heartburn
I) Wild Horses

Toward the right side of the main wall is a vegetated corner system. The next two routes lie right of this corner system.

BITCH *   25 m, 5.11b
A.Genereux and J.Jones, 1986

Climb the bottom part of the corner system, which arches left, to a bolt. Pull over a bulge and climb a steep, sequency wall on small edges past two more bolts. Above, follow an easier groove to a two bolt belay.

STICKY FINGERS ***   25 m, 5.10c
W.Rennie and A.Skuce, 1986
Direct Start: A.Genereux and J.Jones, 1986

This excellent climb can be started from several places near the right side of the rock. Gain a left-trending ramp of clean gray rock and follow it to a bolt. Work up and left past a second bolt and then move up and right to a third bolt. Go up and left to a final bolt and make a strenuous move past it to easier ground. An easier exit to the left is possible. Continue to the belay of Bitch. The direct start climbs a steep, somewhat loose wall past one bolt directly up to the first bolt of the original line.

To the right of the main area and separated from it by a gully is a steep slab cut off at the bottom by a line of overhangs. The remaining routes at First Rock lie in this area.

DIRTY WORK *   15 m, 5.10a
J.Jones and D.Poley, 1986

Climb up the gully past the line of overhangs. Step right to clip a fixed piton, move up to an overlap, and pull over it. Above, finger jamming in solution cracks leads to easier ground and a two bolt belay.

DANDELIONS *   15 m, 5.8
J.Jones and A.Skuce, 1986

Start as for Dirty Work but move up and right from the fixed piton to a bolt. Continue past another bolt to the belay of Dirty Work, or move up and right past the bolt to the belay of Dead Flowers.

DEAD FLOWERS *   20 m, 5.10a
A.Skuce and A.Geoffrey, 1986

Start near the left side of the steep lower wall. Climb the wall past two bolts and continue up lower-angled rock past a third bolt to a belay with fixed anchors. A better finish is to move up left from the third bolt and finish as for Dandelions.

BROWN SUGAR   15 m, 5.10a
J.Martin and R. MacLachlan, July 1986

Climb a short bulging wall past two bolts. Continue up easier rock and then climb a short vertical wall (bolt) to a two bolt belay at a small ledge.

Heart Creek

HEARTBURN   15 m, 5.9
J.Martin and R.MacLachlan, July 1986

Climb a steep break past a bolt immediately right of an overhanging section of rock. Above, move up left on easier rock and pull over an overhang (bolt) to the Brown Sugar belay.

WILD HORSES   15 m, 5.9
J.Martin and R.MacLachlan, July 1986

Climb the face right of Heartburn past a bolt. Continue up and slightly right on easier rock, and then work left up a steep break in the overhang above to easier ground. Belay at a tree.

HEART AND SOLE

Heart and Sole is a small, steep slab directly across the valley from First Rock. It can be reached in three minutes from the trail at a footbridge. A few wired nuts are needed.

SOLE FOOD   12 m, 5.9
J.Martin, S.Dougherty and L.Heidt, July 1986

Starting near the left side of the slab, climb up and traverse right to a bolt. Step up and left, then go up and right, passing a shrub on the left. Continue straight up to the top.

HEART AND SOLE   12 m, 5.9
J.Martin, S.Dougherty and L.Heidt, July 1986

Make a couple of tricky moves to reach the bolt. Move right and up, pass the shrub on the right, and continue to the top.

MR. PERCIVAL   8 m, 5.10a
S.Dougherty and J.Martin, July 1986

Make a long reach and high step to gain the first of three slots. Jam up these and continue up the slab above, joining Heart and Sole near the top.

JUPITER ROCK

A short distance further up the west side of the valley is Jupiter Rock, a steep, black crag rising 50 m directly out of Heart Creek. A large circular hole (the Cyclops Eye), approximately in the centre of the main face near the top, is a prominent feature.

S.U.M.C. BUTTRESS   40 m, 5.10c
D.Morgan, A.Skuce and S.Worthington, 1986

This route (not pictured) climbs past three bolts and a fixed piton to the top of prominent pillar well left of the main wall. The crux is at the top where the pillar narrows.

Heart Creek

DARK CHOCOLATE 50 m, 5.9
B.Wyvill, C.Quinn and A.Bryden, 1985

1) 30 m, 5.9. Starting below a ledge with a dead tree, just left of the point where Heart Creek abuts against the base of the cliff, climb up to a break in a slanting band of overhangs. Gain a small ledge above and move up left over a second overhang. Follow a rising traverse line left to a short, right-facing corner. Climb the corner, moving left at the top, and then go right up a slab to the ledge with the dead tree.
2) 20 m, 5.7. Move up right to the circular hole. Make an awkward step out left and then climb the wall to the top.

RIPARIAN * 55 m, 5.10a
A.Skuce and R.Lanthier, 1986

1) 30 m, 5.9. Start as for Dark Chocolate. Where that route traverses left, climb straight up to the right of a bolt, step right, and then go up and left past two bolts to a big ledge.
2) 25 m, 5.10a. Climb a steep wall past a bolt, traverse left past a fixed piton, and move up and left past a bolt (crux). Pull over a roof and continue easily to a belay.

VENUS *** 30 m, 5.10a
J.Jones and W.Rennie, 1986

This excellent climb is the best and most popular on Jupiter Rock. Jump across the creek to start at a thin crack right of Riparian.
Climb the crack past a fixed piton to a flaky overhang. Pull over this and climb a flake to a bolt. Continue past another bolt to a two bolt belay in the Cyclops Eye.

BRONTES * 30 m, 5.10b
J.Jones and W.Rennie, 1986

Start just right of Venus, midway between two willows. Climb straight up past a fixed piton to a bolt above an overhang. Move right and up to a second bolt. Continue up a steep wall, move left to a bolt, and then climb up and right to a little ledge. Continue up to the Cyclops Eye.

CALLISTO ** 50 m, 5.9
C. Perry and J. Firth, May 1983

Callisto begins to the right of the Cyclops Eye at a break in the lower bulges below an area of shattered, ochre-colored rock. Three bolts were inadvertently added after the first ascent, changing the character of the route.
1) 30 m, 5.9 Climb up to the right end of the ochre-colored rock and traverse left. Pull up left over a bulge to small ledges below an overlap. Move up to a bolt and make a hard step up right over the overlap onto a steep wall. Climb the wall on pockets to a bolt. Continue up left of a left-facing corner past another bolt to the Cyclops Eye.
1a) 30 m, 5.10a Alternatively, climb up to a fixed piton, step left, and continue up to a second fixed piton at the left end of the ochre-colored rock.
2) 20 m, 5.8. Move out right and climb a short wall. Continue, trending left higher up, to fixed anchors at the top.

JUPITER ROCK

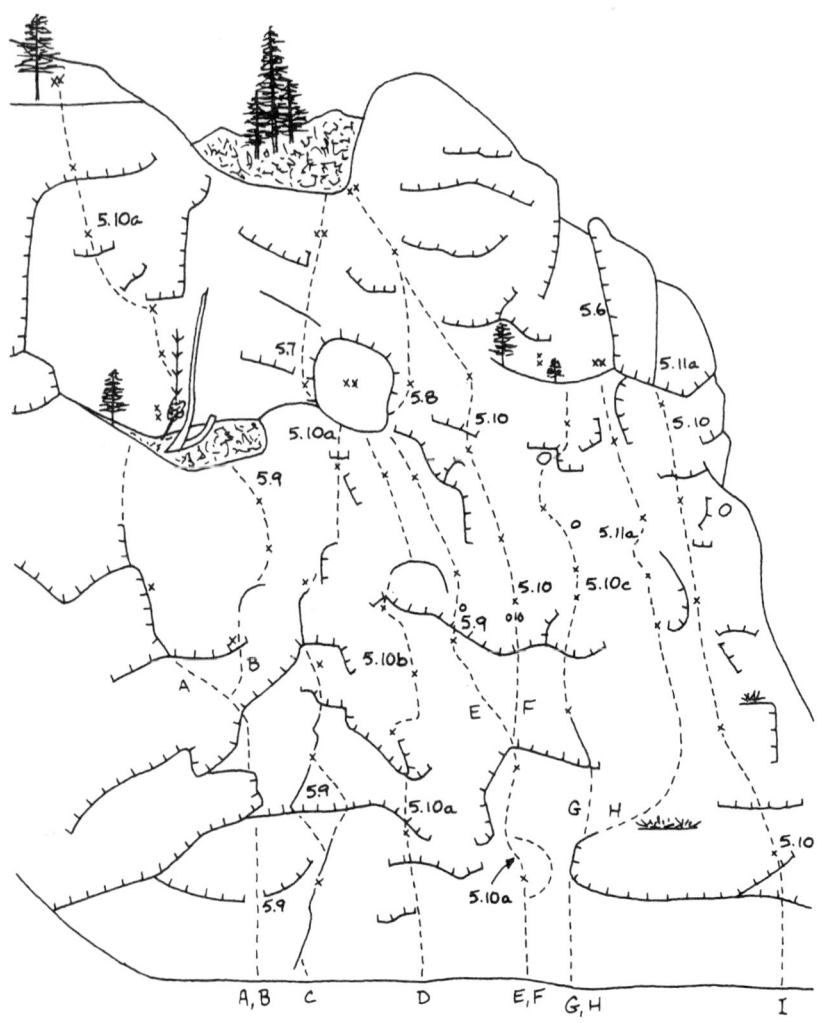

A) Dark Chocolate
B) Riparian
C) Venus
D) Brontes
E) Callisto
F) For your Eyes Only
G) Puppet on a Chain
H) Heart of Darkness
I) Heart of Gold

FOR YOUR EYES ONLY   50 m, 5.10b
A.Genereux and F.Sutherland, 1986

Follow Callisto to the second fixed piton. Move up right and make a difficult move over a bulge past twin holes (The Eyes) to a bolt. Continue up past two bolts, an overhang, and a third bolt, and then trend left to the top of Callisto.

PUPPET ON A CHAIN *   35 m, 5.10c
A.Genereux and F.Sutherland, 1986

Start just right of Callisto. Pass the ochre patch on the right and slant left up a crack (piton). Continue up past a hole (bolts and piton) to a roof. Pull over this on the right (bolt) and continue up to a ledge.

† HEART OF DARKNESS **   35 m 5.11a
J. Jones and W. Rennie, September 1987

Start as for Puppet on a Chain, but after the initial few metres move right to a vegetated ledge. Climb solid rock right of a dirty corner and continue up a steep and strenuous pocketed wall to a vegetated alcove. Steep but easier climbing above leads to a stance on a sloping ledge.

† HEART OF GOLD   45 m, 5.11a
A.Genereux and J.Jones, 1986

This strenuous climb takes a steep face with widely spaced bolts topped by an overhanging crack. Start just left of a birch tree near the right end of the crag. Climb a strenuous bulge (bolt), move up and left past a second bolt and then climb a steep yellow wall past three more bolts to the leering exit crack. Watch for loose rock.

NORTH RIDGE   45 m, 5.7
M. Whalen and M. Peckham, July 1978

The route follows the sharp ridge on the right-hand side of the rock and is mainly 5.5 except for a short wall of 5.7 (piton in place). The lower section is vegetated and can be avoided by traversing in from the right at about one-third height.

LOWER HEART CRAG

Further up the west side of the valley, directly above the creek, is Lower Heart Crag, a big rambling cliff about 200 m high with an extremely steep, bowl-shaped central wall. The quality of the rock, and of the climbs, is variable and on the south side much of the rock is lichen-covered. However, there are excellent individual pitches on some of the routes.

BLACKHEART *   40 m, 5.10b or 5.11a
J.Martin and L.Howard, May 1986
Direct; J.Martin and L.Ostrander, July 1987

This route follows the prominent corner directly above the bridge at the far left end of Lower Heart Crag.

Climb moderate rock to a little ledge where the cliff steepens. Continue up prickly dark rock to a fixed piton slightly right of the corner. Make a few moves up and right. Move up and back left across a steep wall past two bolts to the upper corner and follow this to a two bolt belay. The direct variation stays in the corner and is protected by three bolts.
Rappel or scramble down to the left.

HEART CRACK   70 m, 5.10b
B.Keller, S.Dougherty and J.Martin, June 1985

Heart Crack is the obvious right-slanting crack just right of Blackheart.
1) 40 m, 5.10b. Climb as for Blackheart as far as the fixed piton. Traverse up right to the base of the crack and then follow the crack to a sloping belay beneath an overhang.
2) 30 m, 5.9. Move right to the continuation of the crack. Make a few steep moves and then climb an easy ramp beside the crack. Where the crack and the ramp end, traverse right until it is possible to climb up a short layback crack. At its top, step left and climb a steep little wall to trees.
Descend by rappel.

STYX *   125 m, 5.9
C. Perry, G. Powter and J. Sterner, 1979

Styx follows a rising traverse line across the steep central bowl. It begins at the top of easy slabs on the left where the lower overhangs peter out.
1) 35 m, 5.7. Bypass an overhang on the left and climb up to a prominent fault that slants up rightwards across the face. Follow the fault on dusty, lichen-covered rock to a bolt belay in a scoop.
2) 45 m, 5.8. Continue along the fault to a big tree ledge below a steep wall (junction with Grovel).
3) 35 m, 5.9. Traverse left onto a slab and climb this to a short groove on the left side of an overhang (fixed peg). Swing up right onto a ledge and then make a difficult move over a bulge onto easier rock above. Continue to a belay on a slab.
4) Scramble off left.
To descend, follow the ridge south from the crag and then drop down into a side valley which leads back to the Heart Creek Trail.

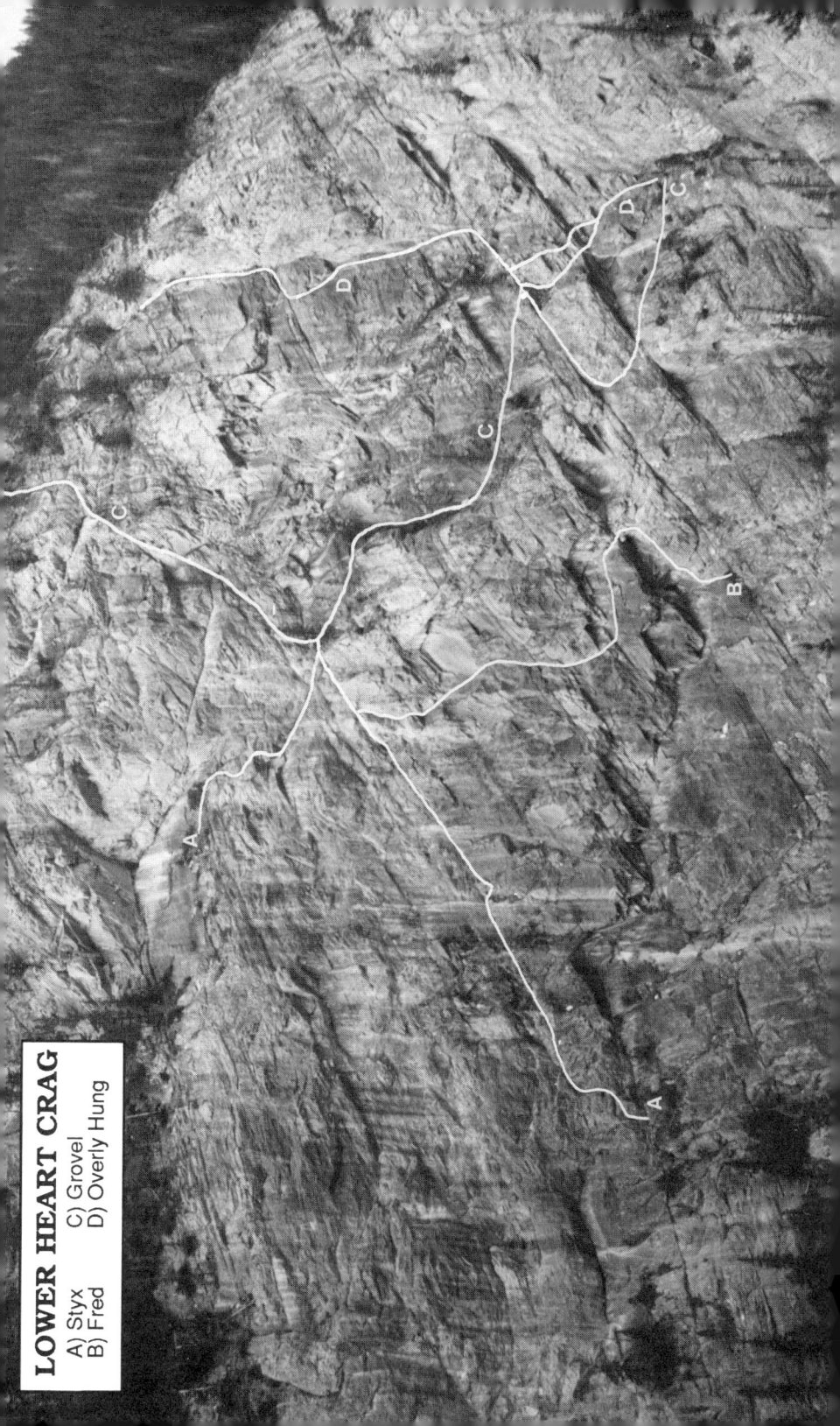

Heart Creek

† FRED 80 m, 5.9
J. Blench and J. Lauchlan, July 1980

Fred climbs directly through large roofs to join Styx near the end of the traverse. The climbing is good except for a dangerously loose pillar near the start. Approach from the left via slabs, and belay in a scoop below a large roof.

1) 40 m, Traverse up right across a steep slab to a loose pillar that leads to a break in the roof. Gain the slabs above the roof, traverse left, and climb a small groove that goes up through the next band of overhangs. Belay on small ledges.

2) 40 m, Climb an obvious groove line that leads up and slightly left to join pitch 2 of Styx.

GROVEL 130 m, 5.6
N. Helliwell and C. Perry, 1978

Follow easy, treed ledges from the stream bed up right to a belay below large overhangs in a prominent corner.

1) 45 m, Traverse left across a slab past an old bolt to a break in the lower roofs. Climb a groove to a higher roof, then traverse up right to a large tree.

2,3) 60 m, Follow broken ground up left to a tree ledge below a steep wall.

4) 45 m, Gain a ledge that slants up across the wall to the right. Follow this to a groove and corner system, exiting right to easy ground.

5) 25 m, Scramble to the top.

Descend steep treed slopes to the north of the crag.

OVERLY HUNG * 105 m, 5.10a (or 5.9)
M. Whalen and W. Faryna, August 1978

Overly Hung follows the prominent left-facing corner in the upper section of the face at the north end. It is probably the best route on the cliff, the rock in the upper corner being unusually good. Start as for Grovel, about 5 m below the roofs.

1) 30 m, 5.10a. Climb the corner to the roof and make a few difficult moves up and to the left to gain a scoop above the overhangs. Climb the wall above to a tree belay.

1a) 30 m, 5.9. Traverse a short distance left under the roof and climb an easier break to the tree belay.

2) 30 m, 5.9. Drop down and traverse right 5 m to a short overhanging crack. A few awkward moves lead to a ledge on the right at the base of the upper corner. Climb the slabby left wall past a protection bolt to a bolt belay in the corner just below a small roof.

2a) 30 m, 5.10. Step up and traverse right across an overhanging wall to gain the ledge above the crack.

3) 45 m, 5.8. Climb up past the roof on the left, following a crack in a corner to an obvious traverse line. Traverse right into the main corner and follow it to the top.

Descend steep treed slopes to the north of the crag.

North Wing

At the north end of the crag is a smaller, triangular buttress of rock separated from the main face by the easy approach gully of Grovel and Overly Hung. The next four climbs are located on this buttress.

PATRIOT'S GROOVE   60 m, 5.7
J. Martin, C. Perry and M. Talbot, April 1980

On the left side of the buttress is an obvious open groove which begins about 18 m above the ground. Start below and slightly to the right of the groove at a break in the lower overhangs. The initial section is a little loose, but higher up the rock improves.
1) 40 m, 5.7 Climb the broken face to a steep section and then traverse up right on a ramp a short distance until it is possible to make a few moves up to easy ground. Move left and up to a bulge at the base of the groove. Climb the bulge and the groove above to a small stance in a scoop.
2) 20 m, 5.6 Continue up the groove and where it splits follow the right branch a short distance to easy ground.

To descend, climb down left to the gully below Overly Hung and continue down on ledges and slabs to the creek.

† HEARTBEAT   60 m, 5.8
J.Martin and L.Howard, June 1986

Heartbeat is a nice face climb on the wall left of Patriot's Groove.
1) 30 m, 5.6. Start as for Patriot's Groove and after about 12 m traverse left to a big ledge with trees.
2) 30 m, 5.8. Starting behind the rightmost tree, work right up a slanting break to a thin flake crack. Climb this to a sloping ramp. Move up and right on the ramp and then climb up past a bolt to the top.

To descend, downclimb slabs to the Patriot's Groove descent.

† HEARTLAND   80 m, 5.8
W. Lee and J. Martin, June 1983

Initially, the route takes the same line as Patriot's Groove, but soon swings right in a slanting traverse to an exit up the wall. Care is required on account of loose rock in a few sections.
1) 30 m, 5.6. Climb the first 12 m of Patriot's Groove to an easy-angled area where that route moves left. Slant up to the right on a ramp until it is possible to move right past a rounded edge. Step down to a good ledge with a bolt.
2) 23 m, 5.8. Just above eye level is a faint fault line, masked by a small discontinuous roof, that slants up to the right. Move up to the fault line and follow it rightwards, staying below the little roof and passing a small inside corner and pillar, to an obvious horizontal slot about 6-7 m past the pillar. Make an awkward step onto the wall above, avoiding a small loose block, then work up left a few moves. Step up right and climb straight up to a big tree on a ledge.
3) 25 m, 5.6. Climb a short slanting corner to easier ground and continue up to a big ledge with trees.

Descend as for Patriot's Groove.

Heart Creek

† HEART OF THE PATRIOT   90 m, 5.7
J. Martin and R. MacLachlan, August 1981
This route traverses further right and lower than Heartland to an exit groove.
1)   30 m, 5.6. Climb the first pitch of Heartland.
2)   35 m, 5.7. Traverse right past a short corner and onto a steep wall. Work right and slightly up to sloping ledges below a bulge, then go right to a faint groove that splits the bulge. Climb the groove, then go past two small trees and continue up a short wall to a good tree.
3)   25 m, 5.6. Climb the groove directly above to easy ground. Continue up left to a good tree.
Descend as for Patriot's Groove.

HEART SLAB

Heart Slab is a pleasant, sunny and popular climbing area on the lower west slopes of Heart Mountain. The slabs are formed by exposed bedding planes of limestone tilted at about 55 degrees. A prominent feature, near the centre, is a smooth, roughly circular slab which starts at a treed ledge about 20 m above the ground and is bounded at the top and left by a long curving overlap. The rock in this area is exceptionally good and gives a number of outstanding one pitch slab climbs. Small pitons, wired nuts and Friends are useful, except on the smooth central slab where most protection is from bolts.
Approach: Continue up the valley past Lower Heart Crag until a cliff band is reached where the creek emerges from a small canyon. Heart slab is then visible high up on the hillside to the left (east).   Cross the creek and locate a trail which starts about 25 m downstream from the cliff band. Follow the trail up through woods to a ridge, turn left along the ridge and climb the hillside to the south end of the slabs.
Descent is normally by rappel, either from trees or from one of two anchors at the top of the central slab. Alternatively, it is possible (but tedious) to walk off to the south after ascending through trees.

MIX-UP   115 m, 5.8
J. McIsaac and D. McNeil, 1979
Start on the slab left of the obvious gully (North Gully).
1)   10 m, 5.6. Climb a short pitch to two trees on a ledge.
2)   50 m, 5.8. After making a couple of tricky moves above the trees, work up and right to reach a ledge. The steep top part of the slab is crossed diagonally.
3)   10 m, 5.0. Move the belay right to a large ledge.
4)   45 m, 5.7. Climb moderate rock to the left to a layback flake. From the top of the flake move up and right to a short steep crack which leads to trees.

HEART SLAB LEFT

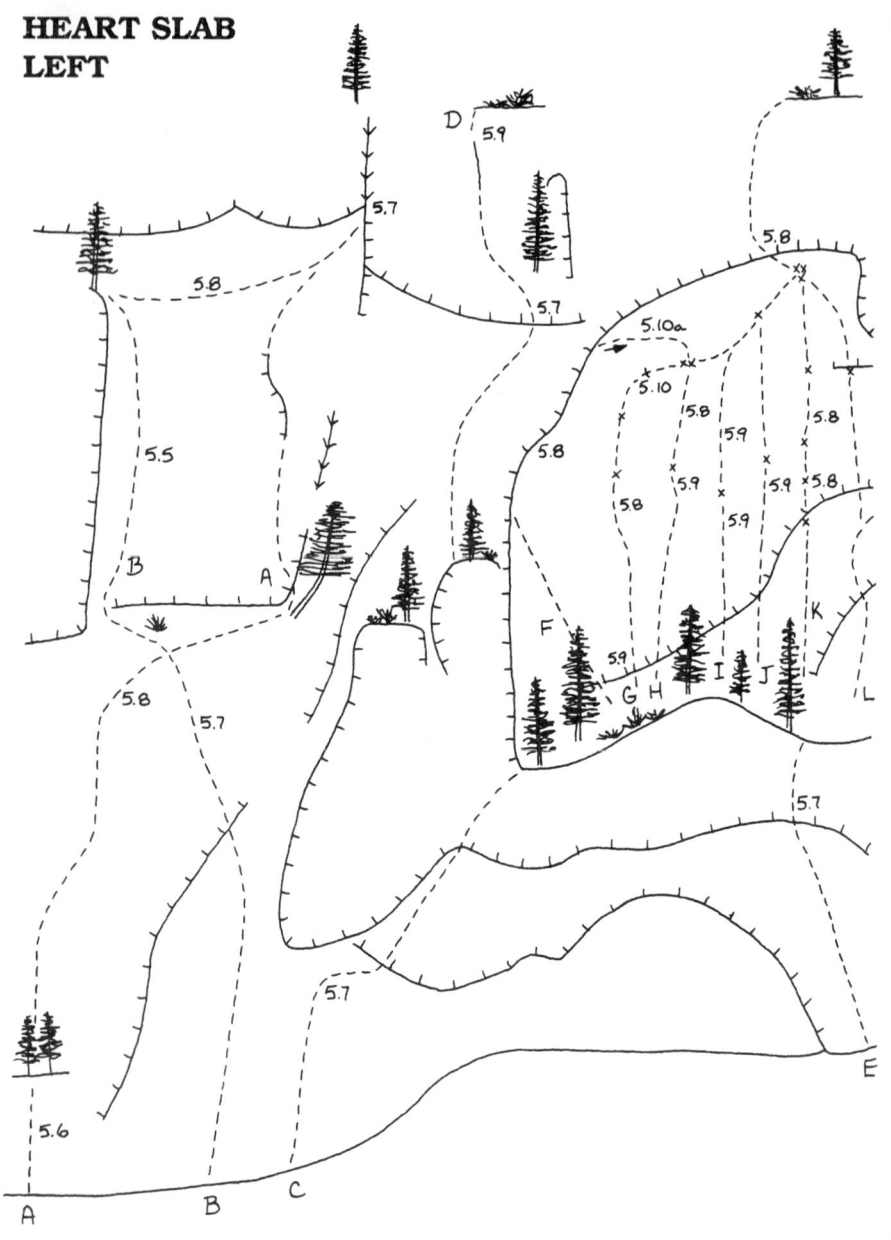

A) Mix-up
B) North Slab
C) Slanting Slab
D) Trident
E) Arch Slab
F) The Hook
G) Skid Row
H) Rough Mix
I) White Line Special
J) A Touch Soft
K) Soft Touch
L) Bad Habits

Heart Creek

NORTH SLAB   125 m, 5.8
U. Kallen and R. Mitchell, 1978; L. Howard and J. Martin, 1981

This climb combines the best features of two routes with a common start that were climbed on separate occasions. Start below North Gully.

1) 50 m, 5.7. Climb the slab to the base of the gully, then move left into a shallow right-facing corner that trends left. Follow this to a ledge (junction with Mix-Up)

2) 40 m, 5.5. Climb the bulge above on the left, then step right and climb an unprotected, pockmarked slab to a tree. An easier alternative is to climb the corner on the left.

3) 35 m, 5.8. Traverse right to the exit of Mix-Up to finish the climb.

SLANTING SLAB   50 m, 5.7
J. Martin and L. Howard, August 1981

This climb provides an alternative route to the large treed ledge at the base of the central slab.
Start on the slabs to the right of the preceding routes and climb up to a roof near its lowest point, then slant up to the right until it is possible to step over an overlap (loose rock) onto a small ledge leading to trees.

† TRIDENT   45 m, 5.9
J. Martin and R. MacLachlan, August 1981

The start of this route, on a small tree ledge, is gained by scrambling up and left from the ledge below the central slab.
Climb up and then trend right to a bulge. Pull over the bulge, then work left and up past the end of a second bulge to a small ledge below three short solution cracks. The cracks provide an entertaining finish up a steep slab.

ARCH SLAB   30 m, 5.7
J. Jenkins and C. Perry, 1979

Arch Slab is another alternative route to the ledge below the central slab. Starting left of a left-facing corner, slant left up a well textured slab to the high point of an arching roof. Pull over the overlap and continue to the trees.

Heart Creek

The following 8 climbs are situated on the smooth central slab, which is reached by climbing the first 20 m of Plimsoll Line (5.0) to the right end of the large ledge. Alternatively, Slanting Slab or Arch Slab can be used as more technical approaches. Several of the climbs reach a ledge at the top of the slab on the right, but only Rough Mix continues over the overlap to the top of the cliff. Rappel anchors are in place at the ledge and at the top of Skid Row and a descent can conveniently be made from either point.

† THE HOOK   45 m, 5.10a
C. Dale and J. Martin, July 1980

The Hook climbs the corner on the left side of the slab.
Slant left up slabs to gain the corner above the loose lower section. Climb the easily protected corner until it becomes necessary to traverse right. Move right and slightly up across the slab, difficult and unprotected, to a point about 1 m above double bolts. A piquant moment now occurs in descending to these bolts.

SKID ROW *   30 m, 5.10b
J. Martin and L. Howard, June 1982

Skid Row tours the steepest part of the slab and is well protected at its crux section.
Climb the bottom overlap just left of the faint ripple that marks the line of Rough Mix, continue past a small flake, and then work up and slightly left to a tiny scoop (bolt). Climb up and then right past two more bolts to a double bolt belay.

ROUGH MIX ***   70 m, 5.9
B. Keller, M. Sawyer and C. Perry, 1978

The first pitch of this climb, which starts at a faint, right-slanting ripple, is a classic friction test-piece. The crux is unprotected and occurs just before the first bolt, some 20 m off the ledge. The moves over the overlap on the second pitch are also interesting, making the climb one of the best in the valley.
1) 45 m, 5.9. Step over an overlap to gain the base of the ripple and follow it until it begins to fade out, not far from the first bolt. Move left and then up to the bolt. Continue up to a second bolt (doubled) and then make a rising traverse past a fixed pin in a small corner to the ledge at the top of the slab.
2) 25 m, 5.8. Traverse horizontally left, and then move up and back right slightly to reach the start of a thin crack which slants up left through the overlap (piton). Climb the crack past a second piton and make a strenuous pull up to gain the easy slabs above. Move up left into a corner and either belay at a tree on the left arete or traverse up right to a larger tree.
Descend by rappel (45 m) to the ledge at the base of the slab.

Bruce Keller on the first ascent of Rough Mix ⇨ pitch 1, photo Chris Perry

HEART SLAB - RIGHT

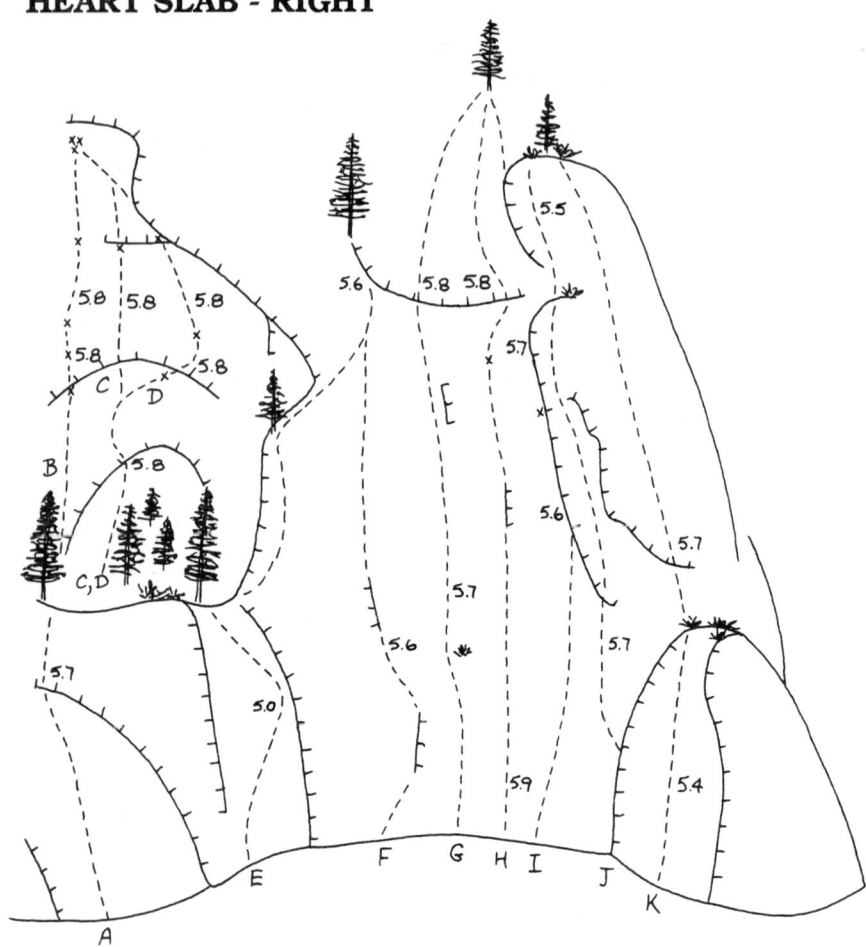

A) Arch Slab
B) Soft Touch
C) Bad Habits
D) Original Sin
E) Plimsoll Line
F) Bluebell Way
G) Red Slab
H) White Slab
I) The Scoop
J) Black Slab
K) Passing Slab

Heart Creek

WHITE LINE SPECIAL *   45 m, 5.9
C. Dale, L. Howard and J. Martin, July 1980

This sustained and poorly protected route follows a pale streak to the right of Rough Mix. Follow the streak to a bolt, then continue up to the top traverse of Rough Mix (no protection), finishing as for that route.

A TOUCH SOFT   40 m, 5.9
J.Martin, L.Howard, C.Perry, M.White, J.Jones and W.Rennie, 1978-1986

The line described here is a combination of three climbs done on separate occasions.
Climb up left of a small right-facing corner and make thin, runout moves to a bolt. Continue up a line of small holds to the fixed piton near the top of pitch 1 of Rough Mix. Climb up and right to the belay ledge.

SOFT TOUCH **   40 m, 5.8
C.Perry and M.White, July 1978.
J.Martin and L.Howard, June 1980.

Soft Touch, the most popular climb at Heart Slab, starts below a faint groove just left of a broken, right-facing corner. As described, it comprises the original start of Soft Touch and original finish of A Touch Soft. Climb the groove to an overlap (fixed piton), move right slightly, and then make some awkward moves up to a bolt. Make a couple of thin moves up, step right to flakes, and then continue straight up past a fixed piton to the belay ledge.

BAD HABITS   40 m, 5.8
J.Jones, 1986

This climb is essentially a direct finish to Original Sin. Start as for that route, but instead of traversing right, make a long runout straight up a nice slab to a little overlap with a fixed piton. Move up and then trend left to the belay ledge.

ORIGINAL SIN *   40 m, 5.8
J.Martin, C.Dale and L.Howard, June 1980

This pleasant climb is the best protected of any in the central area.
Start just left of some small trees and climb up to a break in the first overlap. Move up left over this and continue to a second overlap (piton). Diagonal up right to a bolt and then climb straight up to the base of a left-facing corner (piton). Move over an overlap and climb a slab left of the corner to the top ledge.

PLIMSOLL LINE   65 m, 5.6
N. Helliwell and M. Talbot, 1978

The first pitch of this climb is the normal approach to the central slab.
1) 45 m, 5.0. Starting directly below the right end of the large ledge, follow a faint, right-trending ramp to its top, and then move up and left on slabs to the ledge. Continue right and up on easy rock to a second ledge with a small tree.
2) 20 m, 5.6. Move up and right to a scoop, which is climbed trending up and left to a big tree. Watch for loose rock at a bulge near the top.

Heart Creek

BLUEBELL WAY * 45 m, 5.6
First ascent unknown
This climb, which starts at a small left-facing corner often sporting bluebells, provides a more direct approach to the exit of Plimsoll Line.
Climb the corner to a ledge, move left, and climb an obvious right-facing flake. Above, climb slabs straight up to a piton belay (regular angle) at a small spruce tree on the second pitch of Plimsoll Line.

RED SLAB * 75 m, 5.8
D. Reid and A. Sole, 1978
Red Slab starts directly below a small (50 cm) fir tree about 15 m above the ground.
1) 50 m, 5.6. Climb an obvious flake system and then continue over slabs to the fir tree. The line above is not compelling; climb more or less straight up the centre of the slab to a piton belay below a bulge.
2) 25 m, 5.8. Climb over the bulge and continue up a slab, trending right near the top to a tree.

† WHITE SLAB 75 m, 5.9
J. Martin and L. Howard, May 1983
This eliminate line stays midway between Red Slab and the Scoop. Start at an almost blank slab (the crux) immediately right of a peculiar detached flake about 8 m above the ground.
1) 45 m, 5.9. Climb the smooth slab and continue up easier rock to a belay ledge (bolt) just left of The Scoop.
2) 30 m, 5.8. Continue up the slab to a bulge. Step left and move up over the bulge, then climb straight up to a tree.

THE SCOOP * 65 m, 5.7
C. Perry and S. Climson, 1978
The Scoop climbs a clean, left-facing corner which begins part way up the cliff. It is an enjoyable route with moderately good protection.
1) 30 m, 5.6. Climb up to a faint solution runnel and follow this up to the main corner. Continue up the corner to a bolt belay.
2) 35 m, 5.7. Climb the corner, which bulges near the top, and continue up past a ledge to a big tree.

† BLACK SLAB 70 m, 5.7
J. Martin and L. Howard, June 1983
This climb follows the edge of the slab overlooking The Scoop and just right of that route. Start at an easy groove.
1) 50 m, 5.7. Climb about 7 m up the groove, step left on to a slab and continue up past a little overlap to gain the rounded edge overlooking The Scoop. Climb the edge, staying left near the top to avoid loose rock, to a belay ledge with a dead tree.
2) 20 m, 5.5. Continue up the edge to the top.

PASSING SLAB 70 m, 5.7
J. Martin and L. Howard, June 1980

The line of this route can be varied considerably and the crux section near the bottom can be avoided by staying to the right.
1) 20 m, 5.5. Begin just right of the start of Black Slab and climb a short slab to ledges. Alternatively, scramble up to the ledges from the left or right.
2) 50 m, 5.7. Climb up past an overlap located slightly to the left, and then follow the centre of the slab to tree ledges.

Several climbs have been done on the broken slabs and corners south of the routes described above. They are mostly 4th class with the odd move of easy 5th.

UPPER HEART CRAG

Upper Heart Crag is a steep, west-facing slab of sound rock (Livingstone Formation) partway up Heart Mountain just below the ridge trail.
Approach: Walk up the ridge trail to a small flat area with a large solitary spruce tree, at the top of a broken slabby buttress (about 40 minutes from the bridge across Heart Creek). From here, the main part of the crag can be seen in profile. To reach the three leftmost routes, traverse at this level along a scree covered ledge to a double bolt station at its end. Rappel 30 m to a ledge and ramp system at the foot of the climbs. To reach the remaining routes, continue up the ridge trail, which climbs steeply up just right of a slabby rib of light gray rock for 3 or 4 minutes. Cut over right to a cairn that marks the top of the main part of the crag. Just below this is a small ledge with three double bolt anchors. Rappel from the first of these to a big ledge at the foot of the climbs (45 m).
Take a small rack of wired nuts and Friends. With the exception of Fear of Flying, cruxes are short and moderately well protected, although easier sections are often runout.

† FEAR OF FLYING ** 30m, 5.10d
J.Jones and A.Genereux, May 1987

A serious and sustained route. Climb up past two bolts to a ramp leading right beneath a hanging slab. Follow the ramp (difficult) to a third bolt. Climb onto the slab and make a few difficult moves left and then up to a small break near the left edge of the slab. Move back right (bolt) and climb straight up to the belay.

† QUICKSILVER * 30 m, 5.10c
A.Genereux and J.Jones, May 1987

Climb up, via a short corner, to a bolt. Move up and left to a short ramp. Follow this up and right, and then climb over a small bulge to a bolt. Continue on nice rock to the belay.

UPPER HEART CRAG

A) Fear of Flying
B) Quicksilver
C) Warm Heart
D) Windbreaker
E) Nerve Gas

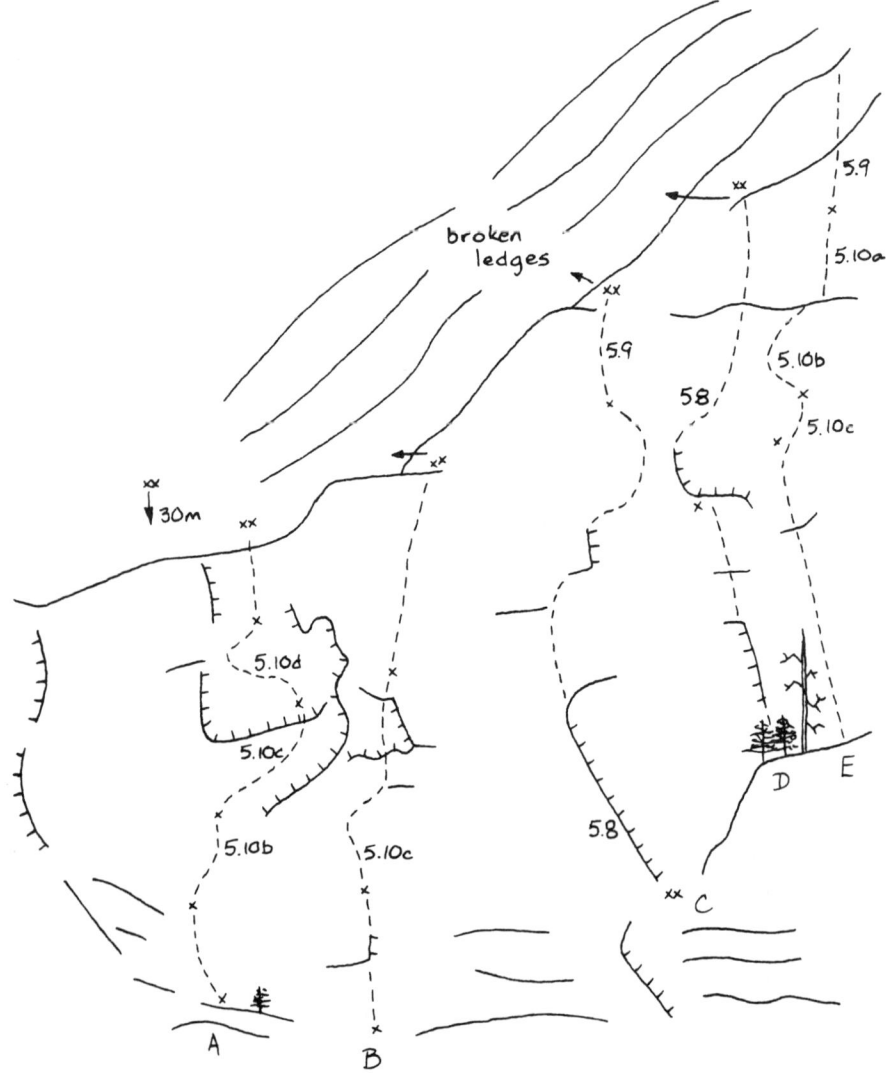

Heart Creek

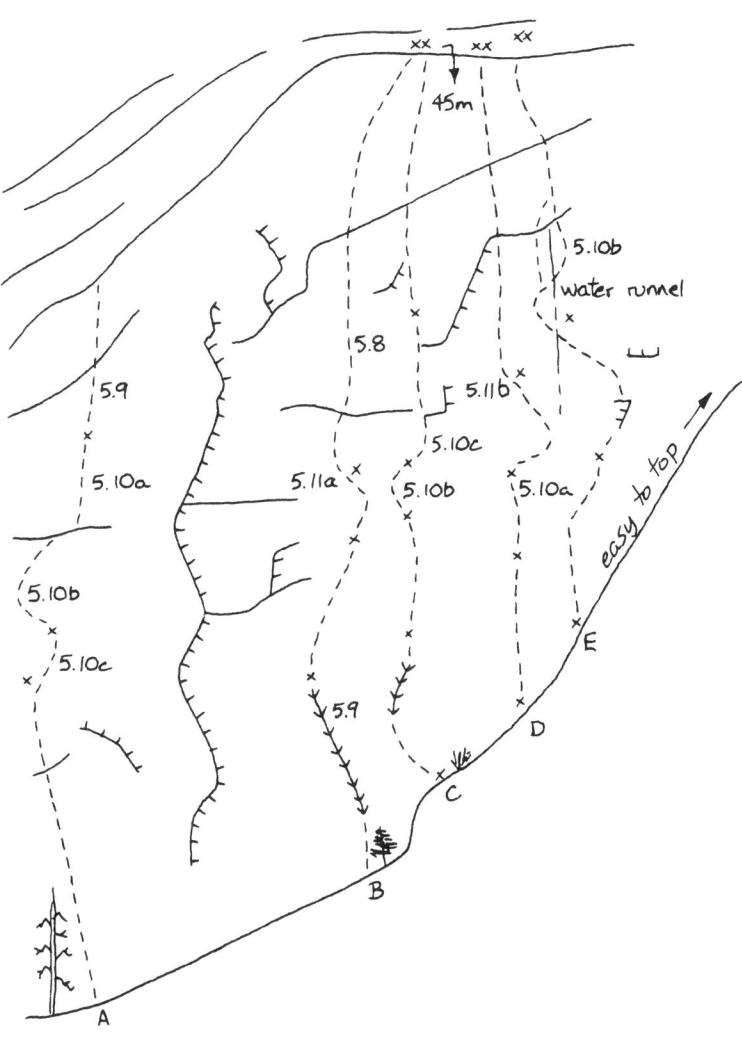

A) Nerve Gas
B) Livingstone Falls
C) Darkest Africa
D) Touch and Go
E) Purple Haze

Heart Creek

† WARM HEART   35 m, 5.9
J.Jones, J.Martin and L.Ostrander, February 1987
Rappel from bolts to the base of a left-leaning corner (belay bolts). Climb the corner and continue up easier rock to a good ledge (optional thread belay). Move easily up and right below a steep section, which is climbed past a bolt at a shallow depression. Continue to the rappel anchors.

WINDBREAKER   40 m, 5.8
C.Yonge and J.Jones, February 1987
Climb a short corner behind a large dead tree near the left end of the main starting ledge. Continue to an overlap, pass this on its left and follow a line of flakes up and right across a steep wall to a fluted ledge. Climb an easy groove to the top.

† NERVE GAS   40 m, 5.10c
C.Yonge and J.Jones, October 1986
Starting a short distance right of Windbreaker, climb a slabby wall to a ledge below a steeper section. Climb up to a bolt then head up and right to a second bolt. Move out left and go up to a fluted ledge. Move right a short distance and climb the steep wall above past a bolt to the top.

LIVINGSTONE FALLS *   45 m, 5.11a
J.Jones and A.Genereux, July 1986
Climb a groove above a shrub for about 10 m to a piton (runout, 5.9) and continue to a ledge (bolt). Go up and right on steep rock and make an awkward move to stand in a small hole from which another bolt may be clipped. Move left with difficulty and go up to a ledge. Easier but runout climbing leads to the belay.

† DARKEST AFRICA   45 m, 5.10c
J.Jones and K.Williams, June 1986
Starting at a belay bolt, angle up leftwards to gain a shallow groove just right of Livingstone Falls. Easy climbing up and right leads past a bolt to a piton. Above and to the left of this is a shallow niche which is awkward to gain (bolt). Difficult moves out right and up lead to a ledge. Climb the unprotected face above (just left of a short broken corner) to a small ledge with a bolt (5.10a), and then continue easily to the top.

TOUCH AND GO   40 m, 5.11b
J.Jones and R.Lanthier, September 1986
Start at a belay bolt just right of some solution pockets. Climb to the second of two bolts, move right (awkward) and go up to a third bolt. Make difficult moves left and up to a small ledge above which easier climbing leads to the top.

PURPLE HAZE   30 m, 5.10b
J.Jones, R.Lanthier and W.Rennie, October 1986
Start at a belay bolt farther up the easy break and right of Touch and Go. Climb up to a bolt, trend right to a small overlap, and then angle back left to a bolt near a prominent black water runnel. Climb up first slightly left of the runnel and then on its right to reach a ledge above. From here, easy twin runnels lead to the belay.

ROSE AND CROWN CRAG

The ridge on the east side of Heart Moutain curves up to a higher, unnamed summit and then bends round to the north, finally droping down towards the highway. The Rose And Crown crag is situated high on the northern section of the ridge, facing west and overlooking the large cwm formed on the east side of the mountain. It is not visible from the Highway but is located a short distance beyond a broken, slabby buttress. Only one route has been climbed to date, up the centre of a smooth slab of good gray rock situated right of a deep corner. Other route possibilities are limited and the existing route is good but hardly worth the walk.

Approach: Take the Quaite Valley trail from Heart Creek or bushwhack directly from the highway. Gain the ridge (good trail higher up) and follow it to a point above and immediately south of the crag. Scramble down to a ledge at the base of the slab.

HAPPY HOUR   70 m, 5.7
C.Perry, V.Powell and G.Smith, July 1985

1)   45 m, 5.7. Follow faint water runnels directly up the centre of the slab (natural and piton protection) to a ledge at the top.
2)   25 m, 5.4. Continue more easily to regain the ridge.

McCONNELL RIDGE

The Diamond Cross Face is a large cliff situated high on the north side of McConnell Ridge directly across the Bow Valley from Yamnuska.
Approach: Access is from the Yamnuska Centre, previously part of the Diamond Cross Ranch, and takes about 1 1/2 hours.

† DIAMOND CROSS FACE   330 m, 5.8 A0
D.Vockeroth and K.Hahn, August 1963

The only climb done to date follows an obvious rising traverse line up and right across the centre of the face and then diagonals back left to the summit. It is reported to be quite loose and probably has not had a second ascent.

1-3) 100 m. Follow an easy traverse line up and right to the base of a steep crack.

4) Climb a short distance up the crack and then move left and go up loose rock to easy ground. Move right along a rising ledge to a belay above a hole.

5) 30 m. Continue right along a grassy ledge to a large boulder.

6) 35 m. Move right and make a rising traverse to the foot of a short wall. Climb the wall to easy ground above.

7) 15 m. Traverse up and back left over grassy rock to a large cave.

8) 35 m. Use the rope to descend 30 m down and to the left and then climb an easy ledge system to a good belay.

9,10) Follow ledges up and left over easy ground.

11) 35 m. Climb a short corner and then move up and right to a ledge. Traverse up and back left to a cave.

12) 15 m. Climb steep rock left of the cave to join the east ridge 30 m below the summit.

McGILLIVRAY SLABS

The Palliser Formation outcrops on Mt. McGillivray in a long line of cliffs punctuated by several buttresses. All the climbs described here lie on McGillivray Slabs, the portion of the cliffs closest to the road. The rock is moderate-angled with occasional steep walls and overhangs, and tends to be friable where it has not been waterworn. The climbing history is poorly documented and the exact locations of some of the climbs are unclear. The lines marked on the photograph are approximate only.

Approach & descent: From the parking areas on the Trans-Canada Highway there are two separate approach and descent routes.

For climbs at the eastern end of the slabs, approach by a 4th class gully (or through nearby trees) that drains the snowmelt waterfall in a large cirque, and descend by means of easy ledges on the cliffs east of this cirque.

For the other climbs, walk up a road which slants up rightwards to a tunnel at the base of the slabs near Kahl Crack, or bushwhack directly upwards. To descend, walk west along the top of the cliffs and follow an intricate but easy descent down cliff bands on the east side of a gully.

GOLLYWOG   225 m, 5.7
R. Howe and C. Smith, 1971

Gollywog climbs the wall just left of the big waterfall in the cirque at the left end of the slabs. From a large pillar that marks the start of Pythagoras, continue left and go up slabs and grooves for about 60 m to the base of a brown streak level with a large tree-covered ledge and 30 m below a dead tree. A cairn marks the start at a groove.

1) 45 m, Climb the groove, then trend left to a ledge.
2) 35 m, Climb the slab and groove above, then move left onto a left-slanting slab and belay at a water hole.
3) 45 m, 5.6. Climb a smooth runnel on the left and continue up a slab past a large block to a grassy ledge.
4) 35 m, 5.7. Continue on grass ledges and go up to the base of an overhanging groove. Climb the groove, then go up a wall a short distance and traverse down left to a tree belay in a shallow cave.
5) 35 m, 5.7. Reverse the traverse and go straight up the wall, then trend left up loose rock to belay at three large trees.
6) Traverse about 15 m left to the base of a steep wall. It is possible to exit left here.
7) 30 m, 5.7. Climb up the wall, making two short leftward traverses, to a small slab. Climb the slab over a block, then continue up left on a slab to the top.

McGILLIVRAY SLABS   NOTE: Lines on photograph are approximate only

A) Pythagoras   C) Imagination   E) 7-Up   G) Rubble Without a Cause   I) Kahl Crack
B) Pixie   D) Tony's Route F) Pitter Patter H) Hiatus

McGillivray Slabs

PYTHAGORAS * 265 m, 5.7
R. Howe, J. Martin and J. White, 1971
This relatively popular route has some good climbing in pleasant surroundings. It is located near the centre of the big cirque, to the right of the waterfall. Begin at a groove on the left side of a large pillar.
1) 35 m, 5.6. Climb the groove to a large ledge.
2) 20 m, 5.4. Climb the slab above and a short corner.
3) 45 m, 5.6. Climb up a few metres, then traverse up right until it is possible to continue over slabs and groove to a ledge.
4) 30 m, 5.4. Scramble up left to ledges, then traverse up right along a ledge to two trees.
5) 45 m, 5.7. Climb a bulge to the left to gain a crack. Follow the crack to a roof, traverse left, and climb a corner to a small pinnacle.
6) 45 m, 5.6. Continue up the corner about 12 m, then traverse left and go over a slab to a big ledge in a bay.
7) 45 m, 5.7. From the right side of the bay climb a steep wall on small holds to a short corner. Climb the corner and continue a short distance up the wall above, then traverse right to another corner which leads to easy ground.

A more difficult variation (5.8) climbs the left-hand of two grooves above the first ledge reached on pitch 4, then traverses right to a belay on a small ledge with trees. A step right leads to the regular route at the corner near the top of pitch 5.

† PIXIE 5.6
R. Howe and J. Martin, 1971
Pixie takes an ill-defined line of corners and grooves up the right side of the waterfall cirque. Many variations are possible. Start at a short corner at the top left edge of the bay of trees extending into the cliffs.
1) Climb the corner and slabs above to a ledge.
2) Walk left to an obvious corner and climb to its top.
3) Climb the corner on the left; near its top move right and up to a ledge.
4) Climb a shallow corner to a tree, traverse right, then go up right to a bulge. Slant up left under the bulge to a ledge.
5) Continue up a groove and the wall on the left to a tree ledge.
6) Walk 15 m left and climb a broken slab to a tree.
7) Climb the slab above to a flake, traverse right to a shallow bay and go up this to easy ground.

† IMAGINATION 5.7
J. Martin and G. Rathbone, 1968
Starting in a gully system below a large tree-covered ledge, climb up easily to a steep section. Traverse left under the tree-ledge, then climb four slabby pitches which trend left and end below a steep slab capped by a roof. Follow a grassy ledge rightwards until it ends at a small tree, then move up a short distance and make a friction traverse right (5.7) to a corner. Climb the corner to a ledge, then continue past a bulge to a final polished exit groove.

McGillivray Slabs

TONY'S ROUTE 5.5
A. Shaw and F. Williamson, 1969

Tony's Route follows a prominent left-facing corner which slants steeply up to the right from the large tree ledge. Start as for Imagination, but instead of traversing left below the tree ledge, continue up until it is possible to traverse left to the base of the upper corner. Follow the corner to the top in several pitches. Steep sections of the corner can usually be avoided to one side or the other.

7-UP 5.7
First ascent party unknown

This route takes the line of least resistance to a prominent corner and slab formation near the top of the cliff. Starting near the centre of the cliff, scramble up past trees and short walls to a treed ledge about halfway up, then walk right along the ledge to the base of the corner. Climb the corner (5.7) and, at its top, move right to a belay. Above, follow broken slabs to the top.

† PITTER PATTER * 5.8
I. Stewart-Patterson and M. Toft, 1982

Start at the first weakness left of Kahl Crack. Climb up past the right end of a long horizontal roof and continue up a broken corner to a belay just below a second long roof. Climb up to the roof, traverse left immediately under it to a weakness, and then climb up 10 m to a belay. Follow easy ground to a tree ledge and walk left to a major right-facing corner. Climb a short wall to reach the corner and continue up this (5.8) to a tree belay. Move easily up to a large ledge, then climb one more pitch past an overhang to the top.

RUBBLE WITHOUT A CAUSE 95 m, 5.5
G.Powter and D.Chandler, June 1983

This variation start to Pitter Patter starts left of the prominent upper corner of that route and just right of 7-Up. Follow the base of the cliff for about 225 m left from the mine entrance and scramble up to the highest, easily reached tree island with a shallow corner above.
1) 45 m, 5.5. Climb to the top of the corner and then move up and left (poor protection) to a bolt stance beneath a notch in a steep wall.
2) 50 m, 5.5. Go up through the notch to a good ledge (a belay here reduces rope drag) and then move up and right across clean slabs to reach the ledge at the base of the upper corner of Pitter Patter.
Continue as for Pitter Patter.

HIATUS 70 m, 5.8
B.Wyvill and G.Powter, June 1985

Hiatus is a second variation start to Pitter Patter. It begins at the left end of a long, horizontal overhang that extends across the lower part of the cliff. Scramble up to ledges below a break that leads up and right to a very short, flared chimney.
1)   45 m, 5.8. Climb up through the break to the chimney. Exit right onto slabs and go up to a second overhang 10 m higher. Move left and follow a left-facing corner for 10 m to a stance below an overlap.
2)   25 m, 5.7. Move left and climb a slab to the foot of the upper corner. Continue as for Pitter Patter.

† OVERHANG ROUTE   5.7
B. Davidson and L. Drews

Details of this route are lost. Apparently it follows the first pitch of Pitter Patter and then continues more or less directly to the top.

KAHL CRACK *   200 m, 5.5
H. Kahl and party, c.1963

Kahl Crack is a deservedly popular easy climb which follows a prominent groove near the right end of the slabs. Begin more or less directly under the groove and climb over slabby rock to its base. Climb the groove in three pitches; at the top, either climb a bulge directly or outflank it to the right on slabs. Above the groove two more easy pitches lead to the top.

STUDENT'S ROUTE   5.5
A. Derbyshire and party, 1980

Starting right of Kahl Crack, follow a groove in a slab to a ledge. Walk left to the end of the trees and climb broken slabs for two short pitches to a second tree ledge. Climb an obvious corner in two more pitches to a third tree ledge, then walk right and climb an obvious broken exit pitch.

PIGEON MOUNTAIN

Pigeon Mountain is located south of the Trans-Canada Highway to the west of Mt. McGillivray. Two prominent buttresses on the north side of the mountain provide the only climbing routes established to date.

Approach: There are no trails up to the cliffs but the forest is not difficult to walk through.

Descent: It is probably easiest to climb up a short distance from the top of the cliffs to the easy, west sloping side of the mountain.

† NORTHEAST BUTTRESS   5.5, A1
G.Crocker and H.Gude, 1967

This is the very sharp buttress that is so prominent from the Trans-Canada Highway. Moderate climbing left of the buttress crest leads to the steep summit wall. This was climbed on the first (and only) ascent by aiding up a short overhanging crack about 10 m left of the buttress crest.

† TV BUTTRESS   5.7.
C.Perry and J.Martin, August 1977

This is the rounded buttress right of the northeast buttress and closer to the road. Third and fourth class climbing leads up the buttress crest to the first steep band, which is detoured on the left. A wide ledge then leads back right to a break, which is climbed past a few 5th class moves to the base of the steep upper headwall below a crack on the prow of the buttress. Climb up and left for about 25 m to an indistinct groove which leads in two pitches (5.6 and 5.7) to a large ledge. Make a long traverse left to gain the top by an easy break in the steep wall above.

WIND VALLEY

In the past, the climbs at the head of Wind Valley have been reached from the Trans-Canada Highway via a tedious 3-4 hr approach up West Wind Creek. However, a trail from the Spray Lakes road up Spurling creek to West Wind pass provides a better means of access, being shorter and more convenient for descent from the summit. This is probably true for all climbs including the Northeast Ridge on Windtower.
Approach: Start 4.8 km past the Spray District Office (at the Three Sisters dam) and walk up the west bank of a dry creek bed a short distance west of Spurling Creek. The trail stays on the bank above the creek for the lower third of the route and then moves away onto steeper hillsides in the middle and upper sections. West Wind pass can be reached in about 1 hr. Steep game trails lead north from the pass down to the head of West Wind Creek.

WINDTOWER

Windtower, the sharp rocky peak of Palliser limestone marking the most northwesterly extension of Mount Lougheed, is prominently visible from the Trans-Canada Highway at Dead Man Flat. It is located approximately 6 km south of the Highway at the head of West Wind Creek, and forms the south portal of West Wind Pass. Windtower's principal feature of interest is its steep north face which is about 450 m high and is divided by an offset gully into two sections. The eastern section is triangular in shape when viewed from the Trans-Canada Highway and is less steep. The western section overhangs for most of its height and at present is unclimbed.
Descent: The descent from Windtower to West Wind Pass is easy as the back of the mountain is a scree slope.

NORTHEAST RIDGE   5.5
B. Corbeau, G. Crocker and K. Hahn, July 1965

The northeast ridge forms the left (east) margin of the northeast face and provides a worthwhile easy route. The climbing begins to the left of the ridge at the top of a scree slope. Starting on the right side of a gully not far from the ridge, climb up and right to the ridge crest. Continue up the ridge on moderate rock to an easy-angled section. Above is a steep step. Climb the left side of the step by a steep gully to gain a small notch in a narrow section of the ridge. Above the notch climb a short steep wall (which overlooks the north face) to easier ground, and then follow the ridge to the summit of Windtower.

NORTHEAST FACE *** 530 m, 5.10a
G. Homer and R. Wood, June 1972
F.F.A: S.Dougherty, J.Sevigny and C.Yonge, June 1987

The route climbs a crack system on the right-hand side of the face. It is one of the better long climbs in the Bow Valley with mainly good rock and a lot of interesting climbing. Its length gives it an almost alpine character. At the right-hand edge of the face is a large ledge system. Walk left along this until below an obvious parallel crack system. The route starts up an obvious corner with a prominent loose flake about 40 m left of the parallel crack system. Climb up (5.7) to a ledge below the corner.

1) 45 m, 5.9. Step into the corner and go up to the loose-looking flake. Climb over this and continue on good rock to a small ledge. Follow a short crack up to a roof, step left over this and traverse left to belay in a corner.
2) 50 m, 5.8. Move up and right over a small roof to a groove. Climb the groove and continue up to a straight crack. Follow this until the rope runs out.
3) 40 m, 5.6. Continue up the crack until below a horrible, wet chimney. Belay on a large ledge.
4) 55 m, 5.10a. Step left into a corner, follow this for a few metres and then move left again over a roof. Continue up the dihedral above with increasing difficulty until a large ledge is reached.
5) 45 m, 5.9. Traverse left along the ledge for a few metres and then move up and right on sloping ledges to a flake. Climb up and left to ledges and belay on the highest ledge below an obvious dihedral.
6) 45 m, 5.9. Climb the crack in the right wall of the dihedral for 10 m, step right and climb up poor rock to a large ledge. Scramble up to belay on the left.
7) 25 m, 5.6. Climb a short crack to ledges, then trend left to below a prominent crack in the left wall of the dihedral.
8) 50 m, 5.7. Follow the crack to a belay.
9) 45 m, 5.7. Climb a short crack to ledges, traverse left to easy ground, and then scramble up and right to belay at a large, detached flake.
10) 55 m, 5.8. Go up behind the flake to a ledge (no good belays) and continue onto the large slab on the right to a scoop. Traverse right to an easy groove in the middle of the slab and then move up and right to a fixed piton. Climb down for 5 m to a niche and belay.
11) 25 m, 5.10a. Traverse easily right on a ledge until slimy rock allows access to a corner. Follow the corner until below an obvious crack to the right of a wet chimney.
12) 50 m, 5.10a. Climb the crack to a roof and step right onto a ledge. Step back left into the continuation of the crack and go up to easy ground. Easy 4th class climbing leads to the Northeast ridge which is followed to the summit (5.5).

○ *Steve DeMaio exploring the N.W. Face of Windtower, photo Jeff Marshall*

Wind Valley

NORTH BUTTRESS   350 m, 5.6/5.9
F.A. unknown

This poor route climbs the buttress left of the offset gully that divides the eastern and western sections of the north face. The line described here is that followed on a later ascent.
Scramble up to the left side of the buttress. Move up and right onto the edge and climb up (5.6) into an easy gully. Follow this to a low-angled section, then move left and climb a corner crack in two pitches (good rock, 5.9) to slabs. Continue up to the northeast ridge and follow this to the summit. Instead of moving left to the corner crack, an easier alternative is to angle up and right following a series of corners to the summit ridge.

THE RIMWALL

To the northwest of Windtower and separated from it by West Wind Pass is an unnamed peak of roughly the same elevation. The northeast face of this peak, a steep cliff some 400 m high, is called Rimwall. Only two routes have been climbed.
Approach & descent: Rimwall can be reached from the Bow Valley but it is more logical to approach from the Spray Lakes side via West Wind Pass. Descend by scree slopes to the southwest.

† PINKO   5.8
G.Homer and J.Jones, 1973

The route consists of 10 pitches up an obvious system of corners which lead up and left near the left end of the cliff. Descend scree slopes to the southwest.

THE GAMBLER   575 m, 5.11a
S.DeMaio, C.Quinn and J.Sevigny, July 1987

Start about 200 m right of Pinko, below an obvious system of corners running most of the way up the face. Scramble up to the right of the first corner for about 80 m until below a second corner.
1)   50 m, 5.7. Climb the corner and traverse left to belay.
2)   45 m, 5.9. Go up into a steep, parallel-sided groove and climb the left wall to a good ledge.
3)   40 m, 5.9. Move left and climb a right-facing corner. Continue up a second corner for 5 m and then traverse right onto a large ledge.
4)   45 m, 5.9. Move right along the ledge system to a right-facing corner. Climb the corner for 4 m and traverse left on good foot holds across the wall to a ledge. Traverse left along the ledge and climb a short off-width. Continue left and then back right to the base of a loose, left-facing corner.
5)   40 m, 5.9. From the belay, traverse back down and left and then go up into a left-facing corner. Climb the corner and continue up a second one (large ledge on right, blind left-facing corner on left) until it is possible to traverse right along a break for 10 m to a belay.

Jim Sevigny on the first ascent of ↷
The Gambler, photo Steve DeMaio

6) 50 m, 5.10c. Climb the corner to a bolt, move up and then traverse left to good holds. Continue up and left along a ramp system into a large left-facing corner. Climb the corner to a good stance.
7) 50 m, 5.10. Continue up the corner past a ledge to a second ledge below a left-facing corner.
8) 50 m, 5.10. Climb the corner for about 35 m and then traverse right along a break and continue up a second corner to a large ledge. Belay on the right.
9 & 10) 80 m, 5.4. Traverse right along the ledge until below a short, steep crack leading to a ramp.
11) 50 m, 5.11a. Climb the crack with difficulty to gain the ramp. Go up the ramp for about 10 m to good nut placements on the right below a steep wall. Make a few moves down and right and then climb the steep wall for 10m to a resting place. Continue up and right and climb a jam-crack to a ledge.
12) 45 m, 5.9. Go up and left to a loose crack. Continue up a ramp system trending left at the top to a ledge.
13) 30 m, Pull up onto a higher ledge and climb a slab to an overlap. Traverse left along the overlap until it is possible to move up over it and continue to the top.

THREE SISTERS AREA

The Three Sisters are located south of the Trans-Canada Highway just west of Dead Man Flat. Rock-climbing routes have been done on the First (Northeast) Sister and the Second (Middle) Sister, both of which are composed of Palliser limestone. An interesting excursion, yet to be completed, would be a traverse of all three peaks (in a day?).

THE FIRST SISTER

The First Sister (elevation 2700 m) is a prominent, irregular peak that is fairly steep on all sides. Two routes have been climbed.
Approach: The climbs are reached from the Trans-Canada Highway via Three Sisters Creek.
Descent can be made by down-climbing the Grassi Route, missing out the narrow summit ridge by dropping down on to the upper northwest face. Alternatively, descend southwest in loose gullies to scree ledges; below these continue down the right-hand gully and rappel a steep wall to reach the col between the First and Second Sisters.

EAST FACE   5.7
A.McKeith and C.Perry, July 1973

The route up this large and complex face follows a generally leftward-trending line with a rightward traverse at the end. Overall, the climbing is broken and lacks technical interest. Beginning at the left side of a broad, grassy slope beneath the face (easily picked out from the Trans-Canada Highway), follow a series of gullies, traverses and steep walls up and left to the base of a huge dihedral on the upper part of the face. The route goes through a small arch in this lower section. From the foot of the dihedral, make an easy traverse down and left into a broad, steep basin with a cave entrance. Climb the slabs of the basin and then the ridge on the left to reach a ledge system. Follow ledges back rightward to a large notch in the northeast ridge not far from the summit.

GRASSI ROUTE *   5.3
L.Grassi, A.W.Drinnan, M.D.Geddes, and T.B.Moffat, 1925

This climb begins on the right side of the northeast face, moves to the northwest face, and finishes up the northeast ridge. Where the north ridge steepens at a rock buttress, traverse left across the face overlooking the highway to an obvious crack and gully system. Climb slabs to gain the base of the crack and follow it past an overhang, above which it widens into a gully. The gully leads to a large ledge about 100 m above the base of the crack. Now descend a scree slope for about 45 m to a large gully on the left, which forms the general line of ascent on the northwest face. Climb slabby rock to the left to avoid an initial loose section, then continue easily up the gully to the northeast ridge. Follow this ridge past a few rock towers to the summit of the mountain.

THE SECOND SISTER

Approach: The col between the First and Second Sister can be reached either via Three Sisters Creek or from Stewart Creek to the east. Both approaches are equally tedious and take about 3 hours.

NORTH RIDGE   300 m, 5.8, A2
E.Bohren and E.Salzgeber, August 1979

This is the steep ridge rising from the col between the First and Second Sisters. The climb starts on the ridge below an initial steep section. Climb a steep slabby wall trending left (some aid moves), and then move up to a ledge. Continue up the ridge, using aid to surmount a bulge, until the easier-angled middle section is reached. Climb several easier pitches, slightly right of the ridge in places, and then move left below an overhang to the base of the upper corner. Climb the corner past a bolt (5.8) moving left at the top to easier ground. Continue up to the summit.

SHIP'S PROW

SHIP'S PROW *   470 m, 5.8, A2
L.MacKay and C.Scott, 1965

Ship's Prow is the very prominent, sharp buttress between The Three Sisters and Chinaman's Peak. It has a large, steep face on its west side which is about 400 m high. The prow itself is a fine, natural line but the climb is spoilt somewhat by poor rock and the long approach. A prominent feature, near the top, is a steep slab of grey rock undercut by overhangs. To date, this "headwall" has only been climbed using aid but free possibilities exist left of the route described here.

Approach: The best approach is via a wooded ridge which juts out in a northeasterly direction from beneath the prow. This can be reached from the Trans-Canada Highway starting just east of the Bow River bridge, or from Canmore. The latter approach is described below and takes about 3 hrs.

Park at the start of a gated dirt road on the east side of the Spray Lakes Road where it leaves Canmore and bends sharply to the right. Walk east for about 10 minutes to a clear area on the right where the cliff first comes into view. Cross over to the power line (pylon No. 20), and gain a small road which initially angles to the southwest and then resumes an easterly direction. Follow this for about 10 minutes until it crosses the dry, indistinct bed of the stream which drains the valley west of the cliff. Turn right along a road which parallels the stream bed and then contours eastwards to the start of the northeast ridge overlooking Three Sisters Creek (accessible by mountain bike to this point). Climb through open forest on the left side of the ridge and then follow its crest to the prow. Start about 100 m left of the prow below a wide, waterworn scoop. Scramble up for 25 m and belay.

The Three Sisters

1) 45 m, 5.7. Climb the scoop to a bay above a ledge. Move up with difficulty to a narrow ledge which leads left to shattered grooves. Climb these to easier ground above and continue up left to a poor belay.
2,3) 90 m. Scramble up right to an edge, cross a wide gully and move up to a bowl on the left side of a smaller buttress located below and left of a prominent roof.
4,5) 90 m, 5.1. Climb the right side of the bowl and continue up a ridge to a large ledge running out right to the prow.
6) 25 m. Walk right along the ledge and belay at a flake about 20 m before the prow.
7) 35 m, 5.5. Climb diagonally right to the prow and continue up this on good holds to a ledge.
8) 40 m, 5.8. Follow a groove system just right of the prow to a small ledge.
9) 45 m, 5.6. Gain an easy corner above and climb up to a stance directly below a thin crack on the far right-hand side of the headwall.
10) 30 m, 5.7. A2. Climb up to the crack and continue up this using a few points of aid (mainly small) to a thin horizontal crack with a fixed piton. Tension left to a hand crack, free climb up and then left to a second crack and follow this to a sentry box in a higher band of overhangs.
11) 40 m, 5.8. A2. Climb the crack above the belay using aid to start and continue up easier corners above.
12) 30 m, 5.5. Follow loose chimneys to the top.
Descend by scree slopes to the east.

CANMORE WALL

Canmore Wall is a large, flat face midway between Ship's Prow and Chinaman's Peak. It is about 350 m high. Two obvious route possibilities near the west end have been attempted but abandoned on account of poor rock.

CHINAMAN'S PEAK

The impressive north face of Chinaman's Peak is a prominent landmark in the Bow Valley near Canmore. To date, four routes have been climbed on the north face and a fifth on the northeast buttress.

Climbs described in this section are reached from the vicinity of Whiteman Pond, a small reservoir on the Spray Lakes Road, at the top of the hill overlooking Canmore. Cars may be left on the earth dam at the north end of the lake or where the road widens sufficiently as it skirts the lake's west shore.

Approach: Walk across the earth dam, climbing around a gated section, and follow a path up right through trees. After a short distance, cut up left towards the face and as the trees begin to thin locate a path which angles up right towards broken cliffs at the west end of the face. Climb scree slopes and gain a path which runs immediately beneath the face.

Descent: Descend scree slopes on the southwest side of the mountain. Bear left at the tree line and locate a trail which heads directly down the hillside on the right side of a gully. The trail leads to a bridge across the diversion canal and hence to the Spray Lakes Road. It is also possible to scramble down slabs in the bowl to the east of the peak and thus return to the base of the cliff.

NORTHEAST FACE ** 450 m, 5.6/5.7
B.Greenwood, G.Prinz, D.Raubach and W.Twerker, July 1961

The route follows the buttress between the North and Northeast Faces and provides interesting climbing in a fine situation. Two more or less independent lines have been done but the best route is a combination of the two and this is described here as the principal means of ascent. The rock is of reasonably good quality but its compact nature makes it advisable to carry a small selection of pitons. Recently, belay bolts have been added at many of the stances.

Follow the path beneath the face to a cairn on the spur beneath the buttress. Go round left and scramble up to the base of slabs.

1,2) 100 m, Climb easy 3rd and 4th class slabs to a break on the edge of the buttress (piton belay).

3) 35 m. Move left and climb an easy corner to a ledge on the right (bolt belay). Alternatively, go straight up the front of the buttress.

4) 20 m, Traverse right and climb an easy corner on the right side of a pinnacle to a bolt belay on a small platform.

5) 30 m, 5.5. Move up right and climb a shallow corner (piton) to a ledge with two belay pitons in place.

6) 50 m, 5.6. Climb up diagonally rightwards over shattered corners to a ledge below a short corner (piton, 25 m). Climb the left wall and move across right to a ledge above the corner (40 m, two bolt belay). Continue up to another ledge 7 m higher (piton belay)

7) 40 m, 5.6. Move up diagonally left to the foot of a corner. Climb the corner and continue up to a prominent band of overhangs. Move left and climb over the overhangs and up to a large ledge 5 m higher (bolt belay). This is the large ledge also reached by the left variation.

8) 45 m, 5.5. Traverse right and climb a short corner. Move round the rib and up to a ledge at the base of the upper corner (bolt and piton belay).
9-12) 130 m, 5.5. Climb the large corner system above staying mainly on the left wall. Bear left at a fork and continue up to the summit ridge (bolt and piton belays).

Left Variation:
This was the line followed on the first ascent and provides an alternative but not recommended route for the middle section of the climb.
5-7) 140 m, 5.6. From the platform at the top of pitch 4, move left and up over short slabs and cracks to a ledge about 60 m below a large, conspicuous ledge on the left side of the buttress. Bypass an overhang on the right and continue up the wall, trending left (loose rock), to gain the large ledge near its left end. Walk right to the bolt belay at the top of pitch 7 of the normal route where the ledge joins the main wall.

Right Variation:
This alternative finish traverses right below the band of overhangs above pitch 6 of the normal route, breaks through them, and climbs a prominent grey slab to the top of the mountain.
7) 50 m, 5.5. To pass the overhangs above, make a long traverse right to a small belay below a short, steep corner immediately beyond a section of slabs.
8) 55 m, 5.7. Climb the rib on the right and continue up and then slightly left to a short layback crack (The pitch may be split here). From the top of the crack, go up slabs to a big horizontal ledge.
9, 10) 75 m, 5.3. Move right to a pillar, climb halfway up it, then traverse a long way right past a crack to the base of an obvious gully.
11, 12) 100 m, 5.6. Follow the gully which narrows higher up and leads directly to the summit.

NORTH FACE ROUTE * 550 m, 5.9 (A3)
J.Firth, C.Perry and M.Sawyer, August 1976
Left Variation: D.Cheesmond and U.Kallen, July 1983
F.F.A. (by Left Variation): D.Morgan and C.Perry, August 1983

At the top left of the north face is a prominent dihedral that slants to the right. The North Face Route ascends the steep wall directly below this dihedral.
The first ascent took three days and followed a direct line involving some sections of aid. These were avoided on the second ascent by climbing an essentially free line to the left in the middle section of the face. This is now the recommended route and can be completed in one day.
Starting directly below the upper dihedral, scramble up and then right on ledges to below a right-facing groove with steep slabs on the right.
1) 50 m, 5.7. Climb up to the groove, then move up and diagonally right across the slabs to a left-facing corner high up. Follow the corner to a ledge (bolt belay).
2) 45 m, 5.7. Follow loose ramps up leftwards until below a short right-facing corner. Climb up to the corner, follow it for a few moves, then move up left into a groove. This leads left up broken rock to a ledge (bolt belay).

Chinaman's Peak

3) 30 m, 5.9. From the left end of the ledge climb a steep, shallow groove for about 10 m to an overhang. Traverse steeply right to a corner (piton) and climb this for about 6 m, then move right to a shallow groove. Follow the groove to a small ledge with a bolt belay.

4) 30 m, 5.9. Climb the steep wall above the ledge and then make a long, horizontal traverse left to a groove. Climb a bulge in the groove to a belay ledge on the left.

5) 45 m, 5.7. Follow the corner system above to a good ledge.

Left Variation:

6) 20 m, 5.9. Move across to the far left end of the ledge and make a difficult traverse left beneath an overhang (usually wet).

7) 20 m, 5.7. Climb up and then left to the base of a corner.

8) 45 m, 5.9. Climb to the top of the corner to small ledges on the left.

9) 45 m, 5.9. Move right and climb a steep wall to a shallow corner (piton). Follow the corner for a short distance, then climb left and up to a good ledge. Continue to a large ledge higher up.

10) 50 m, 5.7. Make a long traverse down and right, then climb slabs to a ledge (junction with the original route).

11) 30 m, 5.7. Climb the steep corner above the ledge to the base of the upper dihedral.

12-15) 140 m, 5.5. Climb slabs and corners on the right side of the dihedral, finishing well out on the right.

Original Route:

6) 50 m, 5.8 (A3). Move left and up for about 10 m then traverse back right to a small niche (bolt) almost directly above the belay. Climb a faint crack using aid to reach a steep slab above an overhang (3 bolts, 15-20 pitons-mainly small). Free climb up and then right to a ledge below a large corner.

7) 35 m, 5.8 (A2). Follow a short bolt ladder up right to a thin crack. Climb the crack using aid (2 pitons), then follow a groove which slants back left to the main corner. (It may be possible to free climb the corner directly to this point.)

8) 20 m, 5.8. Climb the overhang on its right side (3 bolts for aid) and continue up slabs to a belay in the corner.

9) 45 m, 5.8. Traverse right and up for 15-20 m, then climb a steep corner to a break. Follow the break back left to a good ledge above slabs, left of the main corner. (Start of pitch 11)

Jeff Marshall on the first ascent of ⇨
Remembrance Wall, photo Steve DeMaio

Chinaman's Peak

REMEMBRANCE WALL *   555 m, 5.11a A3
S.DeMaio and J.Marshall, July 1987
The route attempts to climb a major line right of the North Face Route but is forced left onto that route near the top by large overhangs. The rock is variable but often excellent and the climb is reportedly very worthwhile. It is named in memory of D.Cheesmond, I.Bolt, D.Guthrie and D.Monroe, all of whom died in the mountains in 1987.
Scramble up for 10 m to a ledge below a small, right-facing corner.
1)   45 m, 5.6. Climb the corner for 5 m, move left and continue up a second corner to a large ledge. Traverse left to a bolt and piton belay.
2)   55 m, 5.10a. Continue left along the ledge and climb a right-facing corner until it is possible to break out onto the steep left wall on good holds (piton). Climb steeply up and left to gain a slab (piton) and go up this trending right past a large spike to a belay in slings (thread).
3)   45 m, 5.8. Climb moderate ground up and right over two short walls and then move back left to a piton belay below a right-facing corner.
4)   45 m, 5.10a. Climb the corner until a traverse right can be made across the wall to a ledge. Move right along the ledge to a groove and go up this to a short corner. Above the corner climb the right side of a pinnacle to a bolt belay.
5)   50 m, 5.10c A3. Climb the corner to a break, move left with difficulty using 3 points of aid, and continue up the corner to a bolt belay.
6)   45 m, 5.11a. Climb the corner on excellent rock to a belay on the right.
7)   35 m, 5.10c. Continue to the top of the corner and then go up to a bolt below a break in the overhangs. Move up and right and climb a short right-facing corner to a traverse line leading left to a bolt belay.
8)   45 m, 5.9. Make a long traverse left on excellent rock following the lower of two parallel cracks.
9)   50 m, 5.9. Continue left and climb a right-facing corner and a chimney above to gain the upper dihedral of the North Face Route.
10-12)   140 m, 5.5. Climb slabs and corners on the right side of the dihedral, finishing well out on the right.

PREMATURE EJACULATION ***   400 m, 5.10b
D.Cheesmond and B.Gross, July 1985
This superb route climbs the left-hand of the two prominent dihedrals on the right side of the north face. The climbing is sustained and the rock is mainly excellent.
Scramble up the corner for 30 m to a ledge.
1)   40 m, 5.8. Climb the corner to a large ledge with a small cave.
2)   50 m, 5.10a. Continue up the corner with increasing difficulty to a ledge 5 m below an overlap.
3)   40 m, 5.8. Climb up to the overlap and step right to a piton. Continue straight up into a corner and belay at a faint break leading rightwards across a slab.
4)   45 m, 5.8. Traverse along the break to a corner system and climb this to a belay below a steep groove.

5) 35 m, 5.8. Climb a short way up the groove and step right onto the arete. Continue up broken ledges to the highest ledge on the right.
6) 50 m, 5.10a. Climb the right-hand of two shallow grooves to detached blocks and then traverse left on good holds to a ledge (bolt). Go up to another ledge and climb the loose wall above to a break. Traverse right and up to a small ledge immediately below large roofs.
7) 50 m, 5.10b. Traverse left below the roof (bolt) and make a tricky step onto a slab. Climb up to an obvious dihedral and go up this to a piton belay on the left (piton).
8) 50 m, 5.8. Move right and up to the top left corner of a grey slab. Traverse across the top of the slab to a ledge and then go straight up into a corner on surprising holds in an awesome position. Belay partway up the corner.
9) 40 m, 5.9. Continue up the corner to the top.

QUICK RELEASE ** (& FINISHING TOUCH) ***   375 m, 5.9/5.10a
J.Bauer and T.Jones, July 1976
Direct finish (Finishing Touch) and F.F.A: B.Gross, B.Baxter and C.Quinn, July 1985

Quick Release follows the right-hand of the two prominent dihedrals until a steep section is reached at about two thirds height. A traverse right is then made to gain an easy right-slanting exit line. Finishing Touch is a direct finish which continues to the top of the dihedral. The rock is generally very good, and both climbs, particularly the direct finish, are sustained and well worthwhile.

Climb easily up the right side of the dihedral to a ledge. Continue for 15 m to a higher ledge and belay in the corner (bolt).
1) 35 m, 5.8. Climb the corner to an overhang, traverse right on a ledge and make a difficult step up onto the wall. Climb the wall (piton), then move back to the corner and follow it to a bolt and piton belay.
2) 40 m, 5.9. Climb the corner with increasing difficulty past an overhang and then up more easily to a ledge (bolt belay).
3) 20 m, 5.7. Move up right on a slab and climb an overhang formed by wedged blocks to a terrace (bolt belay).
4) 45 m, 5.8. Climb the short groove on the right and then move diagonally left into the main corner. Go up for a short distance and move across left to ledges. Continue up for about 12 m to below a short right-facing corner. Traverse left 3-4 m on a small ledge, then climb up steeply to a bolt belay at the bottom of a long corner.
5) 40 m, 5.9. Climb the corner to a blocky ledge on the left.

Original Finish:
6) 45 m, 5.7. Go up right to a terrace and walk right along this to the end. Move up over a bulge and belay in a small bay.
7-9) 130 m, 5.5. Continue up by a groove, then exit rightwards to gain sight of the top. Continue up and right on easy rock to the ridge.

Chinaman's Peak

FINISHING TOUCH:
6) 45 m, 5.9. From the left side of the ledge, climb a groove for 10 m then move left on to the wall. Work up and right over bulges and then traverse left to a small stance with a bolt.
7) 55 m, 5.10a. Climb up and right past a bolt to a groove. Follow the groove to the main corner and either split the pitch here or continue up the corner to a good ledge.
8) 45 m, 5.9. Climb the corner to the upper roof.
9) 50 m, 5.6. Climb out right past the roof and continue on easy ground to the ridge.

Mitch Thornton on pitch 2 of Quick Release, photo Tom Fayle

MOUNT RUNDLE

The Palliser Formation outcrops along the northeast side of Mount Rundle in a series of buttresses that extend from Canmore almost as far as Banff. They are referred to by number, starting the count at Canmore. The first buttress, or EEOR (East End Of Rundle), is a popular climbing area but the others are seldom visited. Also included under this heading are the lesser cliffs of Grassi Lakes, Whiteman Grag and Kanga Crag.

Approach: All the climbs described in this section, with the exception of The Numbered Buttresses, are reached from the vicinity of Whiteman Pond, a small reservoir on the Spray Lakes Road, at the top of the hill overlooking Canmore. Cars may be left on the earth dam at the north end of the lake or where the road widens sufficiently as it skirts the lake's west shore.

GRASSI LAKES

A number of small cliffs are located close to Grassi Lakes. However, most of the rock could be fairly described as appalling and despite the attractive setting, very little climbing has been done.

Approach: Grassi Lakes can be approached from below via the Grassi Lakes hiking trail, or from above starting at Whiteman Pond.

A small, pockmarked cliff situated immediately above the second (upper) lake on the left or southeast side has two routes, both of which climb a steep wall just left of a rotten corner and end a short distance below the top at a two bolt belay.

GARDENER'S QUESTION TIME ** 17 m, 5.10a
D.Morgan and B.Morgan, 1986

This well-protected and enjoyable route climbs the steep wall on pockets past threads and bolts directly to the belay.

MUD GETS IN YOUR EYES 20 m, 5.9
D.Morgan and B.Morgan, 1986

Start in the corner and follow a rising break up left past bolts and threads to the belay.

Note: A climb has been done on the steep wall above and right (west) of the second lake (80 m, 5.6). It follows the second, fainter traverse line up and right across the wall to a belay and then climbs up to ledges. The rock is poor and the climb is unjustifiable since any rocks dislodged fall directly onto the hiking path below and climbers cannot be seen when higher up on the route.

Mount Rundle

Two climbs have been done in the upper gorge above the second lake. They are on the northwest side of the gorge, a short distance beyond some Indian paintings on a large boulder.

† WHITE IMPERIALIST   20 m, 5.10c
J.Buszowski and party, 1986

Start below a white-streaked wall leading up to overhangs. Climb up trending left past fixed pitons and bolts to the overhangs. Continue over the overhangs to fixed anchors.

† RED MENACE   20 m, 5.10d
J.Buszowski and party, 1986

Climb the wall immediately right of White Imperialist. Runout - grade uncertain.

WHITEMAN CRAG

Whiteman Crag is situated at the south end of Whiteman Pond, just above the road. The rock is generally quite poor but the ease of access has made some of the routes quite popular and these have improved considerably with traffic. Die Young, Stay Pretty is probably the best route on the crag and South Corner is a worthwhile easier climb.

PUSHING FORTY   95 m, 5.8
J.Blench and B.Elkin, July 1983

The route follows the ridge at the left end of the crag and is mainly straightforward except for one short but poorly protected section of 5.8. Start just above the base of the ridge on the right in a scree gully.
1) 30 m, 5.5. Move out left to a groove which leads up to the edge of the ridge (piton). Continue up grooves to a belay in a scoop on the right, below and left of two triangular overhangs.
2) 10 m, 5.4. Climb the groove between the overhangs to a ledge.
3) 25 m, 5.8. Scramble down ledges to the left for about 10 m and climb a steep slab, trending left just before the end of the wall. Belay on the large ledge above.
4) 30 m, 5.6. Move back to the ridge and climb up to an overhang. Bypass this on the right and continue up a crack to large ledges.
Either scramble down ledges on the left and descend to the base or climb two easy pitches to the top and then descend to the left.

SOUTH CORNER *   50 m, 5.7
T. Auger and J. Blench, July 1983
This is the obvious corner between the wall on the right side of the ridge and the main face.
1) 30 m, 5.5. Move out left from the base of the corner and climb up to a wide crack. Follow this back right to rejoin the corner, and belay on a small ledge about 5 m below the large roof.
1a) 25 m, 5.7. Climb directly up the corner.
2) 20 m, 5.7. Climb up to the roof, traverse right, and continue up a corner to ledges on the left.
Descend as for Pushing Forty.

† LIVE NOW, PAY LATER   95 m, 5.9
J.Blench and D.Congdon, June 1983
Start below a steep corner just right of the previous route.
1) 50 m, 5.8. Climb the right wall of the corner (pitons) to small ledges on the right. These may also be reached by climbing the groove which slants up left from near the start of Original Route. Continue right and up on easier ground to a small belay below a prominent roof.
2) 25 m, 5.9. Climb up left to a break on the left side of the roof (piton) and move up with difficulty past a second piton to ledges above.
2a) It is possible to split pitch 1 at the top of the corner and then climb the groove on the left which leads directly to the break in the roofs. However this is loose and not well protected.
3) 20 m, 5.7. Move right and climb the wall to the top.

ORIGINAL ROUTE *   80 m 5.7
B. Greenwood and party.
Start at the right side of a small pillar to the left of an overhung bay.
1) 30 m, 5.7. Climb to the top of the pillar and continue up a steep crack on the right. Climb past a block and into a short groove. At the top of the groove, traverse right and down to a scoop. Cross the scoop and move up and right to a bolt and flake belay.
1a) The scoop near the top of pitch 1 may be reached by climbing directly out of the overhung bay to the right of the normal start. *(5.10. R. Mitten, 1979.)*
2) 25 m. Climb a short, easy pitch to a belay level with a horizontal break leading left below roofs.
3) 25 m, 5.7. Climb up left into an open corner slanting left and follow this to ledges round the edge of the buttress.

DIE YOUNG, STAY PRETTY **   75 m, 5.10a
S. Scott and M. Sawyer, July 1979
From the top of pitch 1 of Original Route, Die Young, Stay Pretty climbs the wall on the left and exits up a steep technical corner.
1) 30 m, 5.7. Pitch 1 of Original Route.
2) 45 m, 5.10a. Move out left and climb the slabby wall to a bolt (the pitch may be split here). Continue up left to the base of the corner and climb it with difficulty to the ledges at the top of Original Route.

Mount Rundle

COUSIN SCHLOMO'S REVENGE   100 m, 5.7
I. Witten, A. Savannah, S. Greenberg and Anon.

This route begins in the right-hand of two broken corners in the rounded buttress right of the overhung bay. In the words of the first ascensionists, one of whom requested anonymity, "Schlomo suffered for 2000 years - this is his revenge!"

1) 45 m. Move up left on easy ground and then climb a steep slab to gain a crack on the right. Follow this through a break in the overhangs to a ledge.

1a) The broken corner and chimney on the left can be climbed to reach the ledge at the top of pitch 1.

2) 35 m. Move right and climb a shallow corner to a large treed ledge on the left.

3) 20 m, 5.7. Follow the obvious groove on the left to the top.

STUDENT'S ROUTE   95 m, 5.8
J Blench and K. Klassen, July 1982

To the right of the rounded buttress is a prominent roof at about one third height. Start in a wide corner directly below this.

1) 30 m, 5.6. Climb the slab on the left of the corner past a fixed bolt and piton anchor to the roof. Move left to a belay near the end of the roof.

2,3) 65 m, 5.8. Diagonal up left following a faint groove system.

THINGS ARE ROOF ALL OVER   75 m, 5.9
G. Powter and S. Wood, June 1983

Climbs the right side of the roof on Student's Route and continues directly up the face.

1) 25 m, 5.6. Climb the first pitch of Student's Route and belay immediately below the roof.

2) 50 m, 5.9. Gain a finger crack which traverses right across somewhat loose flakes under the roof (piton) and go right until a good crack is reached. Climb the crack and then move left and continue up a groove system to the top.

RAT TRAP   45 m, 5.9
J.Kaandrop and S.DeMaio, July 1985

At the far right-hand end of the crag is a large, left-slanting corner. Rat Trap climbs the left-hand of two cracks in the right wall.

1) 20 m. Climb the crack to a ledge.

2) 25 m. Climb the left-slanting corner/ramp above.

Mount Rundle

KANGA CRAG

This is a steep, relatively featureless cliff situated between Whiteman Crag and EEOR. The one route recorded to date climbs an unusual, slender flake located in the centre of the face and continues up the steep wall to the top.
Approach: From the dam, walk a short distance south along the road and then follow an open valley leading directly to the base of the cliff.
Descent: Scramble up through trees to join the alternate descent route from EEOR which leads steeply down right to the main path below the cliffs.

CALIFORNIA DREAMING **   125 m, 5.10b
D. Morgan and C. Perry, August 1983
The first pitch to the top of the flake makes an interesting short climb since the belay bolts can be used for rappel. The remainder of the climb is loose in places but could clean up well with use. Start about 15 m right of the flake below a shattered crack.
1) 45 m, 5.10b. Climb the crack for about 12 m and then go left to a bolt. Step down left and make a hard move over an overlap to reach a hand traverse leading left to the crack on the right side of the flake. Climb the crack to a bolt belay at the top of the flake.
2) 30 m, 5.8. Move up and right to a rotten groove and climb this (piton) to easier ground. Follow a series of good holds diagonally right across the wall to an overhang below a short, left-facing corner. Climb the corner and continue up shattered rock on the left until it is possible to move right round an arete to ledges and a bolt belay.
3) 50 m, 5.9. Climb the groove above the belay and move up left with difficulty to ledges. Continue up the wall, trending back right slightly, to a bolt. Make a long traverse right to a second bolt below and left of an overhang which caps a prominent chimney on the right. Move up and hand traverse right into the chimney. Climb the overhang and continue up and left to trees.

Mount Rundle

5) 40 m, 5.7. Climb to the top of the pillar and continue up the steep wall to a slabby corner which leads up right to ledges. Belay by a small tree on the far right (bolts).
6) 20 m, 5.7. Climb slabs above the belay to a corner and follow this to a ledge below a second corner (bolt and piton belay).
7) 30 m, 5.8. Climb the corner for about 5 m and then traverse right across the slab and make a hard move right into a groove. Continue up to a ledge and then go diagonally right up a groove to a bolt belay at a second ledge.
8) 30 m, 5.8. Follow a slabby ramp up and left below bulges and then climb straight up on solution pockets to the ledge at the base of the headwall (difficult to protect).
8a) 50 m, 5.6. Move right and climb up relatively easily to a ledge system leading back left below the headwall (bolt belay).
Descent: Walk left down a large ledge into the gully. Downclimb the gully moving well out on the south side near the bottom and making two rappels.

REPROBATE *** 465 m, 5.7, A1 or 5.9 free

B. Greenwood, J. Horne, R. Wood and O. Woolcock, 1971
F.F.A: J. Horne and M. White, 1974

Reprobate climbs the large dihedral prominent in the upper section of the face near the south end. The route has a well deserved reputation as one of the best long climbs in the valley since the climbing is sustained (at 5.7), and the rock is generally very good.
Start immediately below the upper dihedral in a chimney on the left side of a 100 m high pinnacle.
1-3) 110 m, 5.5. Climb the chimney and the gully above to a large scree ledge.
4) 15 m. Follow an easy groove up left to a higher ledge, and belay on the left by a small corner.
5) 25 m, 5.7. Make a few moves up the corner, move right and climb to the top of a small pinnacle via its right side. Move up left across slabs to a short groove, and continue up and left to a small ledge at the base of a large, open corner.
6) 40 m, 5.6. Follow the corner for a few metres and then traverse easily left across the wall to a small groove around the arete. Climb the groove until it steepens, then move left and climb a slab to a belay in a corner.
7) 25 m, 5.7. Continue up the corner past an awkward narrow section, then move out left and up to belay.
8) 45 m, 5.7. Climb a narrow ramp until it is possible to move down and right to rejoin the main corner (This point may be reached directly (5.8) by continuing up the corner and not moving out left on pitch 7). Traverse across the slabby right wall of the corner on a good ledge, and continue across rightwards to an easy corner. Follow this to a belay below a steep chimney/crack. (Instead of traversing back into the main corner, it is possible to continue up directly above the narrow ramp, and follow a slabby corner up and right to the top of pitch 9).
9) 30 m, 5.7. Climb the crack and the chimney above to a large ledge.

10) 35 m. Move up into a steep alcove below the start of the upper corner. Either climb the right wall using three fixed pitons for aid (5.7 and A1), free climb directly into the corner (5.9), or free climb past the pitons (5.10c). Continue up the corner on superb rock to a small belay on the right (pitons).
11) 30 m, 5.6. Climb over bulges and slabs trending rightwards to a good ledge under a small overhang.
12) 35 m, 5.6. Move left for about 10 m and climb an inside corner to easy ground.
13,14) 70 m, 5.6. Go up and right to a tree (2-bolt belay), then follow a series of breaks left of a gully through steeper sections to the top.

Original Finish   130 m, 5.7
This variant continues up the large dihedral above pitch 10 and was the route followed on the first ascent. It is reportedly better than the route described above.
11) 20 m, 5.7. Continue up the corner and belay at the first good stance.
12) 40 m, 5.7. Climb the groove above and belay in a broken section.
13 & 14) 60 m, 5.7/5.8. Continue direcrly up the corner to the top.
13 & 14 alt) 70 m, 5.7. Traverse right and up easy broken rock to the base of a solid band. Climb through this via a corner to the top.

Left-hand Finish   160 m, 5.9.
C.Quinn and C.Perry, August 1985

This variant climbs the steep corner on the left side of the upper dihedral. Near the top of pitch 9, move left and down slightly to belay on small, sloping ledges by cracked blocks.
10) 25 m, 5.9. Move up into a short corner capped by a roof, then traverse steeply left to a small ledge. Climb up and slightly left to a fixed piton, then traverse left and up to a ledge below a short finger crack. Climb the crack and belay below a long corner.
11,12) 90 m, 5.7. Climb the corner on mainly excellent rock to ledges below the steep upper section.
13) 45 m, 5.9. Continue up the corner, then move right and up round a bulge. Go up left to a small ledge, then climb over a bulge into a steep groove which is followed to the top.

QUASAR   410 m, 5.9
A.McKeith and C.Calvert, July 1972

Quasar follows an indistinct line of corners on the slabby face to the right of Reprobate. Generally, the climbing lacks interest except for the upper traverse, hence Bugs McKeith's tongue-in-cheek reference to its "astronomical importance".
Start by a small cave directly below a prominent tree on a large ledge about 60 m higher.
1) 25 m. Move right and climb a loose corner to a block belay on the right.
2) 35 m, 5.6. Move up right and then climb a short wall on the left to reach a groove. Climb the groove and then move left to belay on the large ledge at the tree.

Mount Rundle

3) 55 m. Walk left and climb an easy gully to ledges at the top of a pillar.
4,5) 55 m, 5.6. Move up left and climb a steep V-groove. Continue up a corner to a band of overhangs.
6) 20 m, 5.5. Traverse easily left until a break is reached that leads to the upper part of the face.
7-10) 100 m, 5.6/5.7. Follow corners and cracks until the face steepens and becomes blank.
11) 35 m, 5.8. From ledges on the left, follow a faint traverse line left across a steep slab to a right-facing corner. Belay in the corner below a roof.
12) 25 m, 5.9. Climb the roof (piton), and continue up easy ground.
13,14) 60 m. Continue without difficulty to join the right-hand finish of Reprobate and follow that route to the top.

EEYORE'S TAIL ** 310 m, 5.8
R.Nelson and B.Stark, September 1977

Between Quasar and Guides' Route are two spectacular cracks set close together in the top half of the face. Eeyore's Tail climbs the left-hand crack and offers some interesting climbing on generally good rock.
Start directly below the upper crack and scramble up for 40 m to a bolt belay at the top of a prominent buttress.
1) 30 m, 5.7. Climb straight up the break above the belay and continue up a corner (bolt runner). Climb diagonally left over a delicate section to a good ledge and two bolt belay.
2) 50 m, 5.7. Traverse back diagonally right into the corner and follow it to a ledge below a steep section. Move left and climb easier rock up and back right to a bolt belay.
3) 25 m, 5.7. Climb the shattered corner above, moving out right higher up then back left to a bolt belay below a steep vegetated dihedral.
4) 40 m, 5.8. Climb the dihedral. At the top diagonal up left to a sentry box (piton). Follow an awkward diagonal break up and right to a two bolt belay.
5) 35 m, 5.8. Following an obvious flake system, climb straight up the steep wall above to a ledge and a two bolt belay.
6) 30 m, 5.8. Make a delicate rising traverse right into the final chimney and belay about 30 m below the large roof (bolt belay).
7) 40 m, 5.7. Continue up the chimney past the large roof (loose rock) and belay in the gully above (bolt belay).
8) 30 m. Scramble up the gully to a chimney blocked by large chockstones.
9) 30 m, 5.4. Climb the back of the chimney to easy ground.
7-9 alt) 110 m, 5.9. Climb the chimney until a narrow ledge leads out left to an edge. Move left with difficulty into a steep corner and climb this to ledges. Continue more easily to the top.

Mount Rundle

GUIDES' ROUTE ** 655 m, 5.6
A.Cole, C.Locke and L.MacKay, 1970

Guides' Route follows the leftmost of three right-slanting ramps. Much of the climbing is lower fifth class and only in a few locations, principally towards the top, are there areas of technical interest. Nonetheless, the route is justifiably popular since it follows a good, natural line and is reasonably solid. Rockfall by snowmelt or other climbers, however, can be a problem.

There are many possible alternatives in the detail of the route, and a typical pitch-by-pitch description with the major variations is given below. Start at a small gully just to the right of a spur, below and left of the upper dihedral.

1) 45 m. Climb the chimney and follow the first left fork to a block belay on a shattered ledge below a corner.

2) 25 m. Move left round a rib and climb an easier corner to a second block belay.

3) 40 m. Angle right up slabs to large scree ledges. Belay at a tree high up on the right.

1-3 alt) Instead of the start described above, the gully on the left, at the highest point in the scree slopes, can be followed up right to the top of pitch 3.

4) 40 m. Move back down and follow ledges rightwards to a large, easy-angled corner which slants up to the right. Belay partway up the corner.

5) 40 m. Continue to the top of the corner and move up and right following easy corners and ledges to a flake belay at the end.

6) 35 m, 5.5. Climb a short wall to a corner and continue up this to a chimney. Move right at the top of the chimney and climb an awkward wall to ledges. Alternately, the scoop on the left above the ledges can be climbed.

5,6 alt) From partway up pitch 5, the wall on the left can be climbed and a raising traverse made to the right to the belay near the top of pitch 6.

7,8) 80 m. Continue up right towards a prominent chimney following easy slabs and corners to a large ledge system.

9) 40 m. Walk right along the ledge to a point almost directly below the chimney and then move up to a belay.

10) 35 m. Traverse left and climb easy grooves to a small belay.

11) 40 m. Continue up the groove above to a right-angled corner. Climb this and trend up left at the top to a belay about 30 m right of the upper dihedral.

12) 45 m. Climb up diagonally rightwards to reach a long narrow ledge with trees. This ledge is a prominent feature of the upper wall.

9-12 alt) A more difficult alternative begins further left on the ledge system, climbs a steep slab trending left towards the main corner, then continues up and right to the treed ledge.

13) 35 m, 5.6. From a belay further right on the ledge below two right-slanting cracks, move up left into a steep scoop (piton runners in place), and climb this exiting left. Continue up left on easier ground, moving back right to belay. **Note:** an incorrect line leads up right from the top of the scoop.

14) 40 m. Follow an easy crack system up right for about 20 m and then step down and traverse right on small ledges. Climb up easily to a belay in a large slabby corner.
15) 35 m. Traverse right across on scree ledges and climb the left side of a 10 m pillar (pitons) to a belay at the base of a shallow chimney.
16) 35 m, 5.6. Climb the chimney which is awkward at first, to a piton belay.
17) 35 m. Continue to the top.

MISGUIDED VARIATION   150 m, 5.7
D. Pauls and P. Stoliker, Sept 1985

This route climbs the wall left of the huge right-facing corner left of the top third of Guides' Route. Approach via Guides' Route and gain a scree ledge 25 m left of 2 small trees at the base of the huge corner, below a prominent crack and overhanging corner.
1) 45 m, 5.7 Climb over a bulge and move left onto a scree ledge. Walk along the ledge for 15 m and climb a short wall to a ledge and ramp system. Belay in the ramp.
2) 50 m, 5.6 Continue to the top of the ramp and around a corner. Climb grooves right of the main corner on the left.
3) 50 m, 5.6 Climb up to an obvious break in the wall above and pull over a flake wedged in the corner. Climb up and then left to a sloping ledge. Belay at a short corner at the left end of the ledge.
4) 17 m Stem up the corner and continue over loose rock to the top.

BALZAC   450 m, 5.8
U.Kallen and M.Toft, May 1972
F.F.A: J.Martin and C.Perry, August 1979

Balzac climbs the centre of the three right-slanting ramps. Only the first few pitches are difficult and much of the route consists of easy scrambling. Start below a shallow corner just left of a rib, right of which is an area of steep yellow rock.
Scramble up to a ledge below and left of the corner.
1,2) 70 m, 5.7. Climb the corner which slants right at first and then trends left to large ledges.
3) 35 m, 5.6. From the top centre of the ledges, follow an obvious groove which slants up right. Belay below a steep wall.
4) 25 m, 5.8. Climb the right-hand of two steep cracks, and continue up a groove to the top of a block.
5) 35 m, 5.8. Move right to a steep slab and climb up to a wall. Traverse right, then move up past two bolts to easier ground.
5a) 35 m, 5.8. Traverse left from the belay and climb a slabby wall to a steep section. Follow a short, difficult groove up left, and then move back right on easier rock.
The climbing above is much easier and trends up right over broken rock to a tree at the base of a big slanting corner. The first ascent party now traversed right past a gully and climbed a second gully which diminishes to a crack. Above this a rib was followed to the top. A more direct alternative leads up a short steep section above the tree (5.7) to slabs which can be third-classed (isolated 5.5 moves) on sound rock to reach the rib and hence the top.

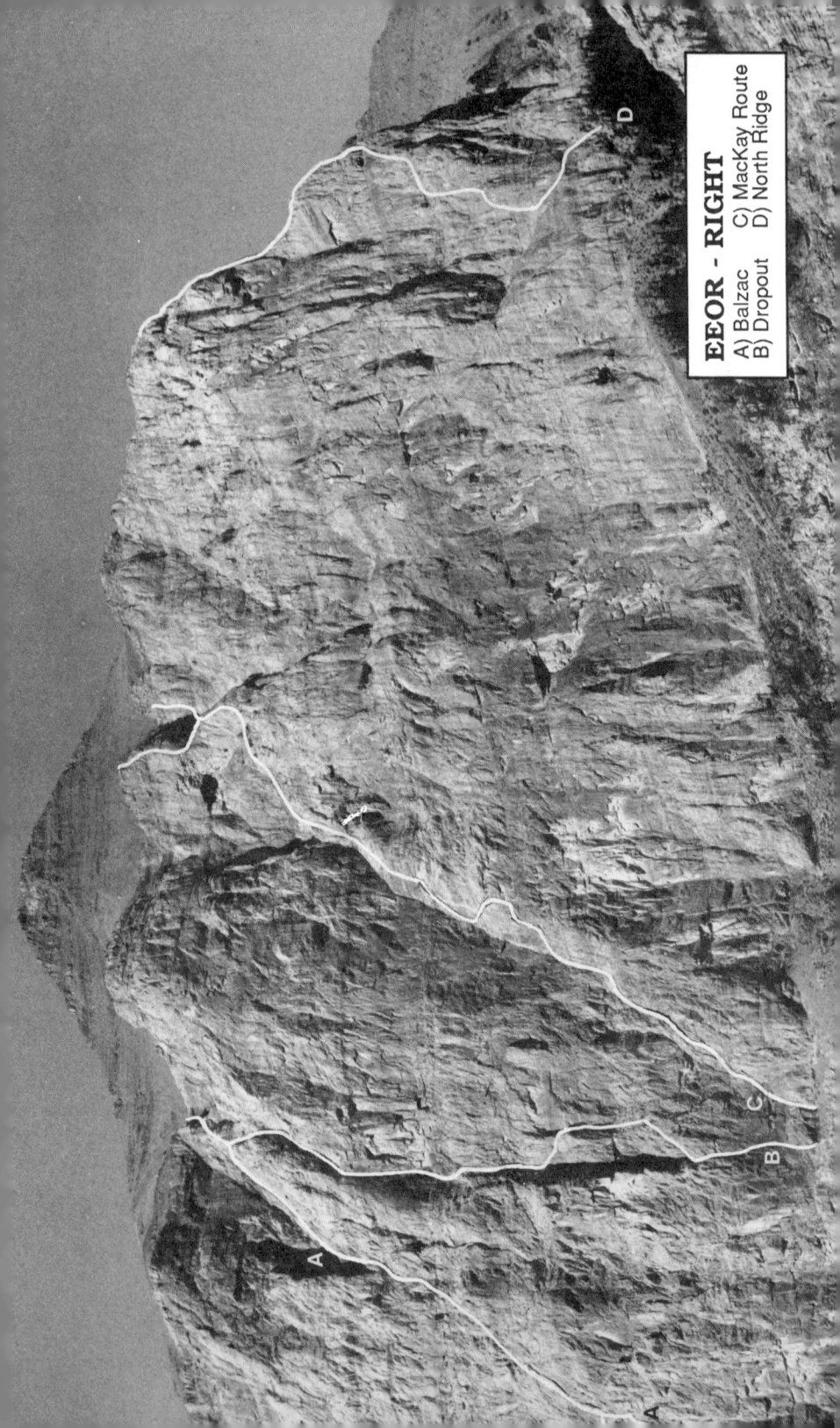

Mount Rundle

DROPOUT *** 450 m, 5.9.
C. Perry and M. White, September 1982

This excellent route climbs good waterworn rock in a large corner system just left of the MacKay Route. However, it is usually wet until midsummer. Climb easy rock for about 15 m to the base of the corner.

1) 30 m, 5.8. Climb the corner to a ledge on the left (old bolt). Continue past a small roof to a second ledge on the left.
2) 30 m, 5.9. Climb the corner above, then move left with difficulty around a roof. Continue to a second roof and then step down and left to easier ground. Belay on ledges a little higher.
3) 45 m, 5.6. After following the corner for a few metres, move up right on easy ground to the right of two short corners. Climb this and continue up the wall to the right to ledges. Traverse right past a shattered block and climb a short corner to broken ledges.
4) 35 m, 5.8. Climb the corner above (this is about 35 m right of the main corner), to a small stance in a steep bay.
5) 35 m, 5.6. Climb up left to the arete and make a long traverse left back to the main corner.
6) 20 m. Follow the corner to a large overhang.
7) 45 m, 5.7. Climb round the overhang and continue up the corner until a traverse left can be made onto smooth slabs below the upper chimney. Climb the right side of the slabs to a ledge about 10 m below and right of the chimney.
8) 10 m, 5.6. Climb the slabby wall to a ledge at the base of the chimney.
9) 40 m, 5.9. The chimney is loose and awkward near the bottom but improves higher up. The crux section round the upper bulge is long but surprisingly well protected. Belay in a cave near the top of the chimney.
10) 45 m, 5.8. Climb the short top section of the chimney and belay high up in an easy bowl.
11) 35 m, 5.6. At the top of the bowl, a hidden ramp leads up left to a ridge (junction with Balzac).
12,13) 60 m. Continue up the ridge to the top.

MACKAY ROUTE   490 m, 5.10a or 5.8, A1
L.MacKay, D.Vockeroth and J.White, 1972
Right Variation: C.Perry and J.Martin, 1981
F.F.A (by right variation): R.Lanthier and party, 1986

The MacKay route follows the right-hand of the three right-slanting ramps. It is named for Lloyd MacKay who pioneered several of the best rock climbs established in the Bow Valley during the 1960's and early 1970's.

Pitches 6 and 7, as described here, deviate right from the original line and are now the normal means of ascent. Several unsuccessful attempts have been made to free climb the original route, a steep, layback crack.

1-5) 150 m. Climb an obvious line of corners and ramps trending up to the right. Pitch 5 is 5.7; the others are easier. Belay from bolts at the base of a slab, above which is a steep section.

Mount Rundle

6) 40 m, 5.10a. Trend right up the slab almost to the steep wall, then make a few moves back left up a short ramp. Starting right of a fixed piton, climb the steep wall past a second fixed piton to gain a short groove. Hand traverse right to easier ground and climb up to a good ledge.
7) 35 m, 5.7. Climb a steep crack to slabs, and work back left into the main corner (poor protection).
6,7 alt) 5.8 A1. Climb the main corner directly, mixed free and aid.
8) 35 m, 5.6. Continue up a steep, rotten groove just right of the corner and belay up and to the right on slabs.
9-11) Traverse right, then climb moderate slabs, cracks and corners more or less straight up to gain a huge scree ledge below the steep upper wall.
12-14) Walk and scramble right on the ledge to its end. Climb a short face to an easy arete and follow this to a final steep wall. Walk right on a ledge into a wide, steep gully.
15) Climb a steep, broken exit crack (5.6) on the right side of the gully, to easy ground.
14,15 alt) 5.10a. Instead of moving right into the gully, climb a crack in the final wall 7-8 m left of the arete.

NORTH RIDGE   400 m, 5.7
C.Scott and D.Smith, June 1972

(Line on photo unverified).
This route starts a short distance left (south) of EEOR's north ridge and climbs several pitches before finishing up the ridge itself. The rock is not very sound in some sections but is excellent on the crux pitch.
Start about 40 m left of the ridge and angle up left over 3rd and 4th class rock for about 60 m. Climb a chimney/corner on the right side of a broad gully, and continue more easily trending right towards the ridge. Follow a steep corner (5.6), then edge right again and climb a corner next to the ridge. Follow a crack which angles right around the ridge, and continue on easy ground to a shallow notch.
Above the notch is a steep tower that constitutes the crux of the climb. Climb a crack in the tower for about 15 m to an overhang, then make a thin traverse right to easier ground (5.7). Continue up and right past a poorly protected 5.6 pitch, above which easier climbing leads to the top of the ridge.

Mount Rundle

THE NUMBERED BUTTRESSES

Long approaches and a general belief that the rock is poor have limited the amount of climbing on these impressive buttresses. However, improved access and the many possibilities for new routes (some good rock seems likely) is sure to lead to a renewed interest in the area.

Approach: The buttress count begins at EEOR and the second buttress is located immediately west of that cliff. The best approach for the Second Buttress is from the Spray Lakes road. Follow an open break up and right through trees to the ridge that descends from the north end of EEOR. Go up the ridge to a rockband, traverse right below it, and then climb easy ledges to gain the gully above. Follow a side gully up right to the base of the second buttress.

The third, fourth and fifth buttresses are best reached from a good trail, accessible by mountain bike, which now runs between the Canmore Nordic Centre on the Spray Lakes road and Banff.

Second Buttress

THE NORTH RIDGE 5.7
L.MacKay and D.Vockeroth, July 1968

The second buttress is characterized by a relatively sharp ridge leading to a thumb-like summit. The route up the north ridge has been climbed only once and the original description, on which this one is based, is very vague.

Start in an easy gully system about 60 m left of the north ridge. Climb about 150 m of third class rock, keeping right at a fork in the gully and heading for a point on the ridge just left of a prominent notch. Reach the ridge 10 m up from the notch below a huge yellow roof.

1,2) 60 m, 5.5. Climb up and traverse left about 25 m below the roof to an inside corner and follow this to its top.

3-5) 90 m. Climb up slabs (5.6), moving right to a nearly vertical gully. Climb out via the left wall of the gully (5.7) and continue to a chimney. Follow the chimney to easier ground.

6,7) 90 m. Follow gray near the north ridge to the top.

Third Buttress

BUDDHA RIDGE 5.5
J.Martin and M.Scott, 1973

This climbs a ridge near the left side of the cliff. Avoid the lower, steeper section of the ridge by traversing left under it past a gully, then climbing straight up on easy rock to a big ledge system. Follow this right onto a face, and when the ledge ends, slant up right to a pillar. Climb down and right through a gully onto the ridge proper. The ridge is now followed over a series of short, steep walls until the angle eases. The final problem is a narrow, almost horizontal ridge with several small towers. An easy descent can be made by the gully between the second and third buttresses.

Mount Rundle

Fourth Buttress

There is no route to the top of the Fourth Buttress as yet. An obvious line on the north face has been climbed as far as a large central ledge but has not been completed. The upper half is steep and loose.

Fifth Buttress

NORTH RIDGE   5.9
L.MacKay and J.White, 1972
F.F.A: G.Homer and J.Lauchlan, 1976

The fifth buttress has sharp prow-like ridge similar to Ship's Prow. It is about 350 m high. The lower section of the climb up the ridge is easy and the crux is a 5.9 jamcrack near the top.

GROTTO MOUNTAIN

There are two climbing areas on Grotto Mountain, They are Grotto Corner on the south side of the mountain and Crag X which lies at the base of the southeast face.

GROTTO CORNER

Grotto Corner is a prominent, slightly S-shaped, open book located in a long cliff band high on the south slopes of Grotto Mountain. It lies to the west of the large southeast face and east of the two deep canyons.
Approach: The best approach is via the stream bed just west of the corner. This takes about an hour, but both climbs are well worth the walk.
Descend by down-climbing and rappel in the gully immediately east of the corner.

GROTTO CRACK * 70 m, 5.8.
B.Greenwood and G.Homer, 1972

This climbs the crack at the back of the corner which is formed by one overhanging and one vertical wall. The first pitch is sustained and quite difficult for its grade. Scramble up the easy, lower corner to the base of the crack.
1) 40 m, 5.8. Climb the crack to a piton belay in a scoop where the left wall eases.
2) 30 m, 5.8. Continue up the crack which widens and becomes less difficult.

JUGHAUL WALL * 70 m, 5.7
M.Sawyer, J.Firth and C.Perry, June 1976

This route follows an impressive line up the right wall of the corner and is much easier than it looks. Climb up to small ledges level with and about 30 m right of the base of the crack. A faint crack system splits the steep wall above and leads to a small tree.
1) 30 m, 5.7. Move up right over a small overlap and climb the crack system, which is discontinuous, to a belay in a groove just above the tree. The section below the tree is steep but the holds are superb.
2) 40 m, 5.5. Continue up the groove until just below a second tree and then move out left and follow a crack system up the slabby wall to the top.

◊ *Chris Perry on pitch 11 of Quasar, photo John Martin*

Grotto Mountain

CRAG X

Crag X is located at the base of the southeast face of Grotto mountain near the mouth of Grotto Creek. It is visible from the 1A highway and can be reached in about 10 - 15 minutes. It's name suggests a secret worth keeping and is somewhat inappropriate since the quality of the rock leaves much to be desired. However, with increased traffic the routes are becoming more solid and Sideline, in particular, is well worthwhile. The proximity of the crag to the road and its sunny and sheltered aspect make it suitable for early and late season climbing.

A prominent corner system, Central Groove, splits the crag into two sections, the left of which is higher and contains most of the routes. The accompanying photograph shows most of the left wing and part of the right wing.

Approach: The easiest approach is to park at the Gap Lake picnic area, walk through trees at the east end of the Rockwool plant and follow an open ridge above a smaller cliff to the top of the descent gully at the south end of the main crag. Here, a grassy platform provides a convenient base and only a short descent is required to reach the start of the climbs. Alternatively, the Grotto Canyon approach can be used and the base of the crag reached directly from the east.

Descent: is to the south via the easy gully described above.

SIDELINE ** 65 m, 5.9
A.McKeith and C.Perry, September 1973
Direct Start: "Main Line" - A.Genereux and W.Rennie, 1985
Pitch 3. alt. P.Lazic and A.C.Gurholt, 1984

The route follows a prominent right-angled corner near the left end of the left wing. It is a deservedly popular climb and has become quite polished in places. The climbing is mainly 5.7 - 5.8 with one move of 5.9 on the third pitch. The corner begins about 15 m above the base of the cliff and the climb starts on the left near a short grassy groove.

1) 15 m, 5.6. Climb steep yellow rock to an overhang, traverse right and then move up to an alcove below a steep crack.

2) 25 m, 5.8. Traverse right, dropping down a move into the corner and follow it to a small ledge with a bolt belay.

2a) 25 m, 5.8. Climb the steep crack above the alcove to its top, traverse right into the corner and follow it to the normal belay.

1,2 alt) Main Line 30 m, 5.10c. Start directly below the corner behind a large tree. Climb a steep wall to a piton in a slanting break. Move up and traverse steeply right past a second piton to a shallow groove. Climb this for a short distance, then traverse back left with difficulty past a bolt to the foot of the main corner. Continue up this to join the normal route, and belay at the top of pitch 2.

3) 25 m, 5.9. Climb the corner past a smooth section to a bulge. Traverse left and regain the corner above. Continue to a large ledge on the left.

3a) 25 m, 5.8. Move left from the belay and climb the wall left of the corner. The climbing eases after an initial awkward section which is protected by a bolt.

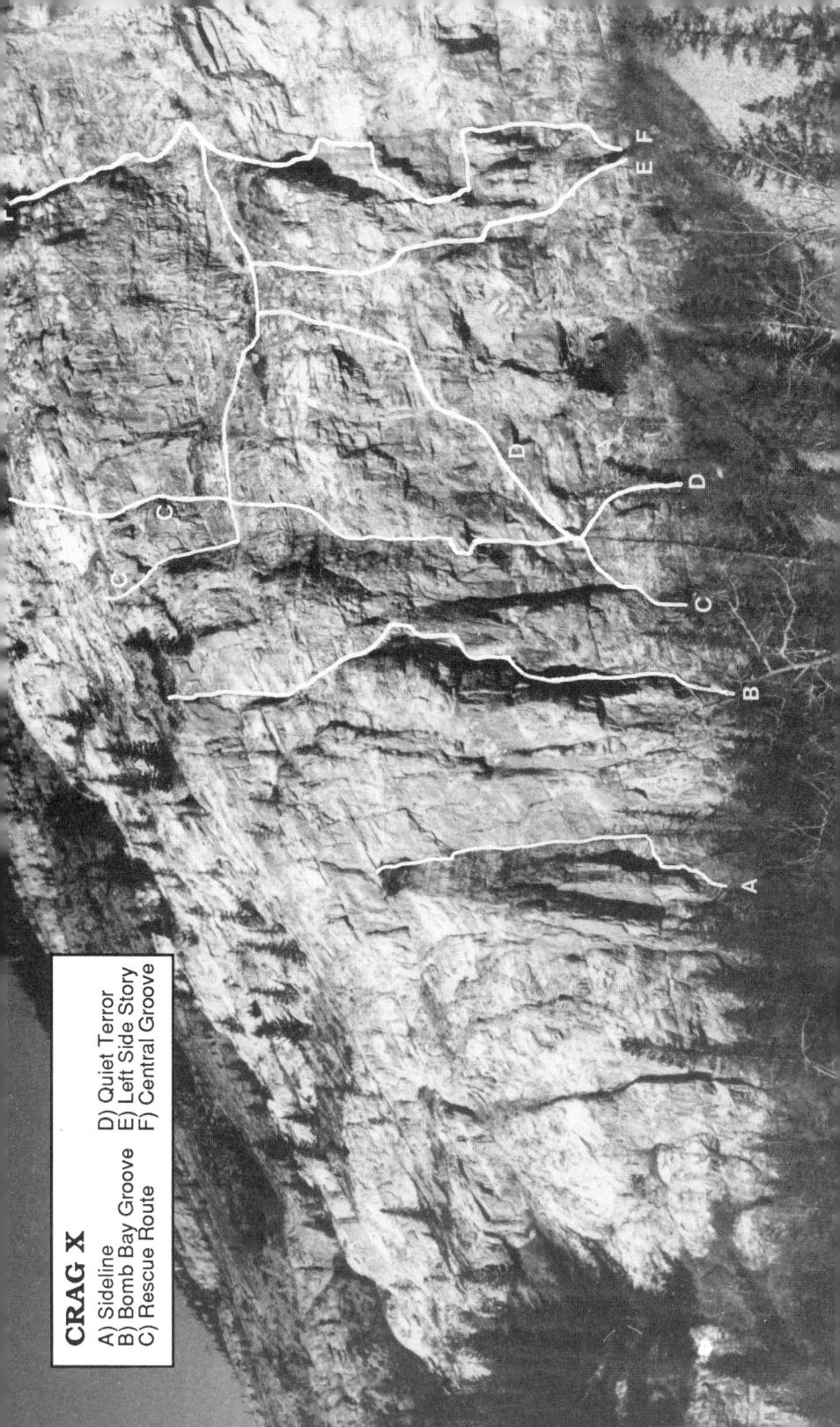

Grotto Mountain

BOMB BAY GROOVE   70 m, 5.7
N. Helliwell, C. Perry and M. Sawyer, 1975

The climb follows a deep groove and chimney system about 30 m right of Sideline. The route was originally menaced by a large block, but now the "bomb" has been dropped and the route is generally sound.
1) 35 m, 5.7. Climb the groove to a belay where it widens below a roof.
2) 35 m, 5.7. Traverse right to a corner and climb this to a second roof. Traverse right again and move up to a corner. Climb the corner (the bomb bay) and move right and then back left to avoid overhangs.

RESCUE ROUTE   115 m, 5.7
K. Bridgens, C. Perry and M. Sawyer, 1975

The route was originally cleaned for rescue practice by members of the now disbanded Calgary Mountain Rescue Group. It climbs a shallow groove system about 20 m right of Bomb Bay Groove and passes a prominent roof on its left side. It is inadvisable to use pitons in either cracks below the roof or at the back of the ledge above the roof as the entire mass of rock appears to be partially detached. Start left of the roof below a right-facing corner overgrown at the base.
1) 25 m, 5.6. Scramble through bushes and move right with difficulty to gain the base of the corner. Climb the corner for about 10 m and then traverse right past two small trees to a ledge below the roof.
2) 25 m, 5.7. Climb the groove to the roof and swing out left with care past a projecting block (this may be dangerously loose). Move up to a small ledge just above the roof (good pitons in the horizontal break a short distance above).
3) 40 m, 5.5. Follow the groove to a large ledge near the top.
4) 25 m, Exit either up the groove above or up the one on the left.

Bugs McKeith on pitch 2 of Sideline during first ascent, photo Chris Perry

Grotto Mountain

QUIET TERROR 5.8
B. Keller and N. Helliwell, 1975

The route follows an interesting line but is reported to be loose and difficult to protect. Start about 10 m right of Rescue Route by a large tree set close to the face.
1) Climb the wall behind the tree and move up left to the first belay on Rescue Route.
2) Follow a ramp diagonally right and continue trending up and right to a belay near a rib located a short distance below some roofs.
3) Move right and up to a shallow groove. Follow this to the large ledge which splits the face.
4,5) Finish as for Rescue Route or Central Groove.

LEFT SIDE STORY 5.7
G. Spohr and party

This route climbs the vegetated corner left of Central Groove. Start in the alcove as for that route and move out left onto the rib. Climb across to the corner and follow it to a belay high up below the steep section. Move up left onto the face and climb a shallow depression to the large ledge. Traverse across to Central Groove and climb the last pitch of that route.

CENTRAL GROOVE * 105 m 5.8
C. Perry and J. Martin, 1976
(Pitch 2 alt. D.Gardner and J.Vader, Aug. 1984)

The route follows the large corner system which divides the crag into its left and right wings. Start in an alcove below and left of a prominent V-corner.
1) 25 m, 5.7. Climb up right to the corner and follow it to a ledge. Move left to a bolt belay.
2) 25 m, 5.8. Climb a corner at the left end of the ledge to a fixed pin. Move up and right on a slab past two more fixed pins, then traverse right into a corner. Follow this a short distance to ledges.
2a) 25 m, 5.8. Climb pitch 2 until a solution pocket with a small bush is reached 6-7 m up the slab. Traverse left with difficulty to the foot of a corner and climb this to a ledge level with the normal belay.
3) 25 m. Climb the groove above to a tree on a large ledge.
4) 30 m, 5.7. Continue up the crack above the belay, making a short detour right to avoid the initial overhang.

HERE AND THERE 105 m 5.7
J. Lauchlan and J. Elzinga, 1975

Probably due to the poor quality of the rock, this is the only route climbed to date on the right wing of Crag X. Start about 25 m right of Central Groove below a broken, slabby wall.
1) 25 m, Climb the wall trending right to a belay below a small roof in a shallow groove.
2) 35 m, Step left and climb a corner, then continue up easy ground, trending left.
3) 45 m, Move right and climb some overlaps, trending right to finish.

79

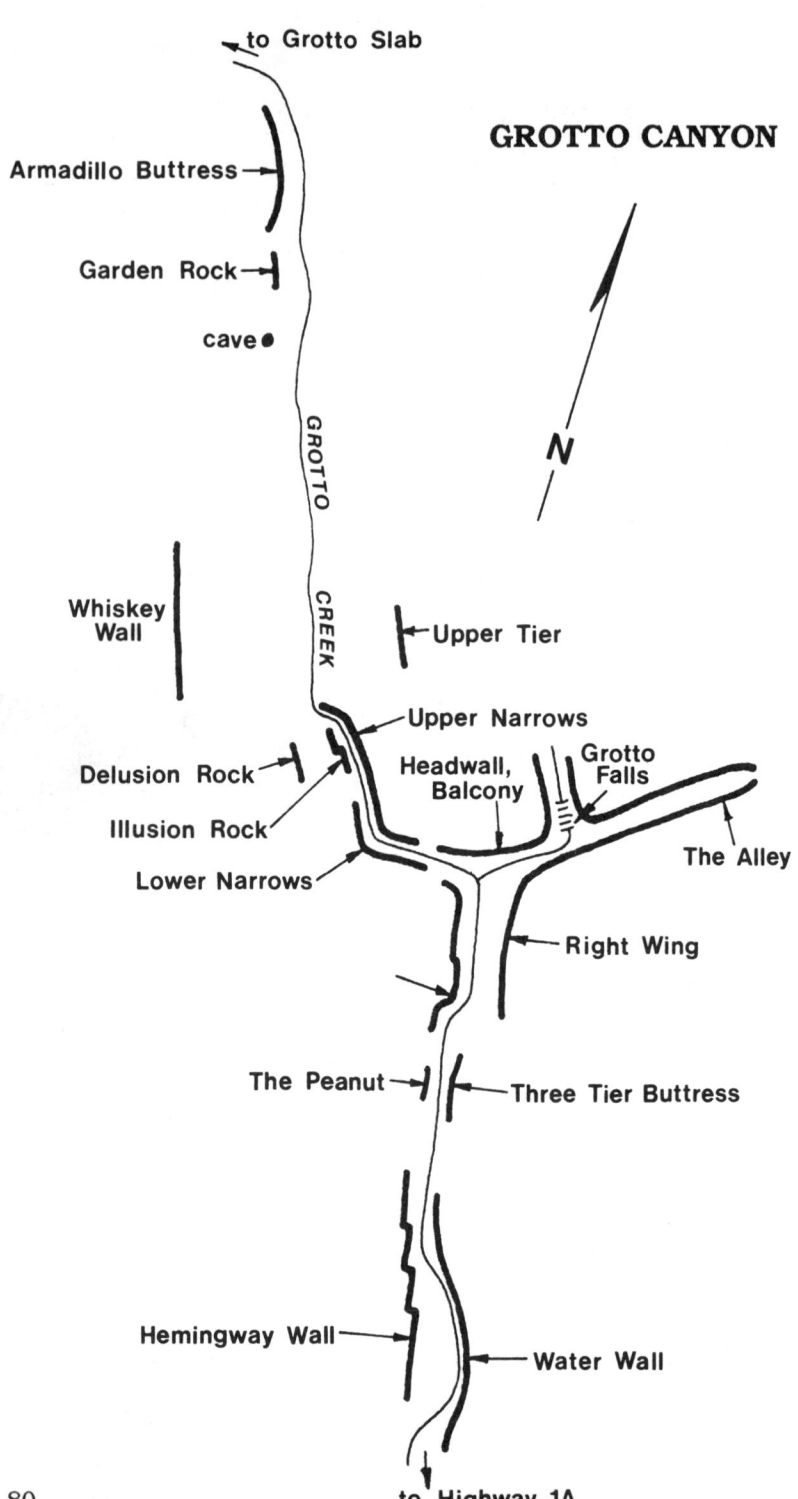

GROTTO CANYON

Grotto Canyon is located in the deep valley immediately east of Grotto Mountain. In the past few years it has emerged as a major climbing locale with the greatest concentration of hard routes in the area. The climbs are generally short, readily accessible and well protected (predominantly by bolts), making it possible to enjoy a considerable footage of good-value climbing in a relatively short period of time. The climbs vary from delicate slabs to steep, fingery face climbs on often excellent rock. Because of its sheltered location it has one of the longest climbing seasons in the guidebook area and is understandably a very popular place to climb.

Approach: The official trail starts at a small lake and picnic area 2.4 km east of Gap Lake on the 1A Highway. However, the canyon can be reached more directly from a gravel parking area north of the highway and about 1.4 km from Gap Lake. A narrow trail starts just west of the entrance (cairn) and heads north through trees toward the canyon. After a few minutes, a power line running east-west is reached and a second trail marked by a cairn continues to the mouth of the canyon. It is currently also possible to drive along the power line to the start of the second trail from an access road 0.7 km east of the parking area.

Sean Dougherty on Scarface, photo Al Pickel

Grotto Canyon

WATER WALL

The first cliff encountered on the east side of the canyon is Water Wall, a long, low cliff situated immediately above the creek. It is about 15 minutes walk from the road. The climbs are described for this cliff from right to left, that is, as one approaches up the canyon.

At the extreme south end of the cliff is a prominent, left-facing corner with a very steep wall on its left side.

THE STING *   25 m, 5.10d
A.Genereux and J.Jones, 1986

Starting just left of the corner, make difficult moves up to a bolt on the left wall. Climb directly up to the top, following a left-facing crack and passing a second bolt below a bulge.

About 35 m upstream past an area of overhanging yellow rock the wall becomes lower and less steep. The bottom of the cliff has been undercut and smoothed by water action, and the lower bulges constitute the crux of most of the climbs. The first line of weakness left of the yellow section is a shallow left-facing corner beginning halfway up the cliff.

ACROSS THE RIVER AND INTO THE TREES   25 m, 5.11b
D.Morgan and C.Yonge, Oct.1984
Direct finish: D.Morgan and S.Dougherty, 1986

This route climbs the wall immediately left of the left-facing corner. Make difficult moves up left past a bolt to reach sloping ledges above the lower bulges (bolt). Move right into the corner and continue up this and easy ground above to the top. Alternatively, continue directly up the wall above the second bolt to a two bolt belay where one's composure can be regained.

CEREBRAL GORETEX   12 m, 5.11c
B.Balazs and B.Webster, July 1986

This fingery test-piece climbs the wall immediately left of Across The River And Into The Trees. Climb with difficulty past a bolt to a ledge. More reasonable climbing past two more bolts leads to the bolt belay on Across The River And Into The Trees.

REFLEX ACTION   12 m, 5.11d
S.Dougherty and D. Morgan, July 1986

Left again is another finger-wrecker. Gain a bolt with relative ease and work up to a ledge. The wall above is somewhat easier though not without interest. Traverse right to belay.

FOR WHOM THE BELL TOLLS   12 m, 5.11b
S.Dougherty and C.Yonge, May 1985

Climb a very shallow groove in the lower bulges 5 m left of Reflex Action (2 bolts). Getting harder as more holds disappear!

Sean Dougherty on The Importance of Being Ernest, photo Dave Thomson

Grotto Canyon

SCARFACE   10 m, 5.11a
S.Dougherty and A.Pickel, Aug.1985

Immediately left of For Whom The Bell Tolls are two small rock-scars. Scarface climbs the wall just left of these past two bolts.

ABLUTOR **   20 m, 5.10b/c
C.Yonge and A.Skuce, Oct.1984

This enjoyable route climbs the wall about 4 m left of Scarface and 5 m right of the prominent slanting groove of Spring Clean.   Climb delicately up right to a bolt above a small overlap. Move up left with difficulty, and then climb up to a second bolt. Continue more easily to the top. The original start is now very polished and it is easier to start further left near Spring Clean.

SPRING CLEAN *   15 m, 5.10a
C.Yonge and J.Rollins, May 1985

The prominent slanting groove left of Ablutor is undercut by a band of overhangs which extends leftwards for about 20 m. Climb over the overhang (bolt runner) and into the groove. Continue up this past a piton to the top. Alternately, the bolt can be reached by climbing the wall left of Ablutor.

The following four routes climb through the lower band of overhangs that extends leftwards from Spring Clean.

POWER PLAY **   15 m, 5.10c
S.Dougherty and D.Morgan, May 1985

A steep and strenuous route on large holds. Climb up to the roof 2 m left of Spring Clean (bolt), and then power through the roof via a shallow groove (bolts) to more reasonable climbing. Continue past a large horizontal break (small Friend) to trees.

LIP SERVICE *   15 m, 5.10d
S.Dougherty, D.Morgan and C.Yonge, May 1985

Make a difficult sequence over the lip (bolt) and continue up a steep wall (bolt) past a large break to the top.

LOOSE LIPS SINK SHIPS *   15 m, 5.10c
A.Genereux and W.Rennie, June 1985

This route is marked by an unusually large bolt hanger on the lip of the roof. Climb up to the roof and step right to the bolt. It is also possible to reach the bolt directly. Struggle over the lip to easier ground and a poor hidden piton up on the left. Continue over another small roof (poor piton) to trees.

DEVIANT BEHAVIOR   15 m, 5.10a
S.Dougherty, June 1985

Climb through the roof past a bolt 3 m left of Loose Lips and wander up easy ground to the top.

Left of Deviant Behavior the roof diminishes in size and becomes a large bulge, below which there is a group of small trees.

CANARY IN A COALMINE   15 m, 5.9
S.Dougherty, June 1985
Start behind the rightmost tree. Climb a short corner and step left and over the bulge (bolt) to easier ground.

ILL WIND   15 m, 5.9
S.Dougherty, June 1985
Three metres left of Canary, surmount the bulge to a shallow groove and easy ground. No protection.

BREEZIN' *   15 m, 5.8
D.Morgan, May 1985
Immediately left of a small conifer make interesting moves up to a large hold. Move up and left to a bolt. Step back right and up a faint ramp line past a second bolt to the top. A more difficult variation (5.9) is to climb directly to the top from the first bolt.

The left end of Water Wall is marked by a right facing, dirty corner.

RAINDUST **   15 m, 5.10c
S.Dougherty, J.Martin and B.Keller, June 1985
Climb the wall immediately right of the dirty corner. Difficult moves above a bolt lead to trees.

Grotto Canyon

HEMINGWAY WALL

Hemingway Wall is a steep, clean-cut wall of excellent rock on the west side of the canyon immediately opposite Water Wall. The main face is marked by several faint, diagonal lines and is bounded on the right by a short, prominent arete. Farther right, the main crag diminishes in size and a larger but more broken upper tier begins above a ledge system that diagonals down to the creek bed.

THE IMPORTANCE OF BEING ERNEST **   20 m, 5.12a
S.Dougherty, M.DeLeeuw, N.Helliwell and A.Hobson, May 1986
Direct Finish: S.Dougherty and M.DeLeeuw, May 1986

This "fun route" starts at a small ledge at the left end of the wall. Climb the steep wall on small holds past ample fixed protection to a ledge. Either climb straight up past a bolt to the top (Lady Bracknell Finish) or step left to large holds and finish more sedately.

FAREWELL TO ARMS ***   20 m, 5.10d
D.Morgan and S.Dougherty, May 1985

This excellent route follows the diagonal break in the centre of the main face. It is steep and strenuous and has become a local test-piece.
Climb up past two bolts to a piton in the break via some long reaches. Run up the break to an awkward rest below a steep bulge (bolt). Delicate moves over the bulge (bolts) lead to a horizontal break and relief. Step right to finish at a tree.

† TROPICANA ***   20 m, 5.12c
B.Howatt, June 1987

This difficult route climbs up to the faint diagonal line immediately right of Farewell To Arms and follows it to a difficult finish up a blank wall.

WALK ON THE WILDE SIDE ***   20 m, 5.11c
S.Dougherty, J.Sevigny and M.Zimmerman, May 1986

A sustained route that climbs the second diagonal line right of Farewell To Arms. Start directly below a bolt. Gain the diagonal line by a difficult move. Hasten upwards to a large foothold (piton) where the final section can be contemplated. Continue over the steep bulge above (#1 1/2 Friend) to a wild dash rightward along a rounded ledge to a "no hands rest" on top.

GREY MATTER *   12 m, 5.10c
B.Balazs and B.Webster, June 1986

Start immediately right of Walk On The Wilde Side. Climb directly up the steep wall past two bolts to a large scoop (bolt). Standing in the scoop constitutes the crux.

GRAND LARCENY **   12 m, 5.10c
A.Genereux and W.Rennie, May 1985

This route climbs the wall a few metres left of the arete at the right end of the main face. A steal at 5.10c! Climb up to the first bolt either by traversing from the arete or directly (harder). Climb the wall above past bolt runners to an interesting finish.

Bruce Howatt on Tropicana, photo Tom Fayle ⇨

Grotto Canyon

FALLING FROM HEAVEN *** 12 m, 5.9
W.Rennie and J.Jones, May 1985

This enjoyable route climbs the prominent arete. It begins on smooth rock just left of the arete and is well protected by a bolt and two pitons.

LITTLE CANADIAN CORNER * 12 m, 5.8
C.Yonge, J.Firth and S.Dougherty, May 1985

Climb the short corner immediately right of the arete.

LIVELY-UP YOURSELF ** 12 m, 5.11a
D.Morgan and J.Firth, May 1985

Lively-up Yourself is an excellent route that follows a thin crack line up the wall immediately right of Little Canadian Corner. Gain the crack which starts 4 m above the ground from the right via some gymnastic moves over slick rock.

FLAKE LINE 12 m, 5.6
S.Worthington and A.N.Other

Climb the corner/flake line right of Little Canadian Corner.

FOOTLOOSE ** 12 m, 5.10d
D.Morgan, J.Firth, A.Skuce and S.Dougherty, May 1985

This sustained and fingery route up the steep wall right of Flake Line is protected by widely spaced bolts. Step left at the last bolt to large finishing holds.

OH NO NOT ANOTHER 10 m, 5.9
S.Dougherty, July 1986

Ten metres right of Footloose is a short wall. Wander up this to the ledge that diagonals down to the creek.

TEMPTRESS * 25 m, 5.10b
A.Genereux, W.Rennie and J.Jones, May 1985

This worthwhile route is situated on the upper wall above and right of the main cliff. It starts behind a large tree where the diagonal ledge system descends to the creek bed. Climb up to a prominent flake (poor wires) and make an awkward move (crux) to gain a bolt and larger holds. Continue straight up (large thread and bolt) to the top.

NYMPHET 25 m, 5.8
A.Genereux and A.Skuce, May 1985

Follow a line of flakes to the right of Temptress past several pitons and a bolt to the top.

Grotto Canyon

THREE TIER BUTTRESS

Just upstream from Water Wall on the east side of the canyon is a smooth bulging wall with a prominent break at half-height. This is Three Tier Buttress.

SHORT AND CURLY *   18 m, 5.10d
D.Morgan and A.Burgess, Sept. 1985
Direct Start: M.Zimmerman and M.DeLeeuw, March 1986
At the left end of the buttress is a small arch at ground level. Start at the right end of this and climb up and left through several bulges to the large break. Move right for 5 m to a bolt. (A much better alternative is to climb directly to the bolt, past a piton and over a large bulge.) Continue right to a second bolt and climb up diagonally rightwards to a slanting groove. Follow this to the top.

TOO LOW FOR ZERO *   15 m, 5.11b
S.Dougherty and M.DeLeeuw, July 1986
This climb, essentially a super-direct start to Short And Curly, starts directly below the final groove of that route. Climb over a small overlap (bolt) to gain a standing position below a huge bulge. Pass two pitons en route to the ledge above. Follow Short And Curly for a few moves and then finish up to the left.

HIGH OCTANE **   15 m, 5.11c
M.DeLeeuw, S.Dougherty and M.Zimmerman, April 1986
This route climbs the steep wall 7 m right of Too Low For Zero. Climb up to a bolt below the lower bulge. Interesting moves gain the break (thread). Continue up past another bolt with difficulty into a short corner. Move left to finish.

MR. OLYMPIA ***   15 m, 5.12a
S.Dougherty and C.Yonge, May 1987
This steep route attacks the left side of the large roof at the right end of the buttress. Climb up to the large break (poor bolt and #4 Friend). Stretch up for a large hold in the lip of the roof and launch upward, passing three more bolts, and hopefully gain the top.

RISING DAMP *   10 m, 5.9
L.Ostrander, August 1985
A pleasant climb with devious protection. At the right end of the wall follow a ramp below a bulge up left to the break. Follow the crack up to the right.

Grotto Canyon

THE PEANUT

Opposite Three Tier Buttress is a small outcrop of rock known as The Peanut.

K.P.SPECIAL * 10 m, 5.11a
S.Dougherty, M.DeLeeuw and M.Zimmerman, April 1986
Strenuous moves over the overhang (bolt) gain large holds to the right and a piton. Continue more easily to the top.

PAINTINGS WALL

Farther upstream the canyon narrows and the wall on the left (west) side becomes steep and continuous. At the start of this section where the T-junction in the canyon first comes into view, are some faint Indian pictographs which give the cliff its name.

FLIPSIDE 30 m, 5.6
R.Howe and R.Lofthouse, 1972
Flipside climbs a prominent, slanting corner with a vegetated and slabby left wall about 45 m downstream of the paintings. It was the first climb in the canyon and quite likely the pioneers did not realize what they had started!

CHANCE IT 16 m, 5.10c
D. Morgan and A.Freeman, 1981
Start a short distance left of the paintings. Climb steep yellow rock to a small ledge below a bulge. Climb over the bulge to a protection bolt and continue up a shallow corner past a small roof to the top. The lower section of the climb is poorly protected and it is advisable to carry pitons.

ARTFUL DODGER ** 16 m, 5.10a
A. Sole & D. Morgan, 1981
The first of the modern climbs in the canyon and one of the best. Not to be missed. Climb the shallow corner just right of the pictographs to the base of a groove. Continue up the groove and a short wall above (bolt) to the top.

† PETER PAN 16 m, 5.11a
A.Sole and C.Perry, June 1987
Climb a shallow corner immediately right of the start of Artful Dodger to an overlap. Move up past a bolt and then go up and right past a second bolt to a third below an overhang with a short, left-facing corner above. Use underclings to gain small holds above the overhang on the left and then lunge up to good holds and the top.

TOWER OF PISA *   17 m, 5.11c
S.Dougherty, B.Balazs, and C.Yonge, June 1985
About 20 m upstream from the pictographs is a steep bulging arete situated immediately left of a prominent corner. Starting on the left, climb up and right to a small foothold on the arete. Strain up and left to a bolt and then improvise over a bulge to relief on larger holds. Continue up the steep wall above, stepping left under a small roof to finish. Crawl to the belay.

RECESS CORNER   20 m, 5.7
First ascent unknown.
At the right-hand end of Painting Wall is a short steep wall behind some pine trees. The climb follows a corner left of this wall and is protected by two bolts.

† CATSENJAMMER   12 m, 5.10b
S. DeMaio, 1986
At the right end of Paintings Wall is a large detached block split by a handcrack on its northeast side. The climb follows the crack over a large roof.

THE RIGHT WING

Opposite Paintings Cliff, about 20 m above the creek bed in trees, is a band of rock that extends upstream to the T-junction. The band is broken into right and left sections by an easy break. Lunatic Madness and Aggressive Treatment are right of the break; the other routes are to the left. The climbs are described from right to left.

† AGGRESSIVE TREATMENT *   40 m, 5.10b
A.Genereux, 1985
Start left of a prominent tree. Climb a steep face 7 m to a bolt. Move right and up on a small ledge to a piton. Climb up over a bulge, continue past another piton, and scramble to trees.

† LUNATIC MADNESS *   50 m, 5.10d
A.Genereux and W.Rennie, 1985
Climb an overhanging face to a piton. Continue up a slanting corner past a bolt and over a bulge to a ledge (piton). Climb up and left past another piton to the top. Sustained climbing and not well protected.

SUPPLICATION *   14 m, 5.10b
J.Martin, S.Dougherty, C.Yonge and C.Quinn, May 1987
Climb a steep wall to the right of a right-facing, arching corner past three bolts to a fourth at the top.

PITRUN ***   16 m, 5.10b
M.Zimmerman and M.DeLeeuw, April 1986
A pleasant pump route with no fixed protection. Climb a steep, right-facing, arching corner to a bolt belay at the top. Take a good selection of Friends and wires.

LEMON PIE *   13 m, 5.10a
J.Martin and L.Howard, July 1986
Start below a wedge-shaped section of yellow rock. Move up and right past a steep ramp, then step left and climb up to a two-bolt belay (three bolts runners, RP's useful).

YELLOW WEDGE **   13 m, 5.9
J.Martin and R.MacLachlan, June 1986
An entertaining climb. Starting just left of Lemon Pie, climb steep rock past 3 bolts.

THE HEADWALL

At the head of the T-junction is a large cliff which faces down the canyon and has a prominent yellow corner on its right side (The Verdict). The corner is about 25 m high and ends at a roof. To the left of this are two small seepages which form the icefalls His & Hers during the winter months. Above the left-hand seepage is a deep, bottomless chimney which splits the crag roughly into two halves.
The left-hand portion of the crag consists of lower angled rock that can be accessed via a ramp system starting below the chimney. The next three climbs are located here.

STAIRCASE   40 m, 5.1
Climb the slab left of a long shallow chimney to gain a tree ledge.

GOFFER GULCH   40 m, 5.3
C.Yonge, May 1987
Climb the obvious shallow chimney to the ledge.

TRAVERSE OF THE MODS   50 m, 5.2
From the top of the last two routes, broken ledges lead right to a tree-filled gully and ledge system known as The Balcony that extends across the top of the Headwall.

† SEA OF DREAMS   45 m, 5.11b
A.Genereux and W.Rennie, June 1985
This sustained route climbs the buttress immediately left of the bottomless chimney to a prominent lone tree. Climb brittle rock past 3 bolts to a crack and small roof. Continue past two pitons to the tree (fixed anchors).

Sean Dougherty bouldering the start of High Octane, photo John Martin

Grotto Canyon

THE VERDICT *** 50 m, 5.10c
C.Yonge and S.Dougherty, May 1987
The Verdict climbs the yellow corner and continues directly up the wall above. It is a superb climb with a big atmosphere and a sensational position.
1) 30 m, 5.10c. Climb the yellow corner to an obvious break just below the roof. Hand traverse right to good holds on the arete and teeter up past a hollow flake to a bolt. Continue more reasonably leftwards to a two bolt belay.
2) 20 m, 5.10b. Move up the wall and traverse right to where the overhang forms a left-facing corner (Friends). Make steep moves up and left over the roof (bolt) to a gain a crack system and follow this to a two bolt belay on a large ledge.
Rappel off (50 m) or continue easily up and left to The Balcony.

CORNER'S INQUEST 40 m, 5.10c
G.Powter and B.Gross, August 1983
Climb to about halfway up the corner of The Verdict and traverse right on loose rock to a bolt on the front face. Continue right and up slightly to join Breakaway.

A short distance right of The Verdict, above the east fork of the creek, is a slanting groove line which leads to the left side of a ledge with three small trees on it. Breakaway climbs the groove and continues to the top of the cliff passing the right end of The Balcony.

BREAKAWAY * 90 m, 5.8
C. Perry and A. Sole, July 1983
A traditional route with a traditional grade. Take some pitons!
1) 35 m, 5.8. Climb up above the creek on steep yellow rock to gain the base of the groove. Continue up the groove, with difficulty at first, and move out left where it ends. Climb up and back right into a short continuation corner which leads to the left side of the ledge.
2) 25 m, 5.7. Climb a steep wall on the right to a traverse line that leads left and ends in a short wall. Climb the wall to a ledge, move right slightly, and continue up a shallow scoop to a second, larger ledge (extreme right end of The Balcony).
3) 30 m, Climb the easy corner on the right and continue on broken ground to ledges near the top.
To descend, traverse round to the right and rappel from a tree to ledges overlooking the upper creek bed on the east side of the cliff. Move right again and rappel down the west side of the waterfall to the base of the cliff. Alternatively, move left and rappel to The Balcony, and then traverse left along this and rappel or downclimb Staircase.

Grotto Canyon

THE BALCONY

The Balcony is the tree-filled gully and ledge system described earlier that extends across the top of The Headwall. It can be gained either via Staircase and Traverse of the Mods or by climbing The Verdict or Breakaway. The following routes are on the buttress at the lower right-hand end of The Balcony. The final pitch of Breakaway takes the corner on the right side of this buttress.

CLEAN LIVING   15 m, 5.4
S.Dougherty, May 1987
Climb the clean ramp of immaculate rock at the left end of the buttress. Rappel from trees.

MAIDEN CENTURY **   15 m, 5.7
C.Yonge and S.Dougherty, May 1987
This airy climb follows the obvious flake on the front of the buttress and is highly recommended. Take a good selection of wires and Friends. Starting from the right end of The Balcony on the front of the buttress, climb up in an exposed position to the flake and continue up this and the wall above to the finish of Clean Living.

THE ALLEY

East of The Headwall is a small waterfall called Grotto Falls and a short canyon blocked by a huge chockstone. Above the chockstone is a wide tree filled gully known as The Alley. This can be reached by scrambling up rocks opposite Grotto Falls. The following routes are on the south side of The Alley near the top end and are described from left to right.

† KNIGHT MOVES *   25 m, 5.10c
J.Jones and A.Genereux, August 1987
Start by a large block 5m left of the prominent flake of Barchetta. Climb the groove above the flake up and left to a bolt. Continue up and left with difficulty, and then move back right and up past a second bolt to a good ledge. Climb a shallow corner past 2 more bolts to the fixed station of Barchetta.

† HOLLOW VICTORY   25 m, 5.10c
A.Genereux and J.Jones, August 1987
Start as for Knight Moves but leave the groove after about 5m following flakes and underclings up and right. Go over two overlaps to reach a ledge below the last bolt on Barchetta and then finish as for that route. Nut and Friend protection.

Grotto Canyon

BARCHETTA ***   25 m, 5.11c
J.Sandford and J.Buszowski, May 1987

The climb starts off a flake just below the top of The Alley. Climb up through a bulge, move right, and then break out left onto the upper slab. Make a few tricky moves left to a small ledge and then go up to a fixed station.

SUBMISSION ***   25 m, 5.11c
J.Buszowski and J.Sandford, May 1987

Start on top of a small pillar near a tree stump and climb up with difficulty past two bolts to a third below a small roof. Traverse left and continue up past bolts to a fixed station.

CROSSROAD **   25 m, 5.11d
M.Dube, June 1987

From the third bolt of Submission make some hard moves up and right over the roof (bolt). Continue through the upper roof and then trend slightly left to a fixed station.

GRACE UNDER PRESSURE **   25 m, 5.11c
J.Sandford and J.Buszowski, May 1987

Start downhill from Submission below a bolt about 5 m above the ground. Climb past the bolt to a second bolt in a left-facing corner. Clip a third bolt on the lip of an overlap and make a hard crank up and right. Technical climbing past bolts leads to a fixed station.

GROTTO FALLS

† END GAME **   20 m, 5.11d
T.Fayle and G.Statham, October 1987

To date, this is the only route climbed in the canyon above Grotto Falls. It goes up a blank, slabby face at the extreme left end of the cliffs on the west side of the canyon, just around the corner from The Headwall. Climb past 4 bolts and one natural runner to reach a narrow groove which leads to the top. The crux is a long reach above the second bolt to gain small handholds just left of a tiny bush.

LOWER NARROWS

The west fork of the creek emerges from a narrow canyon (The Narrows) which farther upstream opens out into a wide valley. The climbs in the Lower Narrows are on the south side where the walls are less steep.

† BOGUS   5 m, 5.10d
T.Fayle, August 1987

This short problem, located a few metres into The Narrows on the left, climbs a scoop and wall above (1 bolt).

† MIGHTY MITE *   8 m, 5.12a
M.DeLeeuw, August 1987

Climb the steep arete immediately left of The Midden (2 bolts).

THE MIDDEN   8 m, 5.9
C.Yonge and I.Phillips, 1982

A short distance into The Narrows, a right-facing corner splits the left wall and leads to a large tree. Balance up a scoop into the wide corner/crack and continue up this to finish.

† STORMY WEATHER   30 m, 5.11a
D. Morgan and A. Sole, 1981

About 50 m into The Narrows, the canyon curves to the right and on the left (south) wall a thin fault line slants up rightwards to a short corner. Starting about 3 m left of the fault, make some difficult moves up to a bolt about 6 m above the ground. Climb the bulge on the left past a fixed piton and continue up left to an obvious crack (bolt). Climb the crack for 5 m and then take the left wall to the top.

WEST COAST IDEA **   40 m, 5.10c
M.DeLeeuw, G.Hill and S.Dougherty, July 1986

This excellent and sustained climb goes up the thin fault right of Stormy Weather. Climb the fault past four bolts and good natural protection (Friends and wires) to a two bolt belay. Rappel off.

BLIK *   30 m, 5.10b
S.Dougherty, J.Martin and C.Yonge, May 1987

A fun outing in a good position. Follow West Coast Idea past the first bolt (crux) to where the crack widens. Traverse left on large footholds to a bolt. Interesting moves lead up and left across an overlap to a huge foothold. Climb straight up to a bolt belay. Rappel off.

MOONABAGO   25 m, 5.10b
D. Morgan, S. Buroker and K. Doyle, 1981

Start about 5 m right of the thin fault and climb through a minor break in the lower bulges onto the slab above. Trend up right to a bolt below a groove and climb the groove (runout) to the top.

Grotto Canyon

BAKER STREET   8 m, 5.10d
S.Dougherty, C.Yonge and J.Martin, May 1987
Start below an obvious, yellow, square-cut hold 12 m right of West Coast Idea. Difficult moves up past a bolt gain a large scoop with a belay bolt.

DOCTER WATSON   8 m, 5.9
S.Dougherty, C.Yonge and J.Martin, May 1987
Starting 3 m right of Baker Street, climb up past a bolt to the belay bolt of that route.

LOST WORLD   20 m, 5.10a
B.Keller and S.Dougherty, Jan. 1986
This route climbs a short wall leading to a treed ridge about 15 m right of Moonabago. It is protected by a bolt which at present has no hanger.

MORIARTY   12 m, 5.9
J.Martin, C.Yonge and S.Dougherty, May 1987
To the right of Lost World is a slender wall. Climb up to some "trees" and continue up the wall above to more trees.

ILLUSION ROCK

Farther upstream on the south side of The Narrows is a small outcrop known as Illusion Rock. The left portion of the cliff consists of a series of small overhangs and bulges that are separated from the smooth right wall by a prominent corner (Jackorner). The routes are short but provide varied and interesting climbing.

HARDER THAN IT LOOKS *   10 m, 5.10c
A.Genereux and J.Jones, Oct. 1985
Follow the left arete past a bolt and a piton.

MONKEY IN A RAGE **   10 m, 5.11a
S.Dougherty and B.Keller, Jan. 1986
To the right of the arete is a rounded scoop in the face. Climb with difficulty into the scoop (bolt) and then surmount the strenuous bulge above (bolt). Finish more easily.

GRAND ILLUSION **   12 m, 5.10a
A.Genereux and W.Rennie, May 1985
Not as hard as its more famous namesake. Start in a short corner. Surmount a small roof to gain large holds at the left-hand end of a second roof (piton). Step left into a shallow groove and climb this (piton) to a large, rounded hold. Step left again to finish.

◁ *Mark DeLeeuw on Mighty Mite, photo Tom Fayle*

Grotto Canyon

THE GRANDER ILLUSION **   12 m, 5.10c
C.Yonge and J.Rollins, May 1985

An excellent route that follows a thin crack high on the front face of the Rock. Directly below the crack is a large corner in the arete. Start at the corner. Move up and left to a large block. Above the block is a second roof (pin). Step over the roof to a large hold in the crack. Continue up the crack to a thin finish.

To the right of Grander Illusion is a large, clean corner. The next route climbs a crack in the left wall of the corner.

GEORGE OF THE JUNGLE **   12 m, 5.10c
B.Balazs, C.Yonge and J.Rollins, May 1985

Make difficult moves to gain the crack (piton). Continue up the crack past two more pitons to the top.

JACKORNER **   12 m, 5.7
C.Yonge and I.Phillips, 1982

Climb the large corner.

The following routes are on the steep face to the right of the corner.

IMPENDING IMPACT **   12 m, 5.10a
A.Genereux and W.Rennie, May 1985

An excellent route that offers sustained climbing with sparse protection. Climb the centre of the wall past the crux to a bolt at mid-height. Continue to the top past a piton.

TINY TIM   12 m, 5.9
A.Genereux and W.Rennie, May 1985

Climb a thin crack and flake line to the right of Impending Impact.

On the right arete of the Rock is a short crack with two groove lines above.

THE ALLEY   10 m, 5.7 or 5.8
C.Yonge and I.Phillips, 1982

This route climbs the arete using a combination of both grooves. The right-hand groove provides the easier finish.

Flexing muscles on George of the Jungle, photo Geoff Powter ⇨

Grotto Canyon

DELUSION ROCK

This steep, slabby cliff lies a couple of minutes scramble uphill from the top of Illusion Rock.

BURNT WEENIE SANDWICH * 15 m, 5.10a
J.Martin and S.Dougherty, May 1987

Start near the left side of the rock at a large tree. Climb the wall past four bolts, traversing right just below the top to exit at a secure pine tree. Rappel to descend.

GRAND DELUSION * 18 m, 5.10d
J.Martin and S.Dougherty, May 1987

Start a few metres right and downhill from Burnt Weenie Sandwich. Climb up past two bolts to a third bolt, staying left of a small tree. Tricky moves lead up to easier climbing and a large pine at the top. Rappel to descend.

UPPER NARROWS

Opposite Illusion Rock, the wall on the north side of The Narrows is smooth and overhanging. At the upstream end of this section is a short ramp below two prominent diagonal lines in the wall above. The following two routes climb these diagonal lines.

TRADING PLACES *** 45 m, 5.10c
C.Yonge, J.Rollins, B.Balazs, and S.Dougherty, May 1985

One of the better climbs in the canyon with sustained difficulties throughout. Climb the ramp to a piton and then step left (5.9) over a bulge onto a sloping ledge. From a higher ledge, follow a thin crack (wires) to a delicate move into a shallow scoop with a bolt. The wall above is climbed past two more bolts to easier ground and another bolt. Climb up, trending left, into a shallow corner with a roof to gain a tree. Rappel off.

TABERNAQUERED *** 50 m, 5.10c
C.Yonge and J.Rollins, September 1986

A superb climb requiring a multitude of skills.
1) 5.10a. Start as for Trading Places and traverse right at the start of the thin crack past a bolt above the small tree. Continue to a bolt belay a short way up a diagonal groove.
2) 5.10c. Follow the diagonal groove until the wall steepens. Traverse to a steep sloping shelf and follow this to a "sentry box". Jam over the roof (large Friend) to two pitons. Rappel or continue to trees.

Grotto Canyon

On the north side of the canyon where it starts to open out is a steep chimney system that slants up rightwards through yellow rock and has a large treed ledge near its base. The next five climbs begin or are reached from this ledge.

GANGPLANK *   30 m, 5.4
C.Yonge, May 1985

Starting at the right end of the treed ledge, climb the obvious ramp to a tree belay. Descend by rappel.

CONNOISSEURS'S CRACK *   20 m, 5.10a
C.Yonge and S.Dougherty, May 1987

This classic limestone line follows an obvious wide crack located about 10 m above the tree belay of Gangplank. Take a good selection of gear. Climb the crack in its entirety, including the off width! Belay down to the left at a large tree. Rappel off.

CODGER'S CRACK   80 m, 5.8
R.Breeze and J.Firth, 1982

This exposed route climbs the wall to the right of the chimney via a wide crack at about half height.
Scramble up to the treed ledge. Continue up the chimney for 6-7 m and then move across to a ledge with a tree on the right wall.
1) 40 m, 5.8. Traverse right on immaculate rock for several metres to a small crack that leads to an easier section. Climb the obvious wide crack above to a ledge and tree belay.
2) 40 m, 5.6. Climb the wall on the right to the top.
Descend by rappel.

PENSIONER'S OUTING ***   40 m, 5.8
C.Yonge and S.Dougherty, May 1985

A highly recommended route with an atmosphere out of proportion with its length. Follow Codgers' Crack until below the obvious wide crack. Move right and follow a crack in the arete to a tree belay. Descend by rappel.

BORBARONOMY   50 m, 5.8
C.Yonge and S.Dougherty, May 1987

This poorly protected climb traverses across a grey slab about halfway up the steep wall on the left side of the chimney. Start in a corner at the left end of the treed ledge below the slab. Climb the corner to some small trees. Continue up on large holds to where the rock steepens (good Friend and wire), and then traverse down and left along a break. At the end of the break, move up and left to the base of a loose, left-facing corner and continue up this to the top. Scramble down the ridge and rappel to the canyon.

Grotto Canyon

THE UPPER TIER

The Upper Tier is a steep, prickly slab high up on the east side of the canyon just beyond The Narrows. It can be reached from the valley floor in about 15 minutes. Walk about 150 m past the upstream end of The Narrows and start up at a little scree slope. Work up and right through small cliff bands to reach the forest below the Upper Tier, then go up and left to reach the climbs. A single 50 m rope is adequate for rappels. Take a small selection of nuts and Friends.

† FAT CITY   22 m, 5.8
J.Martin and S.Dougherty, June 1986

Fat City lies slightly left of the main part of the crag. Start behind a tall shrub at the base of a prominent groove. Climb the groove and continue past bolt to a small ledge. Traverse left to a small shrub and exit past a bolt.

EXCITABLE BOY **   15 m, 5.10d
M.DeLeeuw, S.Dougherty and M.Zimmerman, April 1987

Starting just right of Fat City, climb a short, steep face past two bolts to easier ground. Continue up Fat City to finish.

MANDALA **   27 m, 5.10c
J.Martin and L.Howard, June 1986

This stimulating climb is marked by a roundish depression about 8 m above the ground. Climb up past a bolt into the depression and make an awkward move (5.10c) past a bolt. Continue past a second bolt (5.10a) to a small tree on a ledge. Above the tree, climb past two more bolts (5.10a) to the top.

RAT PATROL *   28 m, 5.11a
J.Martin and S.Dougherty, May 1987

Start just right of a small tree near the base of the slab. Climb past a bolt and a flake to a small ledge and then make an awkward sequence of moves up to easier ground. Continue up past bolts to the top.

SEARCH PATTERN **   28 m, 5.10b
J.Martin and L.Howard, June 1986

To the right of Rat Patrol are two deep water grooves, both of which are cut off at the bottom by a small overhang. Search Pattern climbs the left-hand groove. Starting at a short corner on the left, climb up and right past two bolts to gain the groove. Move right at the top of the groove past a bolt and continue up and left slightly (bolt) to a short leaning corner and the top.

Grotto Canyon

FACELIFT * 20 m, 5.10d**
S.Dougherty, J.Martin and M.Zimmerman, April 1987
Between the two main water grooves is a fainter groove, the line of Facelift. Make a difficult sequence over a small roof past a bolt to gain a foothold below the groove. Interesting climbing leads up the groove past several bolts to a slab. Move up left to the top bolt of Search Pattern to finish.

SQUIRREL BREATH ** 18 m, 5.10b
J.Martin and S.Dougherty, June 1986
This elegant line follows the right-hand water groove. Take some small Friends. Climb a steep wall with little overlaps past two bolts to gain the base of the groove. A third bolt protects the final moves above the groove up to a small tree.

WHISKEY WALL

This large scrappy cliff is located on the west side of the canyon just before a prominent cave in a glacial till formation.

† GLENFIDDICH 175 m, 5.7
G.Smith, L.Heidt, C.Perry and D.Swan, May 1986
The route climbs a prominent slanting corner in the right-centre of the cliff. The corner does not extend to the ground and the climb starts on the right at a short left-facing corner.
1) 35 m, 5.6. Climb the corner and then traverse left along an obvious break to a small corner with a small tree at the bottom. Climb the corner and then move left and up to a two bolt belay.
2) 40 m, 5.7. Climb a steep groove to gain the main corner and continue up this to a scoop on the left with a two bolt belay.
3) 30 m, 5.6. Climb the slabby left wall of the corner until the corner steepens and gets looser. Move left and climb a rib, and then traverse right to a small tree and piton belay.
4) 40 m, 5.7. Move diagonally up and right, first over easy ground, then across a steep slabby break into the bottom of a blank corner (tree runner). Step down and traverse horizontally right across a foot ledge below a steep wall until it is possible to climb up on good holds into the bottom of another corner. Climb the corner and then move out right to a difficult mantelshelf and a tree ledge.
5) 30 m, 5.5. Climb the crest of the rib to the top.
Descend to the south, making a 30 m rappel down a cliff band.

Grotto Canyon

GARDEN ROCK

This attractive little cliff is located in the valley bottom on the west side just beyond the cave. Small wired nuts are required.

PINING AWAY * 8 m, 5.9
J.Martin and L.Howard, June 1986

This fun climb takes the left-hand break on the face. Pull over the initial bulge (bolt) on jugs and then continue up easier rock to the top.

CONIFER CRACK ** 9 m, 5.10c
J.Martin and S.Dougherty, June 1986

Conifer Crack takes an ephemeral crack system just right of Pining Away. Make an awkward move to reach a bolt and continue over a bulge (5.10b) to gain a horizontal break. A second bolt protects the unusual crux sequence above.

CHAINSAW WALL 10 m, 5.11c
S.Dougherty, April 1987

This tendon teaser climbs the wall right of Conifer Crack.

ALL SPRUCED UP * 12 m, 5.10a
J.Martin and L.Howard, June 1986

Climb a discontinuous thin crack system behind a spruce tree at the right side of the rock. There is just enough room behind the tree to climb the route.

Grotto Canyon

ARMADILLO BUTTRESS

A short distance past Garden Rock, the trail passes within a few metres of a steep, high buttress on the left (west) side of the valley. This is Armadillo Buttress.

NO PLACE FOR A FRIEND   85 m, 5.9
R.Baillie and M.Toft, June 1983

This route climbs the left side of the buttress, passing en route a prominent treed ledge at just over half height. It features steep, well-protected face climbing on generally good rock.

From where the trail comes closest to the buttress, walk left to the first large tree growing next to the rock (cairn).

1) 22 m, 5.7. Climb the steep face behind the tree past a bolt to a ledge. The ledge may also be reached by climbing a shattered break a few metres to the left. Move right and climb a shallow corner to a small roof (piton). Climb over the roof and continue on steep juggy rock to a small ledge with two bolts 7 m higher.

2) 25 m, 5.8. Move up, then traverse right to a bolt below and right of a short corner capped by an overhang. Move left and climb the overhang (two fixed pitons). Continue straight up on steep rock to a small ledge (piton), climb up to easier ground, and then slant up left to a big ledge with a dead tree (pitons required for belay).

3) 40 m, 5.9. Move right for about 8 m to a small spruce tree and climb the left-facing corner above (piton). From the top of the corner, angle up left to a bolt and then move up and right to an alcove with a fixed piton. Continue up with difficulty to a bolt, then trend up left to a break in the line of roofs above. Step over the roof (piton), and continue up easier rock to large ledges.

To descend, follow ledges down to the left. No rappel is necessary.

ASYLUM **   100 m, 5.10d
D.Morgan, C.Yonge and C.Perry, July 1984

This recommended route follows the prominent right-facing corner system up the front of the buttress. It is a good testing climb although the blocky corner on pitch 2 demands care (the Limestone Touch!).
Start below and left of the corner.

1) 35 m, 5.10d. Climb up and then make a rising traverse right past several pitons to the foot of the corner. Climb the corner with difficulty (small wires) to a bolt stance above an easier section.

2) 30 m, 5.9. Continue with care directly up the blocky corner above to a large ledge and tree belay on the left.

3) 35 m, 5.8. Make a rising traverse up left, following an obvious line of weakness to a small corner (piton) below the steep upper section. Move left and then climb directly up on surprisingly good holds to reach easier ground.

Descend to the left as for No Place For A Friend.

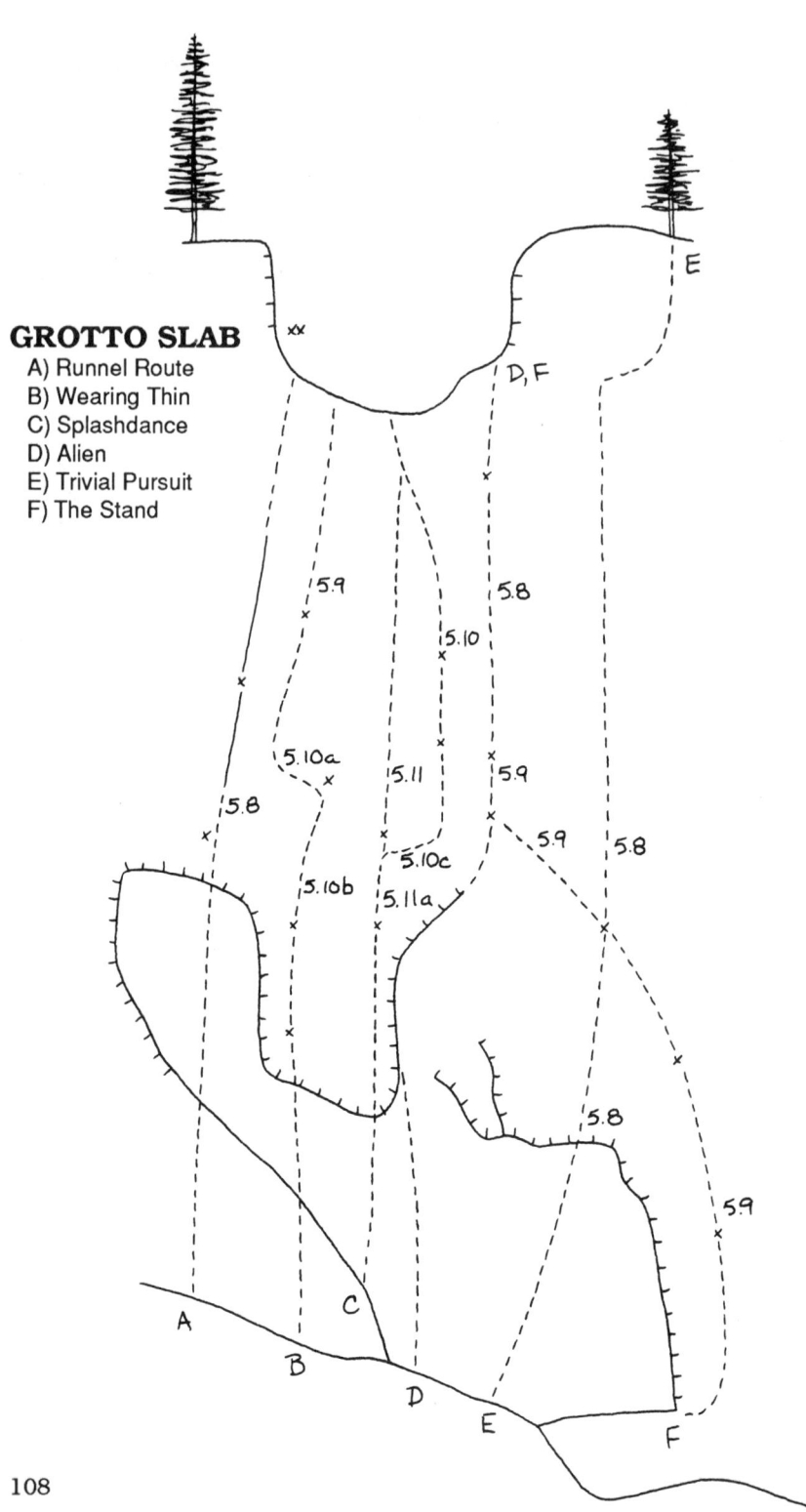

GROTTO SLAB
A) Runnel Route
B) Wearing Thin
C) Splashdance
D) Alien
E) Trivial Pursuit
F) The Stand

GROTTO SLAB

Another 10 minutes farther up the west fork lies Grotto Slab, an excellent friction climbing area. The routes are all one pitch in length and the rock is sound, particularly in the water-worn central section.
Descent: Two ropes (preferably 50 m) should be taken to facilitate descent, which is by rappel from trees or bolts. Many of the bolt hangers have small (1/2 in.) holes.

PRELUDE   45 m, 5.7
G.Smith and A.Savannah, October 1983
Located about 100 m south of the main area, this route climbs a narrow section of rock situated between areas of vegetation at the start of the slabs. Climb a short corner and a thin crack in the slab on the right to a tree. Continue 5 m above the tree, then traverse left on an obvious line to the middle of the upper slab. Climb straight up to the top (unprotected), keeping about 2 m right of the vegetated corner.

The following climbs are situated in the main area as shown in the photo.

NORTH CORNER   50 m, 5.6
P.Walls and A.Watts, 1981
Climb the main right-facing corner at the north end of the cliff (nut protection).

LEFTOVER SLAB   50 m, 5.6
J.Martin and L.Howard, May 1984
Climb the slab right of North Corner, joining the corner near the top at a yellow area just below the point where the corner becomes vegetated.

SPRING THING   45 m, 5.6
J.Martin and L.Howard, May 1982
Climb slabs right of a vegetated corner and left of a shrubby ledge. Small stoppers are useful. A bolt is in place about two- thirds of the way up.

FALL THING   30 m, 5.5
J.Martin, S.Stahl and S.Stahl, October 1983
Climb slabs past the right end of the shrubby ledge. Just below a second vegetated ledge, move right to a small ledge near the water streak. No protection.

RUNNEL ROUTE **   30 m, 5.8.
J.Martin and R.MacLachlan, June 1982
Climb up to and then follow a shallow, entertaining water runnel that is protected by a bolt and a fixed angle.

WEARING THIN *   30 m, 5.10b
J.Martin and L.Howard, October 1983
This eliminate route follows the line of three bolts on the slick rock between Runnel Route and the water streak.

Grotto Canyon

SPLASHDANCE *   30 m, 5.11a
J.Martin and L.Howard, July 1985
Follow the line of bolts in the waterstreak. The climb is slow to dry and normally cannot be done until late summer.

ALIEN **   45 m, 5.9
D.Morgan and A.Skuce, 1981
Climb a short corner to a manky bolt (a second bolt a short distance above was added later). On the slab above, a few thin moves lead to easier, but sustained climbing. Difficulties ease after 10 m at a third bolt.

TRIVIAL PURSUIT   45 m, 5.8
J.Martin and L.Howard, April 1984
Climb a short slab right of Alien, pull over an overlap, and continue to the third bolt of The Stand. Climb straight up to a ledge at the top of the slab, making a short detour right near the top.

THE STAND **   20 m, 5.9
J.Martin and C.Perry, May 1982
Follow a line of three bolts to the right of Alien, then work up left and make a difficult move to reach the first bolt of Alien.

CENTRAL PARK   45 m, 5.5
First ascent unknown
Climb easy rock through the bushes to the right of The Stand.

SPACE CADET   45 m, 5.4
J.Martin, April 1984
Climb the slab between a vegetated break and the bolts of Spacewalk. Near the top, traverse left and continue up on large holds.

SPACEWALK *   50 m, 5.7
D.Morgan and P.Walls, 1981
Climb past two bolts to a station at the top of the slab.

AFTERNOON DELIGHT **   50 m, 5.5
D.Morgan and P.Kato, 1981
Follow the bolts (two) right of Spacewalk.

CRUISIN' FOR BURGERS   50 m, 5.4
J.Martin, May 1982
Climb well-textured rock right of Afternoon Delight. No protection.

PATTY'S CLIMB   50 m, 5.5
P.Kato and D.Morgan, 1981
Climb the left-facing corner which takes small to medium nuts for protection. It is advisable to traverse left near the top to avoid a huge detached block.

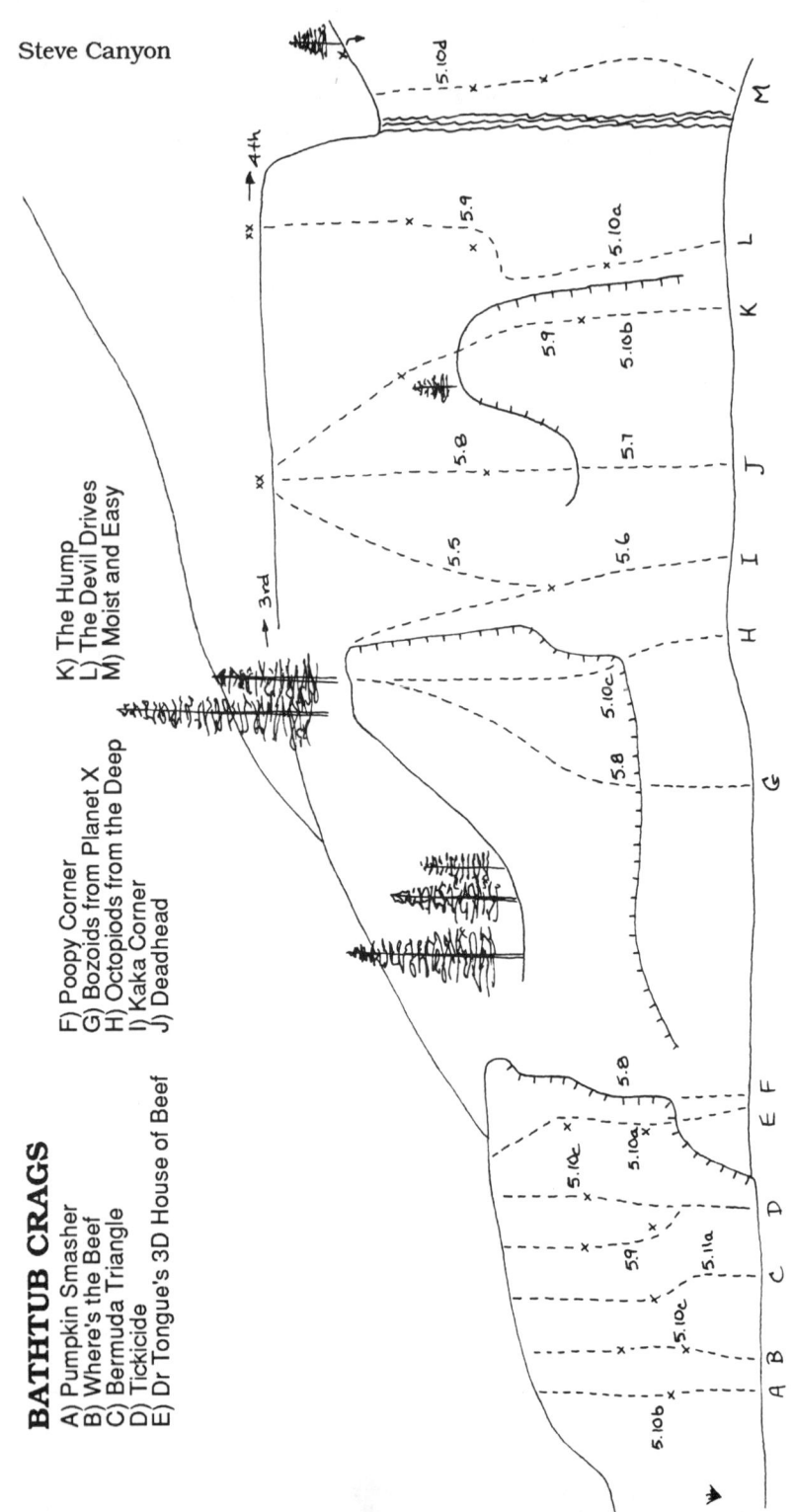

STEVE CANYON

Steve Canyon is the next watercourse east from Grotto Canyon. It offers short, steep, mainly bolt-protected face climbs.
Approach: Park at Grotto Pond Picnic Area 2.4 km east of Gap Lake and start as for the official Grotto Canyon trail. Walk up the trail for a couple of minutes to a watercourse and follow this uphill for 10 -15 minutes to reach the cliffs which start just beyond a nicely sculptured waterslide. There are two main climbing areas separated by a waterfall. Below the waterfall are the Lower, Middle and Upper Bathtub crags; above it is the Main Canyon.

BATHTUB CRAGS

PUMPKIN SMASHER   7 m, 5.10b
J.Martin and L.Ostrander, June 1987

This is the leftmost route on Lower Bathtub Crag, the first climbing rock encountered. A bolt protects the lower moves; a #3 RP is needed higher up.

† WHERE'S THE BEEF? *   7 m, 5.10c
L.Ostrander and J.Martin, June 1987

Climb the wall right of Pumpkin Smasher past two bolts.

BERMUDA TRIANGLE   7 m, 5.11a
J.Martin and L.Ostrander, June 1987

Make a difficult pull off the ground, step left, and continue more easily to the top past a lone bolt right of Where's The Beef?

TICKICIDE *   8 m, 5.9 or 5.10c
J.Martin, L.Howard and S.Stahl, June 1987
Direct Finish: J.Martin and L.Ostrander, June 1987

Climb up the only easy break at the bottom of Lower Bathtub Crag to a bolt. Move left and climb past another bolt by a tiny tree for the regular route. Continue up and slightly right (bolt) for the direct finish.

† DR. TONGUE'S 3D HOUSE OF BEEF   8 m, 5.10a
J.Martin and S.Stahl, June 1987

Climb over a bulge and up a groove near the right side of Lower Bathtub Crag. Two bolts.

† POOPY CORNER   8 m, 5.8
S.Stahl, April 1987

This is the right-facing corner at the right margin of Lower Bathtub Crag.

Steve Canyon

† BOZOIDS FROM PLANET X   15 m, 5.8
J.Martin, L.Howard and S.Stahl, June 1987

This route climbs the centre of Middle Bathtub Crag. Pull over a tricky bulge at a yellow scar, then trend up right to the top. A small Friend protects the crux.

OCTOPOIDS FROM THE DEEP   15 m, 5.10c (toprope)
J.Martin and L.Ostrander, June 1987

Pull over the bulge at the right side of Middle Bathtub Crag and continue to the top.

KAKA CORNER   18 m, 5.7
S.Stahl and S.Slymon, April 1987

Climb the obvious right-facing corner separating Middle and Upper Bathtub Crags. A variant trends up right from a bolt at one-third height on easy rock to a fixed station near the top of Upper Bathtub Crag.

DEADHEAD   18 m, 5.8
J.Marshall, S.Slymon and S.Stahl, April 1987

Climb a slabby wall right of Kaka Corner to a bolt at a ledge. Continue past a short slot to a fixed station. Variations are possible and all are somewhat runout.

THE HUMP   18 m, 5.10b
J.Marshall and S.Stahl, April 1987

Right of Deadhead is a smooth rounded buttress in low relief called The Hump. Climb the right side of this feature past a bolt to a small tree on a ledge. Trend left past a bolt to the Deadhead belay.

THE DEVIL DRIVES *   18 m, 5.10a
J.Martin and L.Ostrander, June 1987

Climb a tricky corner just right of The Hump (bolt). Move right onto a smooth wall and climb to the top past two bolts to a bolt station at a ledge.

MOIST AND EASY **   14 m, 5.10c - 5.11a
J.Marshall and S.Stahl, May 1987

This nice face climb lies immediately right of the small waterfall that marks the end of the Bathtub Crags. Protection is fixed and the difficulty of the climb depends on the height of the climber.

MAIN CANYON

† DREAM WEAVER   30 m, 5.10c
J.Marshall and S.Stahl, May 1987

Above the waterfall is a higher wall. Dream Weaver climbs past five bolts to a fixed station about 12 m past the waterfall near the left side of this wall.

† TAKE FIVE *   25 m, 5.10c
S.Stahl and J.Martin, August 1987

Start as for Dream Weaver, but after clipping the first bolt move up and right, then angle back left to the Dream Weaver belay. All protection is fixed.

† FRIENDLY PERSUASION   20 m, 5.8
S.Stahl, L.Howard and J.Martin, June 1987

This surprisingly moderate route follows a steep left-facing corner about 15 m right of Dream Weaver. Pull over a tricky bulge past a suspect piton and then follow the corner past four bolts to a rappel station.

EXSHAW SLAB

This is a small slab about 5 km northwest of Exshaw near Mt. Fable. The only routes established so far lie on the far right end of the outcrop, on a clean facet of rock to the right of a prominent right-facing corner.

Approach: Turn north off Highway 1A in the town of Exshaw and follow a road on the east side of Exshaw Creek through a residential district to a small parking area by a footbridge that crosses the creek. Go across the creek and head north up the valley, following first a trail beside a wire fence, then an abandoned road, and finally a trail in the creek valley. Walk to a fork in the valley (about an hour), turn left, and continue for about 15 minutes, watching for a large cairn on the right about 100 m past a big treed slab. Exshaw Slab is not visible from this point but is only 5 minutes' walk uphill to the right (east) from the cairn.

STRICTLY FOR BOLTEN **   22 m, 5.10a
J.Marshall and S.Stahl, 1984

This climbs the face immediately right of the prominent corner mentioned above. Climb up with difficulty past two bolts to a little tree. Continue past a fixed piton, step left to avoid a difficult section, and then move up and right to another bolt. Continue up and right to a fourth bolt and exit straight up. Alternatively, from the piton go straight up to the third bolt and continue directly to the top.

† NEANDORCRAWL   22 m, 5.8
S.Stahl and S.Stahl, 1984

Start about 6 m right of Strictly For Bolten. Climb straight up the slab, passing left of a small tree and shrub, to a break below a small overhang. Climb a short, right-leaning corner, traverse left to the final bolt of Strictly For Bolten, and finish as for that route.

YAMNUSKA AREA

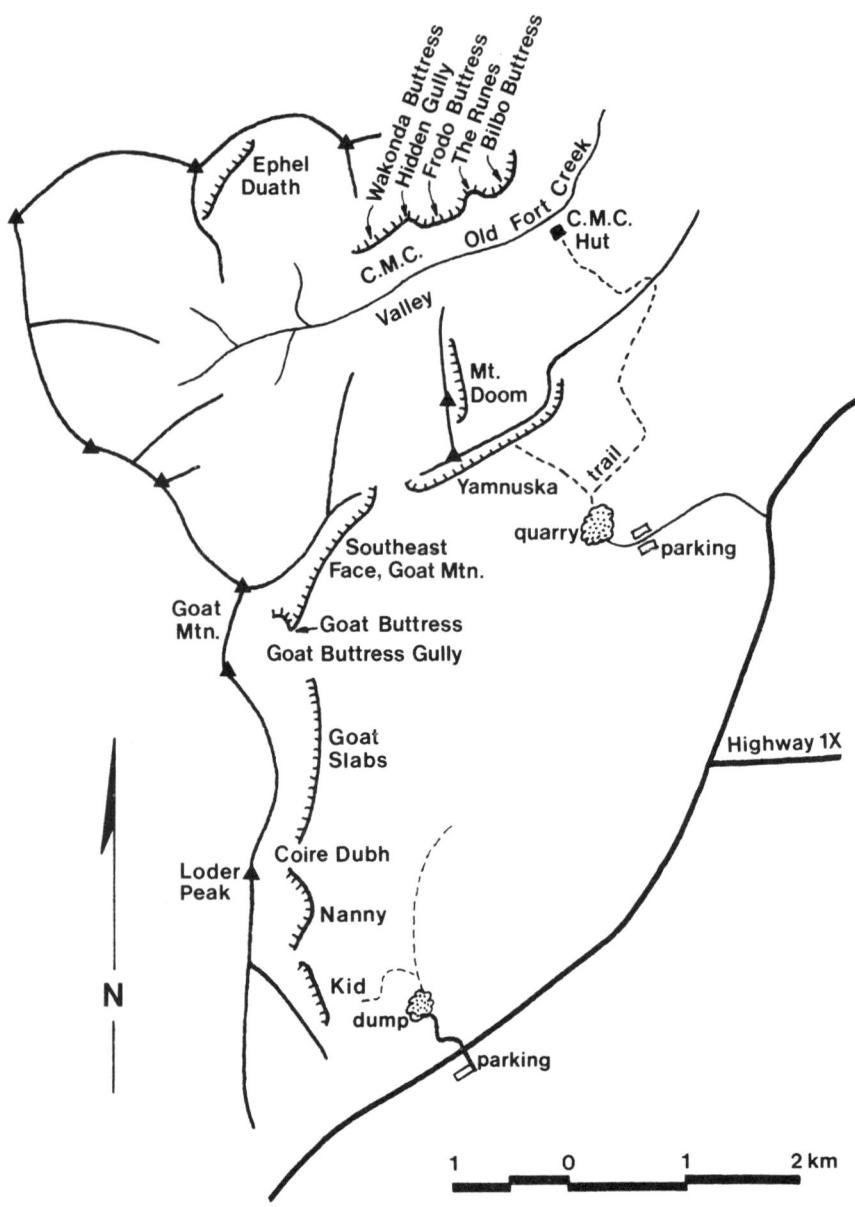

GOAT MOUNTAIN

The east face of Goat Mountain is a huge overthrust mass of Eldon Limestone which marks the southward extension from Yamnuska of the McConnell Fault. The face extends along the long south ridge of the mountain and is broken by major gullies into four sections. These decrease considerably in size from north to south and are called Goat Wall, Goat Slabs, Nanny Goat and Kid Goat (see map opposite).
In addition to the four areas mentioned above, a number of climbs have been done in the two disused quarry slots at the base of the south ridge. However, climbing here is now strictly forbidden since the owners, Steel Brothers, are liable for any accidents that occur. Prosecution has been threatened on a number of occasions and mention of the slots is made here only to inform climbers that this obvious area is out of bounds.

KID GOAT

Kid Goat, the smallest of the Goat Mountain climbing areas, is about 150 m high. The quality of the rock is generally quite good and often excellent. However, some loose rock is found, notably along the top of the cliff. The cliff is characterized by lines of overhangs that run along its length and give a false impression of difficulty. The easier routes typically take lines of least resistance through the overhangs often on moderately-angled slabs. Protection is sparse on many of the climbs although the most recent ones are well-bolted and do not require pitons.
Approach: Park at a paved pull-off on the south side of Highway 1A a short distance east of the crag. Cross the highway and follow a gravel road to a landfill site. From the northeast corner of the site, follow a gravel track for a short distance until it enters a large meadow. Turn left up a fainter side track and follow this to a small gravel pit. Climb the open hillside above and to the right and then near the top contour left (cairn) to join a trail that runs beneath the cliff. The climbs on the south end of the cliff can also be reached by climbing up the ridge directly from the highway, although this approach is now posted "No Trespassing".
Descent: From the top of the cliff, easy descents can be made to the south or to the north via the gully between Kid Goat and Nanny Goat. The first four climbs can be finished by following easy rock to the top of the cliff, or more conveniently by traversing left to trees and scrambling down.

RIPOFF * 30 m, 5.6
J. Martin and M. Sawyer, May 1975
An interesting and well-protected layback problem.

SLIPKID   30 m, 5.8
C. Perry and M. White, 1978
Slipkid follows a moderate corner above a crux start - an unprotected layback sequence up a short bulging wall.

117

BREEZY   30 m, 5.6
J. Martin and L. Howard, September 1979
This short route follows a moderate corner capped by a small roof.

TIP-OFF   30 m, 5.7
G. Spohr and J. Martin, September 1979
Tip-off takes an easy corner capped by an awkward roof. Watch for small loose blocks at the roof.

LEFTOVER GROOVES *   80 m 5.7
C. Perry and J. Martin, April 1979
1)   15 m, Climb to a horizontal ledge and belay at its right end.
2)   30 m, 5.7. Continue up and right on a steep slab, making an ill-protected mantle move at its top. Follow an obvious corner system to a large ledge.
3)   35 m, 5.4. Climb a low-angled layback crack to the top.

NIGHT SHIFT *   85 m, 5.5
C. Dale and J. Martin, April 1981
This spectacular-looking route is easier than it appears, but it has some loose blocks. Start at the left side of a tree ledge.
1)   40 m, 5.5. Traverse right from a large block into a groove, or climb the overhang at the base of the groove (5.8). Climb the groove, traverse right to a break in the bulge above and then move up to the main roof. Traverse left on a slanting ledge, continue left to an easy break in the overlap above, and move up to a small ledge.
2)   45 m, Climb easy rock to the top.

CHEAP THRILLS   135 m, 5.8
J. Martin and G. Spohr, September 1979
1)   50 m, 5.2. Climb an easy pitch to a big ledge with trees.
2)   35 m, 5.8. Make a few steep moves to gain the groove right of Night Shift, then climb more easily to a sloping ledge. Traverse right, climb up to a small birch shrub at a horizontal break, traverse right to a short corner (watch for loose rock), and climb this to a ledge with a bolt.
3)   35 m, 5.7. Step up onto a slab under a roof, move left to a break, and step over the roof. Continue easily to a ledge.
4)   15 m, Climb easily to the top.

SLINGSBY'S OVERHANGS DIRECT   155 m, 5.6
K. Bridgens and T. Jones, 1975
1,2)   80 m, 5.5. Various possible lines on moderate rock lead to a belay below an obvious break in the long roof.
3)   35 m, 5.6. Climb up to a short, steep corner directly below the break in the roof. From the top of the corner make a thin step up left onto a slabby wall. Climb this and then trend left on easier rock to a ledge.
4)   40 m, Continue to the top.

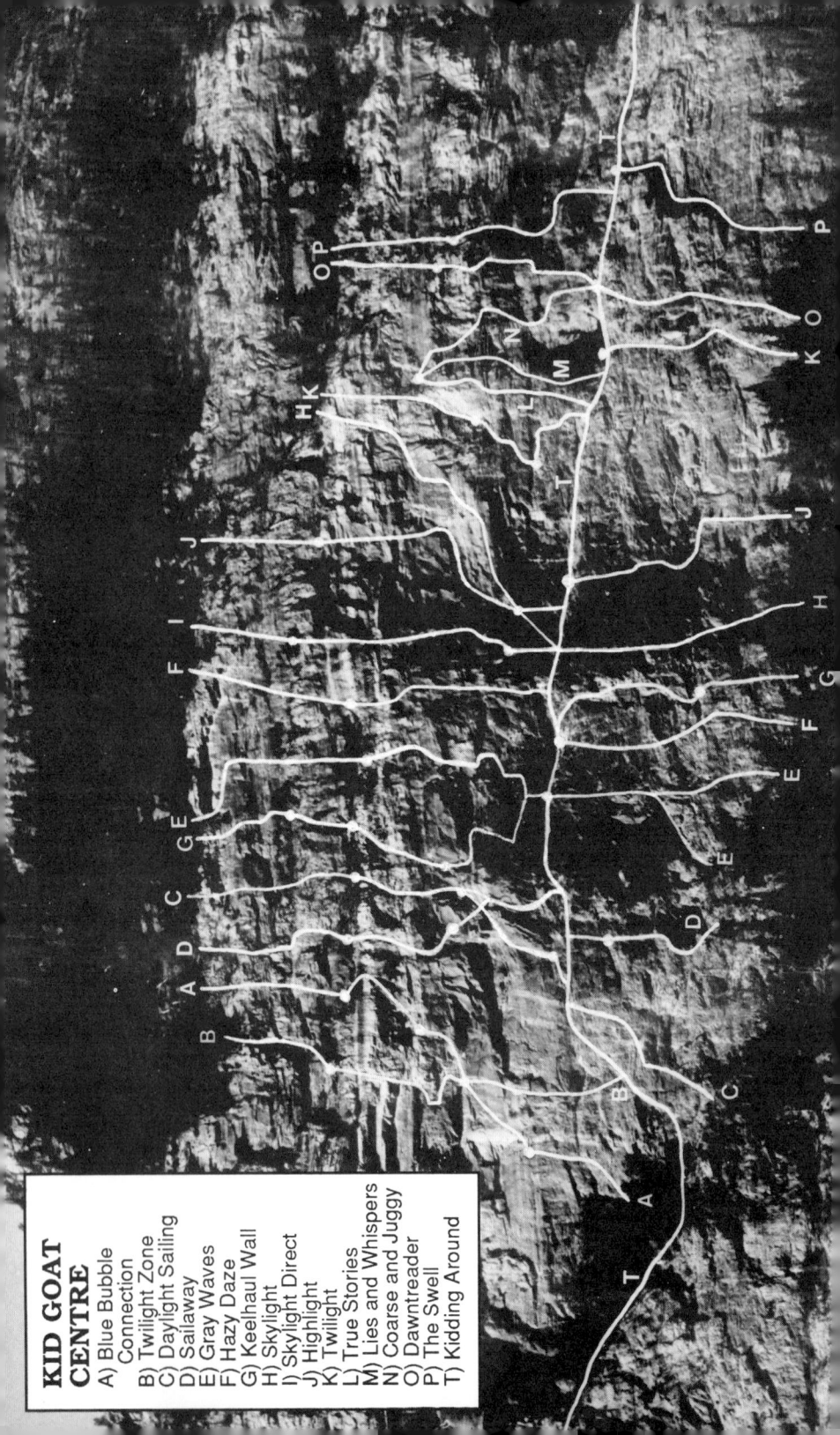

SLINGSBY'S OVERHANGS INDIRECT   110 m, 5.5
K. Bridgens and T. Jones, 1975

This is the easiest climb on Kid Goat. Start by scrambling left from the left edge of the big central tree ledge.
1)   35 m. Climb easy rock left and up to the belay below the roof.
2)   35 m, 5.5. Climb the short corner as for the Direct. At the top of the corner traverse right to a break in the bulge above, then climb up easily to a ledge.
3)   40 m. Climb easy rock to the top.

EDGE OF NIGHT *   155 m, 5.7
J. Martin and C. Perry, October 1979

This interesting route has some steep moves directly above an impressive drop-off.
1,2)   80 m, 5.3. Climb two easy pitches to a good ledge where the rock steepens.
3)   35 m, 5.7. Climb up right on a steep slab. From its top, step right into a little bay and then step up right again. Now move back left, stem up to a narrow ledge, traverse right to a corner and climb easily to a small tree below a roof.
4)   40 m, 5.5. Climb up left onto a rib, surmount a short roof, and then continue by a slab and a short, steep wall to easy ground.

BLUE BUBBLE CONNECTION   140 m, 5.7
J. Martin, G. Spohr and J. Tanner, June 1975

Start at the upper right side of the central tree bay.
1)   40 m, 5.6. Climb up to a steep, narrow ramp. From its top trend right over slabs to small ledges.
2)   35 m, 5.7. Traverse up and right to a corner (Twilight Zone), then continue right by a few awkward moves above a roof to a flaky crack. Climb this to broken blocks.
3)   30 m, 5.6. Climb a short, steep wall and continue to a tree ledge.
4)   35 m. Move left to an easy exit or finish directly.

TWILIGHT ZONE **   135 m, 5.6
K. Bridgens and T. Jones, 1975

Twilight Zone was one of the earliest routes on Kid Goat and it remains one of the best.
1,2)   65 m, 5.6. Two pitches of face climbing, topped by a short finger crack, lead more of less straight up just right of the tree bay to a ledge below the main overhangs.
3)   40 m, 5.6. Climb up right, then move left. Step up, traverse back right to a corner-crack and make a jamming move up to surmount the overhang. Move right and climb a steep little wall, then continue to a tree ledge.
4)   30 m, 5.5. Exit above by face climbing.

Kid Goat

DAYLIGHT SAILING   140 m, 5.6
J. Martin, M. Toft and L. Howard, June 1979
1) 55 m, 5.5. Climb the wall right of Twilight Zone to a bulge at the base of a large slab. Traverse right, layback over the bulge, and move right to belay at the base of a short groove.
2) 20 m, 5.3. Climb the groove a few metres, then traverse right and climb into an easy groove, belaying when convenient.
3) 25 m, 5.5. Face climb straight up to a tree ledge.
4) 40 m, 5.6. Scramble up to a ledge below a bulge. Step right, climb the bulge, then step left and continue to the top.

SAILAWAY   130 m, 5.6
J. Martin and J. Tanner, May 1980
Sailaway starts up the steep wall right of Daylight Sailing.
1) 25 m, 5.6. Beginning from the high point of scree below the wall, move left on a ledge. Climb to a second ledge, move right, climb past a flake, and belay on a ledge.
2) 45 m, 5.6. Climb straight up to a traverse line below an overhang. Traverse right, climb up to the right of the overhang, and then move back left to a short corner. Climb the corner, then move left across the easy groove of Daylight Sailing and continue up left to a ledge below a small roof.
3) 25 m, 5.5. Traverse left by means of a finger crack and climb up to trees.
4) 35 m, 5.6. Climb the slab above, then move left below a steep wall to a right-slanting corner. Climb the corner and finish up over a short but tricky bulge.

GRAY WAVES *   140 m, 5.7
J. Martin and L. Howard, April 1980
Start at a narrow slab with a drop-off on its left.
1) 50 m, 5.6. Climb up the slab a short distance, traverse right and climb a short wall. Slant left up slabs to a large dead tree on a sloping ledge or gain this ledge easily from a treed break to the left. From the upper end of the ledge climb more or less straight up, staying left of some orange rock, to ledges.
2) 45 m, 5.7. Climb up a few moves, then trend up right on slabs. Move back left to climb a short wall to a small ledge below a roof. Traverse right under the roof to a break, then step up and back left. Continue up to trees.
3) 45 m, 5.6. Move the belay 15 m to the highest trees. Climb up slabs to a break in a small overlap (slightly to the right). Climb the break, then traverse back left to an exit at the left edge of a prominent overhang.

HAZY DAZE 140 m, 5.8
B. Keller and J. Martin, July 1979

1) 50 m, 5.6. Climb the wall between Gray Waves and Keelhaul Wall, belaying at the big ledge.
2) 45 m, 5.8. Traverse right to a pale scar and make some tricky moves up a steep section. Continue by sustained face climbing, stepping left at a small overlap to gain easier ground. Climb up to a large ledge.
3) 45 m, 5.5. Continue straight up to the top.

KEELHAUL WALL ** 145 m, 5.6
J. Martin and C. Perry, May 1975

Keelhaul Wall is the most popular climb at Kid Goat and is a good introductory route.

1) 20 m, Climb easy rock to a ledge with a belay bolt below an obvious corner.
2) 35 m, 5.6. From the left end of the ledge, go up and right into the corner. Climb the corner. Just before it closes, move left and up, to a big ledge below a band of overhangs.
3) 30 m, 5.5. From the left end of the ledge, climb a break in the overhangs and move across left to a small, vegetated ledge. Climb up to beneath an overhang, traverse left, and move up to a ledge.
4) 20 m, 5.5. Climb a short wall to easy ground and tree ledges.
5) 40 m, 5.5. Climb slabby rock over a small overlap to the top.

SKYLIGHT * 125 m, 5.6
J. Martin, C. Shank and D. Strand, June 1979

To the right of the corner on Keelhaul Wall is a faint, rounded buttress. Start by scrambling up left 30 m to gain the buttress and belay where the rock steepens.

1) 45 m, 5.5. Climb up the buttress nearly to a line of overhangs. Slant up right to a break and pull over the overhang to a ledge at the base of a slab.
2) 50 m, 5.6. Traverse right, moving up slightly, to a point where the slab steepens. Climb up, traverse right to a rib, then continue up and right to a groove. Climb the groove to easy ground.
3) Scramble to the top.

SKYLIGHT DIRECT * 140 m, 5.7
C. Dale, J. Martin and C. Perry, May 1980

1) 45 m, 5.5. Start as for Skylight, but break through the overhanging band by an obvious short hand crack.
2) 45 m, 5.7. Move right and climb a short, steep wall, then continue right to an obvious groove. Climb the groove and two short walls above it to a ledge.
3) 50 m, Climb easy slabs to the top.

Kid Goat

HIGHLIGHT *   140 m, 5.8
C. Perry and J. Martin, May 1979

Highlight is one of the harder of the earlier climbs on Kid Goat and has an interesting exit sequence. Start by scrambling up to two small shrubs on a ledge right of Skylight.
1) 30 m, 5.7. Climb up and left in a steep groove, then continue by the face above to a good ledge with fixed pitons.
2) 15 m, 5.5. Move left to a break in the overhangs above and climb up to a ledge (the ledge on Skylight).
3) 40 m, 5.8. Climb up to a roof, traverse right, and climb up to a smaller overhang. Climb this and a sustained groove above. Near the top make a long reach left and layback up to easy ground. Continue up a short wall to good ledges.
4) 30 m, Climb easily to the top.

TWILIGHT *   135 m, 5.7
J. McIsaac and R. Coley, 1975

Start at a corner below a bay with big trees.
1) 45 m, 5.5. Climb the corner, detouring left when necessary, to the trees.
2) 30 m, 5.6. Move left and climb up to a small roof which slants up left. Climb up under the roof to its left end, then move up to a bulge and traverse left to a small belay ledge.
3) 15 m, 5.6. Climb the bulge above, then traverse right below a second, larger bulge until it is possible to pull up into a bay. Move up to the base of a groove and belay at a bolt.
4) 45 m, 5.7. Climb the obvious layback crack above and right and then follow slabs to the top (large Friends useful).
4a) 45 m, 5.6. Move left and climb an obvious groove which leads to the top of Skylight.

TRUE STORIES *   35 m, 5.10a
J.Martin and L.Ostrander, June 1987

This fun route climbs the crest of a rounded pillar left of the tree bay of Twilight. Approach from the right by scrambling along a ledge system. All protection is fixed.
Move up left from the tree bay to the left of two bolts and climb a short, tricky wall. Angle up left and then back right to a bolt at an overhang. Pull over the bulge and continue up the crest of the pillar past bolts to a small tree and a bolt belay. Rappel to descend.

LIES AND WHISPERS *   35 m, 5.10b
J.Martin and L.Ostrander, June 1987

Start just right of True Stories on the right side of the rounded pillar. Climb a short, steep wall (bolt), move up past a second bolt, and pull over a bulge (bolt) at a pale grey streak. Climb a short slab (bolt) and break through a roof at an irregular crack with a distinctive cemented block. Above, pull through two more smaller bulges and continue more easily to the belay of True Stories, moving right to avoid some dubious blocks. Take small wired nuts and a #4 Friend. Rappel to descend.

COARSE AND JUGGY **   40 m, 5.9
J.Martin and L.Howard, 1987

This route climbs the back of the tree bay of Twilight. Starting near the right side of the tree bay, slant left up a faint ramp past a bolt to an overhang (bolt). Traverse left and pull up an impending wall past two more bolts. Work up right, then back up left to the belay of True Stories. Take wired nuts. Rappel to descend.

DAWNTREADER   140 m, 5.9
J.Martin and W.Lee, June 1983

The crux of this climb is a steep, rough wall protected by bolts. Start immediately right of the corner of Twilight.
1)   45 m, 5.6. Climb up to a short, left-facing corner. Climb this and follow a discontinuous series of broken corners to a big ledge with trees to the left (the tree bay of Twilight).
2)   30 m, 5.9. Starting from a birch shrub, climb up to a bolt where the rock becomes vertical. Step right and mantleshelf onto a big hold (bolt). Climb the overhang above (piton) and make an awkward exit onto easier rock.
3)   35 m, Climb easily to a ledge with big trees.
4)   30 m, Move left and scramble up to the top.

THE SWELL   145 m, 5.9
J. Martin and L. Howard, August 1980

This climb is easy except for a few moves.
1)   50 m, 5.5. Climb up to a prominent right-facing corner system and follow this to a big ledge.
2)   30 m, 5.9. Continue up moderate rock nearby to a bulge, then slant up left to a short impending wall with a bolt. Climb the wall and bulge above to easier ground.
3)   35 m, Continue easily to a tree ledge.
4)   30 m, 5.5. Finish by a break slightly to the left.

HALF LIFE   35 m, 5.9
J.Martin and C.Yonge, May 1987

Right of The Swell is a yellow wall capped by an overhang. Start at a steep grey wall to its right. Climb the grey wall past three bolts. Move up and left onto a slab and then up and right to a yellow streak in a stepped wall. Climb to a roof (two bolts), traverse left past the end of the roof, and angle up left to a spruce tree. Rappel to descend. A medium size stopper is useful.

SMOKING MIRROR *** 85 m, 5.10a
J.Martin and R.MacLachlan, April 1987

This route follows a water-streaked, right-facing corner. Double ropes and Friends to #4 are recommended.
1) 35 m, 5.10a. Climb a short overhanging wall past a bolt to gain the corner. Follow this past two bolts until it steepens, then traverse right and mantle onto a ledge. Climb up and left past three bolts to regain the corner. Trend right up a ramp. At its top move up and left to a bolt on a sloping ledge.
2) 20 m, 5.8. Climb up on the left to an overhang. Traverse right past a bolt to a break and follow this past another bolt to easier ground.
3) 30 m, Scramble up and right over slabs to the top.

CRUISING 95 m, 5.8
C. Perry and J. Martin, June 1980

Protection is marginal on this steep climb which is hard for its grade. Start below a small spruce about 10 m right of Smoking Mirror.
1) 25 m, 5.7. Climb up a steep, unprotected wall to the spruce. Traverse right, climb up to a roof, traverse right again, and then climb up to a ledge with a second small spruce.
2) 30 m, 5.8. Traverse right and climb up over a difficult and unprotected bulge, then slant up right and pull over a second bulge. Continue up and right to the final bulge which is surmounted just to the right of an irregular crack by a tricky move onto a slab. Continue easily to a small tree.
3) 40 m, Climb easy slabs to the top.

WAVE GOODBYE ** 40m, 5.11a
J.Martin and S.Dougherty, August 1987

This strenuous and technical climb starts just right of Cruising. Climb a short wall past two bolts to a ledge with a small tree (junction with Cruising). Continue up a right-facing corner to the first of several overhangs. Climb past four bolts to the top overhang and make a difficult high step left to reach easier ground. The belay is about 12m higher and slightly left.

MAX HEADROOM *** 40 m, 5.10d
S.Dougherty, J.Martin and M.Zimmerman, July 1987

This recommended climb takes a direct line up the cliff through the first belay ledge of cruising. Climb a steep but broken face past three bolts to the ledge and continue to a large bulge with a bolt. Pull over the bulge on sloping holds and continue up steep, sustained climbing past three more bolts. A final easy runout up a slab leads to the anchors. Protection is fixed. Rappel to descend.

Kid Goat

NEW HOPE FOR THE DEAD *** 40 m, 5.9
J.Martin and L.Ostrander, June 1987
This fun route follows a line of bolts right of Max Headroom. Near the top, the line trends left across the second pitch of Cruising to an unlikely exit through the upper band of overhangs. Protection is fixed. Rappel to descend.

TALK DIRTY TO ME ** 45 m, 5.10a
J.Martin and R.MacLachlan, April 1987
Start directly below a small pine located about 25 m up and a short distance right of New Hope For The Dead. Large Friends recommended.
1) 25 m, 5.10a. Climb up steepening rock towards the pine. Continue up a steep wall past three bolts and step right to the pine.
2) 20 m, 5.9. Slant up right to a roof. Move left under the roof past a bolt and pull over the overhang. Angle up right under another roof, avoiding a dubious block, to a bolt. Step up and follow a ramp up right to bolts. Rappel to descend.

TAKEDOWN ** 40 m, 5.10c
J.Martin and S.Dougherty, June 1987
This sustained route climbs the rounded pillar just right of Talk Dirty To Me. Climb a difficult overhanging wall and continue up the crest of the pillar to the fourth bolt. Move up and right to the edge of the pillar, climb straight up, and then angle up right on a steep ramp, finishing up the last few metres of Feeding Frenzy. Take a #2 Friend. Rappel to descend.

DRIFTER * 70 m, 5.8
C. Perry and J. Martin, September 1979
Drifter is an excellent sustained climb on a steep wall. Start just right of Takedown.
1) 45 m, 5.7. Climb up to a pale gray streak at the right base of an overhang. Climb the gray streak, then move up and right to overhangs. Trending right, surmount the overhangs at a break, then climb up slabs and traverse right to a two bolt belay.
2) 25 m, 5.8. Traverse up right on slabs to a minor break in the roof above (bolt). Make a difficult step over the roof, move right to a short corner, and then climb up steep slabs just right of the corner to a belay at a tree.
3) Scramble to the top or rappel (45 m).

FEEDING FRENZY *** 40 m, 5.10b
J.Martin and C.Yonge, May 1987
This route typifies Kid Goat climbing at its best. All protection is fixed. Start right of Drifter and climb up to a short, right-facing corner near the pale grey streak. Climb the undercut arete left of the corner (two bolts) to a slab and continue to a ledge (intersection with Drifter). Continue up past five more bolts to the belay of Talk Dirty To Me. The upper part of the climb can be combined with the start of Drifter to make an excellent 5.9. Rappel to descend.

Kid Goat

DIVERS FROM THE ANAEROBIC ZONE ** 45 m, 5.10b
C.Yonge and J.Martin, May 1987

Start about 8 m right of Feeding Frenzy. Pull over a difficult stepped overhang past a bolt, move up and left past another bolt, and continue to a bolt at the right end of a big overhang. Move up and left, continue up steep rock past two more bolts, and then angle easily up left to the final wall. Climb this past two bolts and two bulges to a bolt belay on a slab. Take a small wired nut. Rappel to descend.

SHAKEDOWN * 25 m, 5.10a
J.Martin, S.Dougherty and C.Quinn, May 1987

Start about 4 m right of Divers From The Anaerobic Zone. Surmount the initial overhang at a short, right-facing corner (bolt). Traverse right past a bolt and climb a second overhang (bolt). Continue to a roof about 10 m higher and climb it by a flake at its smallest part. Angle up left on easy rock to the bolt belay of Drifter. Take small wires and Friends. Rappel to descend.

BREAKDOWN * 15 m, 5.11a
J.Martin and S.Dougherty, July 1987

Figuring out this roof problem above the belay of Shakedown may give you a breakdown. Tiptoe up a slab to the overhang and then employ similar tactics to swarm over it. Two bolts protect the difficulties.

STICKY FINGERS   75 m, 5.6
J. Martin, June 1979

This route has an amusing start and an unprotected crux. Start at a fir tree just left of an obvious shallow corner which is cut off from the ground by an overhang.
1)   25 m, 5.6. Climb the tree until it is possible to step right onto the rock. Move right, climb up into the corner, and continue to a ledge.
2)   50 m, 5.5. Climb up slabs and a short wall, then scramble to the top.

SLOW HAND   40 m, 5.9
G. Spohr and J. Martin, October 1979

Slow Hand starts in a right-slanting, right-facing corner just right of Sticky Fingers.
1)   40 m, 5.9. Climb up the corner, which is awkward and ill-protected, until it is possible to stand comfortably on a foothold. Step left and go up a short, steep slab to easier ground. Traverse up right across a slab under an overhang, then continue up and right to a tree.
2)   Scramble to the top or rappel from the tree.

Kid Goat

KIDDING AROUND 370 m, 5.6
J. Martin and J. Tanner, May 1980

This girdle traverse follows a prominent, discontinuous ledge system which crosses the cliff at about one-third height.
1) 60 m, Walk out on the ledge under Leftover Grooves, then climb 3rd class to trees. Belay at the right end of the tree ledge.
2) 30 m, 5.4. Drop down about 3 m, then traverse past an awkward corner to ledges.
3) 40 m, Climb 3rd class on ledges to the central tree bay. Belay at the right side of this tree bay near a pale gray streak.
4) 45 m, 5.5. Climb over to a large block (shrubs), then go straight up to an obvious traverse line. Traverse right, then step up over an overlap and belay at the base of a short groove (Daylight Sailing first belay).
5) 25 m, 5.6. Climb down 4 m to a ledge. Traverse right to a larger ledge. From its end angle up right and continue to a niche with a bolt.
6) 20 m, 5.5. Step down from the right end of the niche, then go right to the large ledge of Keelhaul Wall.
7) 30 m, 5.4. Walk right to an awkward corner. Beyond this, climb down 2 or 3 m and continue across slabs to a ledge with fixed pitons (Highlight).
8) 40 m, 4th class. Continue right on a sloping ledge. At its end climb down to a big tree ledge (Twilight).
9) 80 m, 3rd and 4th class. Scramble off along ledges.

NANNY GOAT

Nanny Goat is steeper and less broken than Kid Goat. The quality of the rock is quite variable and the routes vary from mediocre to excellent. As on Kid Goat, the older routes tend to be poorly protected and require pitons. Most of the cliff faces east (this section is shown in the photograph). Prominent features are a smooth, dished wall just left of centre and a rounded buttress on the right with a steep, roughly semi-circular face bounded by overhangs in its lower section. Farther right, the cliff curves round into a gully (Coire Dubh) and becomes less steep.

Approach: As for Kid Goat as far as the gravel pit then head north for about 400 m to a water course descending from the gully between Kid Goat and Nanny Goat. A trail leading up to the south end of Nanny Goat starts on the south side of the water course and crosses to the north.

Descent is to the south via scree slopes and an easy gully.

BLUE MOVIE *   40 m, 5.10b
J.Martin, S.Dougherty and M.Zimmerman, April 1987

This steep face climb starts near the south end of the cliff below the left end of a right-trending ramp in dark gray rock. Climb easily to the base of the ramp. Pass a bolt and trend up right on easy rock to a bolt below an overhang. Climb up and right past two bolts, step over the overhang onto a steep wall, and climb past two more bolts to a third. Step right to a ledge, climb a short corner, and finish up a gray wall (bolt) to a bolt belay. Rappel, or continue to the top by a 5.5 pitch to a big cave and then a left-slanting, slabby class 4 pitch.

PREDATOR ***   45 m, 5.10c
J.Martin and L.Ostrander, May 1987

Predator follows an obvious leaning layback crack which starts about 25 m above the ground and 25 m right of the start of Blue Movie. Climb a steep juggy wall to a small ledge and continue with difficulty to the base of the crack. Make an awkward exit from the top of the crack onto a sloping ledge and then finish up a short corner. The climb is protected mainly by bolts but a range of equipment from small wires up to Friends #3 1/2 and #4 is also required. Rappel to descend.

CRAPULEUSE   140 m, 5.7
C. Scott and D. Vockeroth, 1970

Just left of the smooth central wall is a shallow buttress of broken rock with a small pillar at about one-third height. The route begins just right of the toe of the buttress directly below the pillar.
1) 40 m, Climb up to a tree in the chimney on the left side of the pillar.
2) 30 m, Traverse left a short distance on a steep wall until it is possible to step up to a block. Climb to the top of the block and step up left (5.7), then gain a corner above. Climb the corner to its top and cross a short slab to a big tree ledge.
3) 35 m, Climb up to the right of the ledge to an overhang and pass this by a short steep wall (5.6) on the right. Continue easily to a big ledge.

↶ *Choc Quinn on One Night Stand, photo Brian Wyvill*

4) 35 m, Move left on the ledge and make an ascending traverse left on a ramp. A few thin moves lead up from the ramp to a ledge below a slab. From the right end of the slab, climb a short steep wall and then scramble to ledges.
5) Scramble easily to the top.

Overnight Sensation Area
Near the middle of the smooth wall is a prominent, light-colored water streak which is the line of The Great White Hope. Below the water streak is a water-polished, roughly triangular facet of rock set at an angle to the main cliff and facing south. This is the Overnight Sensation Area, scene of the following seven routes. The climbs here are short and technical, with bolt protection. Several are usually wet until midsummer due to water seepages.

NIGHTLAND   25 m, 5.9
J.Martin and B.Keller, June 1985

Starting below a prominent left-facing corner, climb easily up to a bolt. Make a few awkward moves left and then climb up past a second bolt to a small ledge. Continue up a little corner and a steep wall to another small ledge, then slant right up a ramp to double bolts. An alternative start (S.Dougherty, 1986) begins further left and slants up right without protection to the second bolt. Small wired nuts are useful on the upper section of the climb.

BEDTIME STORY **   25 m, 5.10b
J.Martin and S.Dougherty, August 1986

This excellent climb takes the prominent corner mentioned under Nightland. Start as for Nightland. From the first ledge, move right to the base of the corner and climb it with increasing difficulty past four bolts to the ramp at the top of Nightland.

OVERNIGHT SENSATION *   25 m, 5.10d
W.Lee and J.Martin, June 1983

A serious and sustained climb. Starting in the centre of the rock, climb easily to a bolt (small hole). Climb a difficult section to a second bolt (groundfall potential). Step right to a little ledge and climb difficult rock past three more bolts. Trend left up a little corner to finish.

INTO THE NIGHT *   25 m, 5.10b
J.Martin and S.Dougherty, August 1986

This technical and sustained route lies just right of Overnight Sensation. Climb a tricky slab and steep wall past two bolts to the ledge on Overnight Sensation. Move right and climb a black water streak past two more bolts to the top.

NIGHT SENSATION **   25 m, 5.10d
Not a separate route, this combination of the start of Into The Night and the finish of Overnight Sensation is the best climb on the outcrop.

OVERNIGHT SENSATION AREA - NANNY GOAT

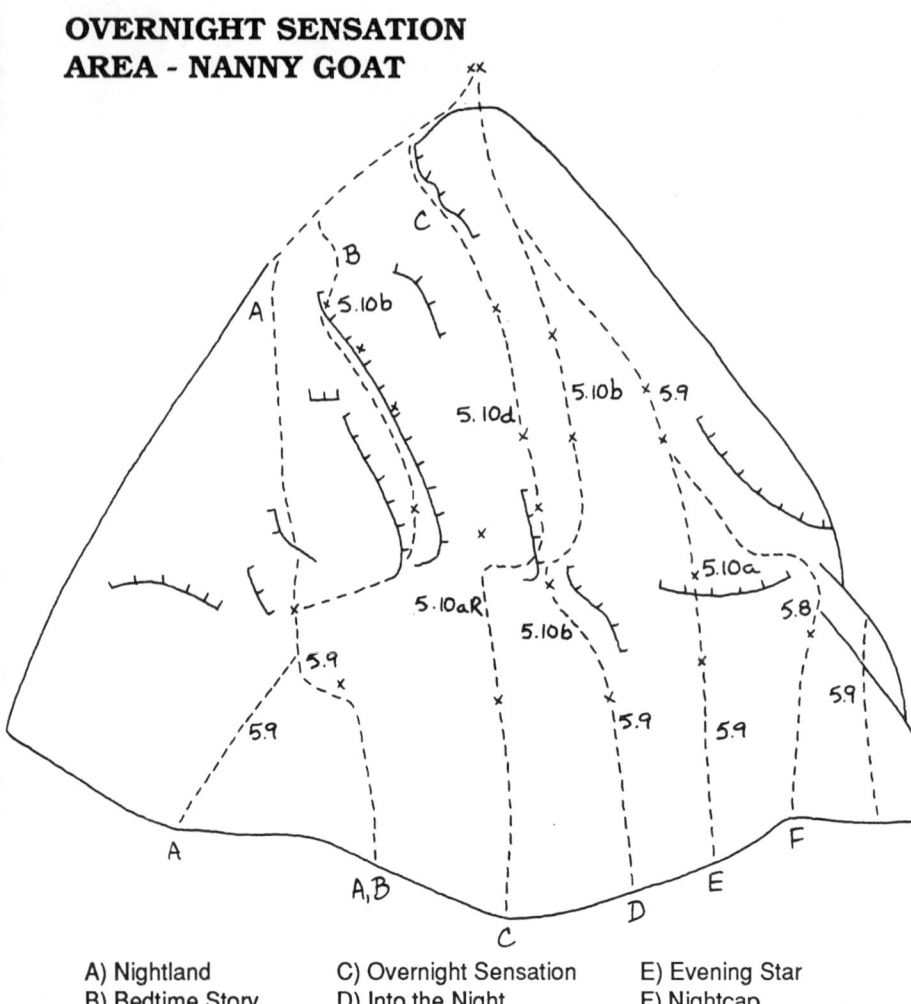

A) Nightland
B) Bedtime Story
C) Overnight Sensation
D) Into the Night
E) Evening Star
F) Nightcap

EVENING STAR 25 m, 5.10a
J.Martin and S.Dougherty, August 1986
This entertaining climb takes the prominent overhang near the right side of the rock. Climb a slick slab to a bolt, grope over the overhang past a second bolt, and then continue past two more bolts, trending left to finish.

NIGHTCAP 30 m, 5.9
J.Martin and S.Dougherty, August 1986
Climb the dihedral at the right end of the outcrop, avoiding the overhang at its top to the right. Move up left across a steep slab to the third bolt of Evening Star and finish as for that route. Take a # 1 1/2 Friend.

† GREAT WHITE HOPE * 185 m, 5.10b
G.Powter and B.Wyvill, September 1987

This serious route climbs the water streak near the centre of the smooth main wall. It remained the "last great problem" on Nanny Goat for many years and, in keeping with its classic nature, was finally led essentially on-sight. The overhanging section at the bottom is avoided by a rising traverse from the right and the climb joins the water streak on the upper wall partway up pitch 3.
Start as for One Night Stand.
1) 30 m, 5.10a. Move up and left to a small ledge below overlapping slabs. Gain the upper slab (piton) and climb up diagonally left to a bolt. Step down and move delicately left around a corner. Go up slightly and continue left to a good stance and bolt belay.
2) 35 m, 5.10b. Reverse the last few moves until directly below a steep crack leading to an overhang (piton left of crack). Climb the crack and traverse steeply right on good holds to a small ledge. Continue up and then step right into a crack. Follow this for a few moves until it is possible to traverse left for about 10 m past a piton to a poor stance and bolt belay.
3) 45 m, 5.10a. Climb up and left to an overhang. Make a tricky move around the left side of the overhang and continue over slightly easier ground to a second overhang (poor protection). Step left and go up a groove to a bolt. Climb right and up until a crack line leads rightwards to an overlap. Climb onto the slab above, move left, and continue up a corner to a belay at its top.
4) 50 m, 5.10a. Climb up to the next ledge and follow a rising ramp line rightwards to a break. Go straight up on small holds to an overhang (piton) and gain the continuation of the ramp. Follow this until it is possible to climb straight up to a groove leading slightly leftwards to a bolt belay.
5) 25 m, 5.9. Traverse left and down to gain a groove capped by an overhang. Climb the groove escaping left to a recess. Climb up and make an interesting move over an overhang. Continue directly to the top.

ONE NIGHT STAND * 170 m, 5.10b
C. Perry & M. Sawyer, 1980
F.F.A: B.Gross and Dougherty, July 1985

One Night Stand climbs the face to the right of the water streak and crosses a prominent band of overhangs in its lower third. The rock is good and the climbing is steep and technical. Pitches 1 and 3 are difficult to protect. Scramble up a rib on the right side of the bowl below the water streak to a small ledge with a bush beneath slabs.
1) 35 m, 5.8. Climb up a short distance and traverse easily right to a corner on the right side of the slabs. Move right again and up into a shallow groove in the rib. Follow this to a bulge, move up, and then step right to a ledge (piton). Follow slabs up and left to a bolt belay below and left of a prominent triangular roof.
2) 25 m, 5.10b. Move out left across the bulge past a piton runner and up to a bolt. Make a hard move left to holds, and continue up and back right on good rock to a ledge below a groove on the right side of an overhang.

3) 35 m, 5.8. Climb the groove to an easier-angled section. Continue to a shallow bay, move right, and climb a steep wall to a bolt belay in an alcove below the upper overhangs.
4) 35 m, 5.9. Make a hard move up left to a bolt runner and then follow an obvious rising traverse line left across the steep face, staying low near the end (piton). Move up and belay where the angle eases.
5) 20 m, 5.6. Climb up left and follow easier slabs and walls to a belay below roofs.
6) 20 m, 5.7. Surmount the roofs on the left and move back right to finish.

DECEPTION *   170 m, 5.7
T. Jones and C. Perry, 1975

Between the central wall and the semi-circular face is a shattered buttress with a slanting, left-facing corner on its left side. The corner begins at about one-third height and is capped by a large roof. Walk left on ledges above easy slabs to a bay just right of a rib below the upper corner.
1) 30 m, Climb up to a short corner and move out left to a ledge on the rib. Follow the rib to a belay by a block about 20 m below and left of the upper corner.
1a) The same point may be reached more easily by scrambling up a gully and ramp system which slants up from the left above the lower slabs.
2) 20 m, Move left to a hidden corner and climb it to a large ledge just left of the main corner.
3) 45 m, Move up right to the main corner and follow it until a steep, loose section is reached. Traverse out left on a ramp between overhangs to a groove. Belay a little higher on the right.
4) 30 m, Climb the slabby left wall of the corner to a small belay about 8 m below the terminal roof. A large overhang is located on the rib to the right at approximately the same level.
5) 45 m, Move up left to a short wall at the side of the roof. Climb this and the easier ground above to large ledges.

HESITATION   205 m, 5.7
J. Martin, C. Perry and M. Sawyer, 1975

This route climbs the shattered buttress between Deception and the corner on the left side of the semi-circular face. The latter is the line of Skywalk. Hesitation follows the first two pitches of that route before moving left onto the buttress. The rock is mediocre and the climbing lacks interest.
1,2) Climb the first two pitches of Skywalk.
3) 10 m, 5.7. Traverse left on sloping ledges (difficult to start) to a good belay below another corner.
4) 15 m, 5.6. Climb the corner/crack above for a few metres and then angle up left on easier rock.
5) 35 m, 5.6. Move slightly right, climb a corner, and then continue up slabs to a big ledge.
6) 25 m, 5.6. Climb a short slabby wall to a ledge and follow it right to a break in the wall above. Climb this to a major ledge system.

John Martin on pitch 3 of Skywalk, photo Chris Perry ⇨

7)   30 m, Walk left and scramble up to a tree ledge.
8)   30 m, 5.7. Climb a short corner to a ledge below a slabby wall. Move left to start up the wall, then after about 5 m traverse right to a rib. Move up, then right into a groove and climb this to the top.

SKYWALK ** 250 m, 5.9
T. Jones and C. Perry, April 1976

This excellent route climbs the corner on the left side of the semi-circular face and traverses right below the roofs, finally breaking through them at their highest point. The situations are good and the overhang move on pitch 4 is memorable. Start on slabs below the semi-circular face.
1)   20 m, 5.3. Move left and climb a slabby wall to a narrow ledge.
2)   40 m, 5.7. Traverse left along the ledge and make an awkward move up left into a shallow groove. Continue up slabs and corners, trending slightly left, to a large ledge on the left below a short wall.
3)   40 m, 5.8. Climb the wall to a ramp which leads up right below roofs. Move right onto a small rib and climb the slabby wall just right of the main corner to a horizontal band of overhangs (20 m). Make a long, rising traverse rightwards below the overhangs until a steep slab leads up to a bolt belay in a scoop below a second band of overhangs.
4)   35 m, 5.9. Move up right onto the slab and traverse right below the overhangs, descending slightly near the end to small ledges below a steep wall. Difficult moves up the right side of the wall lead to a bay below the upper roofs. Climb up right to a second bay, with a slab at the base, and from its lower left side make a hard move left over the roof (crux). Continue left just above the lip of the roof to a bolt and piton belay in a shallow corner.
5,6)   50 m, Climb past a large block immediately above (5.7) and continue up and right over easy ground to large, vegetated ledges on the north side of the buttress.
7,8)   55 m, 5.6. Follow slabby rock up and left to an obvious shallow corner which leads to the top.

THIRD DEGREE   215 m, 5.9
T. Jones and J. McIsaac, October 1979

Instead of making the long traverse right on pitch 3 of Skywalk, this route climbs up to the upper roofs, moves out left onto the buttress, and finishes as for Hesitation.
1,2)   As for Skywalk.
3)   35 m, 5.9. Climb the third pitch of Skywalk to the traverse right below the overhangs. Climb the groove that cuts the overhang at the start of the traverse and continue up a crack. Traverse right following an overlap to a belay at a large block with a solid horizontal crack in the wall above.
4)   35 m, 5.8. Go up and left following a line of small holds around a corner (no runners), then follow easy ground to a good ledge with small trees.
5-7)   85 m, Follow the easiest line up from the left end of the ledge, finishing as for Hesitation.

WAGES OF THIN   35 m, 5.10b
J. Lauchlan, A. McKeith and M. Sawyer, 1977

This is a variation to the fourth pitch of Skywalk. Climb as far as the first bay, but instead of moving up right to the second bay, traverse left on a slab between two lines of roofs to an edge. Climb over the roofs (difficult to protect) and continue directly to the fourth belay of Skywalk.

CHOCOLATE FROG   170 m, 5.7
A. McKeith and J. Sterner, July 1971

This route climbs the rounded buttress to the right of the semi-circular face. The first ascent party continued up the low-angled buttress above the cliff to the south ridge of Goat Mountain (Loder Peak). This provides an enjoyable finish for those of mountaineering bent. Scramble up to a ledge below an open, slanting corner just right of the semi-circular face.
1) 40 m, 5.6. Climb up a short distance and then move left over a small bulge into the corner. Continue up the slabby right wall, trending right to a belay at the start of a narrow ramp below a yellow, overhanging wall.
2) 15 m, 5.7. Move left up the ramp to a sloping ledge, climb the overhanging wall and then go right to a ledge.
3,4) 45 m, Climb easily to a broad alcove with trees.
5) 25 m, 5.3. Climb straight up from the right side of the alcove to the base of a right-facing corner.
6,7) 45 m, Two more pitches, first up the corner (5.6) then more easily up slabs, lead to the top.

BLUE THREADS   255 m, 5.7
J. Martin and B. Stark, 1979

The route starts below and immediately right of a square gray rock "window" toward the right side of the cliff. The easiest descent is to the south as for the other Nanny Goat climbs.
1) 50 m, 5.4. Climb to an obvious tree belay below a steep wall.
2) 30 m, 5.7. Traverse right under the wall about 8 m, then step up and continue to a large alder above a short crumbling bulge.
3) 50 m, 5.5. It is now possible to scramble up and left for several pitches to the exit of Chocolate Frog. Blue Threads continues straight up over walls, slabs and shallow corners toward blocky overhangs near the top of the cliff.
4) 45 m, 5.7. Continue easily to a large ledge and climb an obvious right-facing, steep corner to another large ledge with a small tree.
5) 30 m, 5.2. Make a gently-rising traverse left to a small tree and horn belay near a small broken pillar.
6) 50 m, 5.6. Climb the pillar, then continue up and slightly right over compact slabs to the top.

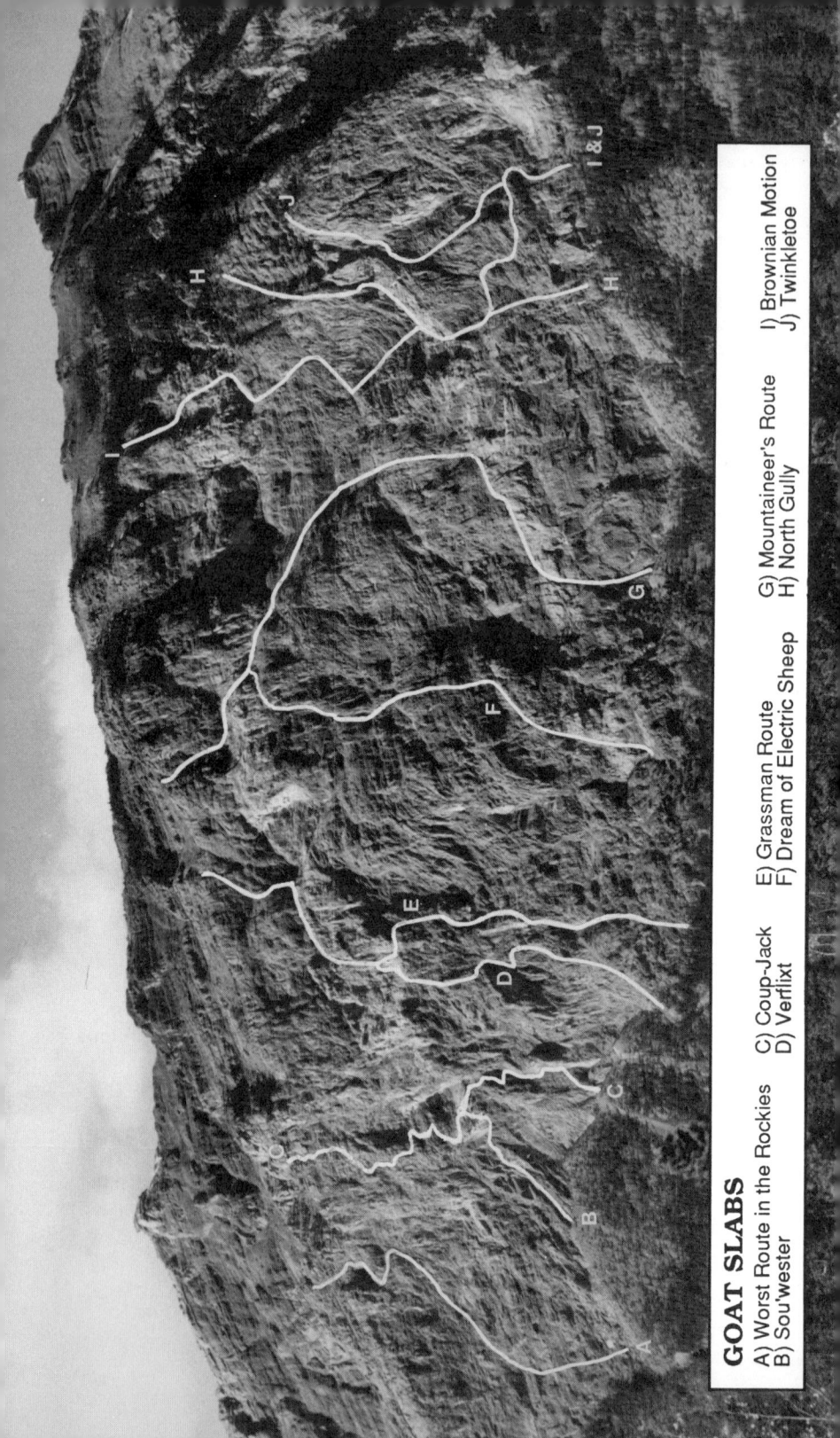

GOAT SLABS

The large cliff that extends from Goat Buttress Gully to Coire Dubh is known as Goat Slabs. It is about 600 m high. The most prominent features of the cliff are two roughly horizontal pale grey bands (one near the top of the cliff and one near the bottom) and two water streaks (one in left-centre and another further left). The water streaks normally dry up by midsummer or earlier. Generally, the cliff is relatively low-angle and broken, lacking obvious natural lines, but the rock is of reasonably good quality. Although they are long, all climbs can be easily completed in a day.

Approach: Start as for Kid Goat. When the track to the gravel pit swings left for a short distance, head right through open forest toward the cliff, staying left of a prominent esker that parallels the mountain.

Descent can be made by Goat Buttress Gully or by Coire Dubh. The latter is the most convenient descent route from most of the climbs, but the bottom has some tricky downclimbing on waterworn slabs.

COIRE DUBH 5.4
R. Allen and J. Martin, 1965

This climb begins in the gully at the left end of Goat Slabs and continues directly to the ridge top at a saddle above a wide, shallow bay. Coire Dubh is a good winter climb with optional ice pitches.

At the base of the rock several possible lines can be followed into the gully, which soon narrows to a slabby, waterworn chute (5.4). The gully then opens out into a wide scree bowl with a steeper rock section above. The easiest line through the rock section follows a vague, left-facing corner toward the right (north) side of the bowl. An easy 5th class pitch is encountered near the bottom of this section after which 4th class climbing leads to the top. A short distance to the south lies the bump of Loader Peak, from the top of which an easy walk down the ridge leads to Hwy. 1A.

WORST ROUTE IN THE ROCKIES 350 m, 5.7
C.Perry and M.White, 1975

This aptly named route climbs an obvious slanting line near the south end of the cliff.

Climb easy slabs up and right to gain a prominent, slanting crack system. Go up this on poor rock and continue above in the same general line. Higher up, a steep section allows access left to a prominent depression and hence the top.

SOU'WESTER 5.9
T. Jones and P. Littlejohn, August 1976

This route, an alternate and harder start to Coup-Jack, follows an obvious line of blocky corners angling up rightwards from the high point of the scree slope near the left-hand waterfall.

1,2) 5.7. Climb the corners until a large, unpleasant-looking yellow dihedral looms above.

Goat Slabs

3) 5.9. Turn the dihedral by moving out on the gray wall to the right, taking the line of least resistance to a pocket to the right of the base of a 6 m groove.
4) 5.9. Climb the groove and turn a roof on a rib to the left. Above, easier climbing leads to the big ledges lying above pitch 6 of Coup-Jack.

COUP-JACK ** IV, 5.9
R. Howe, A. McKeith and I. Rowe, July 1974

Midway between the two waterfalls on Goat Slabs is a prominent cave-like feature set in a system of left-facing corners. This fine route follows corners and cracks almost to the cave, then trends left and finishes up slabs and walls. Start about 20 m left of a left-facing corner capped by a large roof.
1) 45 m, 5.7. Go up and right past a short steep wall to a ledge which leads into the corner.
2) 35 m, 5.8. Climb the corner to the roof.
3) 25 m, 5.5. Traverse left under the roof to ledges.
4) 30 m, 5.8. Climb an overhanging crack in a short corner (5.7), then move up and left to another corner with a few awkward moves (5.8) to start. Belay in the corner near a small tree.
5) 25 m, 5.7. Climb up and left past the tree to a short corner. Climb this and then continue easily to an obvious overhanging crack in a right-facing corner.
6) 10 m, 5.9. Climb the crack which is well protected.
7) 40 m, Move up and left over easy slabs and ledges, trending away from the main corner system to a bolt belay in a shallow corner.
8) 40 m, 5.8. Make a long traverse left on smooth slabs, then climb a short steep wall and continue to a bolt belay.
9) 45 m, 5.7. A few thin moves lead to a right-trending ramp. Follow this until it is possible to climb up and left to easier ground.
10) 40 m, Traverse left on easy slabs and ledges below a huge overhanging yellow corner to the foot of a right-facing gray corner.
11) 35 m, 5.5. Climb the corner, step left and continue to a ledge below a V-chimney.
12) 40 m, 5.7. Move up into the chimney and then traverse across the steep left wall about 5 m below a large roof. Climb up and right to a belay.
13) 35 m, Follow an easy gully up to the right.
14) 35 m, 5.6. Climb steep slabs above to a ledge.
15) 35 m, 5.6. Continue above on steep slabs, then move left and up to finish.

VERFLIXT 685 m, 5.7, A1
W. Batzhuber and U. Kallen, 1974

The route starts slightly left of the lowest part of the face in a gully and crack system and curves up to the right aiming for a waterfall high on the face. This is the right-hand of the two waterfalls on Goat Slabs. The Grassman Route provides an alternative start.

1) 45 m, 5.4. Climb up the gully.
2) 45 m, 5.6. Head up toward a smooth waterworn gully. When this becomes difficult, climb up left in a corner system and belay at its top.
3) 35 m, 5.5. Go up and left over a faint ridge into some cracks (15 m), then left and down to an obvious corner.
4) 45 m, 5.6. Climb an easy jam crack, then go up the corner until it becomes difficult. Go left to a diagonal crack, follow it to the top of a corner and continue up an obvious chimney.
5) 45 m, 5.6, A1. Climb overhangs blocking the chimney to reach the top of a pillar. Climb 10 m, angle up left to a short steep wall and climb the wall (1 point of aid) to a good ledge.
6) 35 m, 5.4. Climb straight up on slabs then go left into a corner and chimney.
7) 45 m, 5.6. Go up the corner over a steep section with overhangs. At the top, go right up a ramp to a stance.
8) 45 m, 5.6. Ascend 10 m, then step around to the right and go up to an arch. Exit on the left, then climb back right to a good ledge.
9) 45 m, 5.5. Go straight up 20 m then traverse easily to the right. Climb a short wall and go right again to a small stance. From here, an obvious rock "ear" can be seen up and to the left.
10) 45 m, 5.7 Climb 35 m to a roof, traverse left 6 m on a slab to a crack and follow this 3 m to a stance.
11) 35 m, 5.6. Go up a bit then drop left into a gully to reach a big scree scoop.
12-14) Follow the gully easily up right for about 100 m. At its end traverse right onto low angle slabs near the waterfall.
15) 45 m, 5.7. Above is a steep wall, the crux of the climb. Head for a small pillar and from its top climb left on small holds to an easy crack. Climb the crack and traverse right to a belay.
16) 35 m, Climb easily up toward a tree in the exit crack and belay in a niche.
17) 40 m, 5.6. Climb over the niche and up to a steep groove. Climb the groove, then go up and right over slabs to reach the top of the face.

GRASSMAN ROUTE *   625 m, 5.7
E. Grassman and M. Sawyer, 1976

This climb is named for Eckhard Grassman who died on the north face of Mount Edith Cavell. It follows a line close to and left of the big waterfall, then moves left to intersect Verflixt at the base of that route's 10th pitch. The Grassman Route is now the usual approach for parties wishing to climb Verflixt. After scrambling up to the highest scree ledges, begin in an obvious gully and groove system a short distance left of the waterfall.

1-2) 100 m, 5.4. Climb two long and mostly easy pitches up the gully.

3-4) 90 m, 5.6. Move left and follow a discontinuous series of short corners and cracks to a tree on a large ledge behind a big rectangular pinnacle.

5) 35 m, 5.7. Climb the steep wall above and then slant right up a ledge to a tree belay.

6) 40 m, 5.6. Walk to the right, then slant left and up to a belay in a wide, shallow gully.

7) 30 m, 5.4. Traverse left on a ledge into the pale gray band. Climb up a few feet and belay.

8) 30 m, 5.6. Climb straight up to the stance at the base of the 10th pitch of Verflixt.

DREAM OF ELECTRIC SHEEP   5.8
B. Greenwood and A. McKeith, 1971

This route has not been repeated and the line marked on the photo is approximate except for the exit pitches. In general, it follows a shallow buttress in the central area of the cliff. The main feature of the route is a shallow, 90 m left-facing corner, with a dogleg to the right, in the centre of the buttress. Start left of this feature where a gully can be seen leading up and right onto the buttress. An initial 12 m wall leads over a bulge (5.7) onto smooth slabs and then into the gully which is followed easily for three pitches to a ledge at the right end of a line of overhangs. The next four pitches, culminating in the crux, lead first up and right, then up and left to an area of ledges. An easy pitch and a loose wall on the left (5.3) lead to a crack about 30 m left of the corner. Above the crack (5.6) a ledge leads right to the corner, which is followed for about 60 m until it is possible to move out left into a smaller corner. Steep broken rock now leads to an obvious break in the upper light gray band which is climbed (5.5) to a broad scree ledge. Above the ledge, a corner with a thin crack (5.6) is climbed to easier rock which leads up in two more pitches under an overhanging yellow arch to the finish.

MOUNTAINEER'S ROUTE   5.6
R. MacLachlan and J. Martin, 1981

To the right of the buttress followed by Dream of Electric Sheep is a shallow scoop. This rambling climb starts on a scree ramp which leads up right to a point below the shallow scoop. Climb one pitch up dark shattered rock (5.4) to a ledge, then move right and climb a slabby pitch (5.5) up the light gray band above to a major ledge system. The ledge is followed right for several pitches to prominent shattered pillars. Some short 5th class walls and traverses are encountered in this section. Climb moderate rock left of the pillars to a stand of conifers in a big scree bowl. Wander up and left to a large ledge below the upper light gray band, climbing this by an obvious left-slanting crack to another large ledge. Slightly further left are the 3 exit pitches of Dream of Electric Sheep which are followed to the top.

NORTH GULLY   5.8
J. Jones and J. Robson, 1967

Details of this climb, the first route on Goat Slabs, are lost. The route begins at a fairly obvious break and after a difficult first pitch leads more or less straight up on easier ground to the left end of a huge gully. This gully is at the base of the lower pale gray band. It then follows the gully (which is easy at first) up right for several pitches to a steep, difficult section and after breaking out on the left wall continues up easy rock to trees.

BROWNIAN MOTION   5.4
M. Bowen and J. Martin, 1969

This wandering climb has some enjoyable 4th class and easy 5th class pitches. Considerable variation is possible. Start at the only easy break near the right side of the cliff. After climbing up a few metres, make a long traverse left and then climb up to a large scree-filled gully below the lower pale gray band. This is the same gully utilized by the North Gully Route. Follow the gully right to the first break in the pale gray band, then climb first up and right, then up and left for several pitches in cracks and corners to a huge scree bowl with a few trees. From the top of the bowl, another corner system leads in two or three pitches to a scree ledge below the upper pale band. Walk right to a break in this band (it is possible to continue right and off the cliff from here), climb it, and then traverse back left to a shallow gully which is followed to the top of the cliff.

Goat Slabs

TWINKLETOE 5.6
B. Budd, J. Martin and S. Slymon, September 1968

Start as for Brownian Motion but instead of traversing left, scramble up to a bowl with a slanting slab on the left.

1)   20 m, 5.2. Climb up left on the slab and belay around a corner.
2)   30 m, 5.3. Climb an inside corner on the left, then continue to an obvious belay stance.
3)   Climb up broken rock to a big ledge below a large slab.
4)   30 m, 5.6. Climb the slab, trending toward the right to a small stance. Poor protection.
5)   35 m, 5.4. Traverse left about 12 m to a slanting, blocky ledge. Climb this to a crack in the smooth wall on the left, continue up the crack and then traverse left to a tree belay.
6)   25 m, Follow broken rock with a very smooth wall to the left to a small stance.
7)   30 m, Traverse right and up into an obvious chimney.
8)   35 m, 5.5. From the chimney, traverse a few metres right then climb up slabby rock past a crack to a steep wall. Traverse around a corner on the left to a tree belay.
9)   20 m, 5.6. Follow an obvious inside corner on the left to a ledge.
10) Climb diagonally right over broken rock to a large tree.
11) 35 m, 5.6. Make a descending traverse right, then climb up to an obvious overhanging wide crack which is followed to easier ground.
12) A short scramble leads to the trees.

GOAT WALL

The southeast face of Goat Mountain is the huge wall that extends from the Yamnuska col southward to the prominent prow-like outline of Goat Buttress. Much of the face is extremely steep and continuous natural lines are few. With the exception of Goat Buttress, the existing routes are confined to lower-angle areas. The rock is comparable in quality to that on Yamnuska although it is less jointed and generally there is more face climbing and less natural protection.

Approach: The best approach for most climbs is from the south. Start as for Goat Slabs and follow a trail along the top of the esker until it turns eastwards away from the cliffs. Drop down left into the valley between the esker and the cliffs and continue in an easterly direction through meadows for about half a kilometre. At a clump of large poplar trees on the left, head north towards the Goat Mountain-Yamnuska col and follow an intermittent trail to reach the dry bed of the stream that drains the gully left of Goat Buttress. Continue up the gully over several rock steps to the base of the cliffs. The Ramp, and possibly also Wendigo, can be reached more easily via the Yamnuska col.

Descent: is made via the east ridge to the Yamnuska col. In places, traverse slabs on the north side of the ridge, and near the bottom, move left (north) and downclimb a broad, easy gully leading back to the col. From the top of Goat Buttress, it may be easier to descend the treed break to the south (Goat Buttress Gully).

GOAT BUTTRESS *** 375 m, 5.10d
C.Perry and T.Jones, July 1977
F.F.A: S.Dougherty and C.Yonge, June 1987

This classic route follows an superb natural line up the prominent prow-like buttress at the southern end of the face. The rock is generally good and the situation on the upper headwall is exceptional. The long approach and descent necessitate an early start.

The climb begins in the large gully west of the buttress above a lower cliff band. Bypass the cliff band on the left via an open slope which leaves the stream bed about 200 m below the cliffs. Cross the gully and scramble up easy slabs to a long ledge left of a bottomless chimney that leads up to an obvious break on the edge of the buttress.

The route described below varies slightly from that of the first ascent which involved short sections of aid. Consequently, fixed equipment can be seen right of pitch 8 and left of pitch 9.

1) 40 m, 5.7. Climb a shallow, right-facing groove about 40 m left of the chimney and continue up and left to a belay at a small tree below overlaps.
2) 40 m, 5.7. Move up and climb easily through an overlap onto a slab. Walk right on the slab and follow a groove up and then back left. Continue up to a short V-corner to a ledge system that angles down rightwards across the face.
3) 15 m, 5.4. Climb easy rock up and right and then traverse back left to a belay below a long corner with a slabby right wall.
4) 45 m, 5.7. Follow the corner to a small belay about 5 m below a large roof that arches rightwards above the slabby wall.

5) 40 m, 5.8. Move up and across the left wall of the corner to the arete. Climb this past the left end of the roof to gain a curving slab above. Follow the slab to a large sloping ledge below a formidable, overhanging crack, the "Fissure Firth". Bolt belay.
6) 7 m, 5.10d. Either climb the corner (large Friend) or the overhanging right wall on widely spaced holds with no protection (the "Gross Wall") to gain a good ledge above. Bolt belay.
7) 33 m, 5.6. Move right onto a higher ledge and continue right to a corner. Climb the corner, moving out onto the left wall to reach a ledge on the prow of the buttress (used as a bivouac on the first ascent). Bolt belay.
8) 20 m, 5.9. From the left end of the ledge, climb a loose ramp up and left to a bolt. Continue up and left to larger holds and then traverse right to a sloping ledge and a bolt belay.
9) 40 m, 5.10b. From the belay, make some tricky moves up and right (the "Cheesmond Step") to easier ground. Continue right to the top of a crack and then move back left to an obvious ramp. Climb this (5.8) past a piton to a crack that leads to a bolt belay in a small alcove.
10) 45 m, 5.10a. Move up and go across right on good holds to a crack. Climb this and then angle up and left (5.7) to a bolt below a steep, shallow groove. Climb the groove and move left past a bolt into the base of the exit gully.
11) 50 m, 5.5. Climb the gully and exit left just below the top of the buttress.

OREAMNOS *   450 m, 5.8
J.Firth and J.Jones, June 1973

To the right of the buttress is a slanting system of corners and slabs that leads up right to a prominent ramp near the top of the cliff. This is the line of Oreamnos which is perhaps the best of the three major climbs on this section of the face.
Scramble up left following easy corners and ledges to a large pinnacle below the main corner. Start about 30 m right of the pinnacle below a short right-facing corner.
1) 5.6. Climb a short wall and then move up and diagonally right to a corner. Follow this to ledges on the right.
2) 5.4. Angle back left and up on easy ground to a belay in the main corner.
3) 5.6. Continue up the corner and belay below a small roof level with a traverse line leading right.
4) 5.7. Traverse right to a belay ledge.
5-7) 5.7-5.8. The exact route taken on the next section is uncertain. The steep slabs above the belay are climbed for a short distance and then a long traverse is made to the right. Slabs and corners are then followed, trending slightly right towards a prominent exit chimney. Finally, a traverse right is made to a ledge beneath a steep section, below and left of the exit chimney.
8) 5.8. Climb steep loose rock following a thin crack diagonally up right. Continue on easier ground to good ledges at the foot of the chimney.
9) 5.8. Move up into the chimney and then make an awkward descending traverse right round the corner on a ledge.
10-12) Follow corners and chimneys to the foot of the ramp.
Continue up the ramp to join the east ridge of Goat Mountain.

Goat Wall

MANITOU 580 m, 5.8
J.Martin and C.Perry, 1980

About 100 m right of the easy beak where Oreamnos starts is an area of large blocks on the scree below the cliff. Start in the first obvious corner right of Oreamnos near the middle of these blocks.

1) 50 m, 5.7. Climb the corner, which faces right, for about 40 m to a steep section. Hand traverse left using an obvious crack to gain a good ledge.
2) 40 m, 5.5. Climb up to a bulge, step right to a break and then climb the groove above. Belay near the top on a small ledge.
3) 40 m, 5.6. Finish the groove and then go easily up and right to an easy gully.
4) Go easily up a gully leading left, then cut up to the right to large ledges. Above are easy-angled gray slabs below a steep, dark, shattered wall. To the right of the wall is a pillar with slanting grooves on its left side.
5) 35 m, Climb easily up slabs for about 15 m, then traverse right and belay near the rightmost slanting groove.
6) 40 m, 5.7. Climb the groove to its top. Step left and continue by short walls and corners to an alcove.
7) 40 m, Moderate climbing leads to the top of the pillar.
8) 45 m, 5.6. Continue above and slightly right by a thin slabby wall leading into an obvious gully which slants up left.
9) 40 m, 5.4. Climb the right-hand of the two grooves. Near its top traverse up to the left along a ledge.
10) 40 m, 5.2. Climb left and up along a discontinuous but obvious break and belay at a ledge.
11) 40 m, 5.2. Continue left and up to a ledge at the end of the ascending traverse line.
12) 25 m, 5.6. Go straight up the slabby wall above to a poor belay on a sloping slab below a steeper wall.
13) 25 m, 5.6. Traverse left across the slab, step onto a second slab and traverse left across it, passing below the base of a slabby groove. Step left onto a wall and climb up into the base of a groove with a good crack.
14) 35 m, 5.8. Climb the groove to a traverse line just below a prominent small roof which blocks the groove. Traverse upward on steep rock into a groove on the right. Climb this a few metres, then traverse back left across a steep, improbable wall to a good belay in the original groove just above the overhang.
15) 40 m, 5.7. Move left, then back right and up the groove above on awkward, sloping rock. Belay where the groove becomes easy.
16) Easy rock now leads into the exit ramp of Oreamnos.

John Martin on the first ascent of ⇨
Manitou - pitch 8, photo Chris Perry

Goat Wall

WENDIGO 535 m, 5.8
J.Lauchlan and C.Perry, 1974

Wendigo follows a major right-facing corner system leading up to a huge ledge high on the face, traverses left across this ledge, then climbs up to the prominent exit ramp of Oreamnos. Start at the first right-facing corner left of a large black water streak.

1) 45 m, Climb the corner to a ledge on the left.
2) 35 m, Follow the right-hand crack for 15 m, then move left into a chimney. Belay at its top.
3) 30 m, Scramble up and left along ledges to an arete.
4) 30 m, Traverse left into a corner and climb this to a ledge.
5) 45 m, Move diagonally up left to a piton and continue up to a ledge.
6) 15 m, Follow the ledge up right to the foot of a smooth corner.
7) 15 m, 5.6. Climb the corner for a few metres and then go diagonally left across a slab to a large ledge and bolt belay.
8) 20 m, 5.7. Traverse left for 10 m along the ledge until it peters out beyond a small rib. Climb steep rock up and then right to a ledge. Diagonal up left to a corner and follow this to a niche.
9) 40 m, 5.8. Follow a ramp right for 15 m to a small bay. Climb this on the left side, and then move right and make a difficult move onto the continuation ramp above.
10-12) 135 m, Traverse left along the big ledge to a belay on the far side of a pinnacle.
13) 35 m, Trend up and left toward an obvious exit groove, then step down to a poor belay on a sloping ledge.
14) 45 m, 5.7. Climb up and across to the exit groove. When the groove blanks out, traverse left around a corner and belay in a scoop.
15) 45 m, Ascend a shallow scoop to gain the exit ramp of Oreamnos.

THE RAMP 5.6
B.Greenwood, R.Lofthouse and J.Steen, 1961

This is by far the easiest route on the face but to the editors' knowledge it has yet to be repeated. Follow the huge slabby ramp that slants across the face from lower right to upper left and belay at its very top. The climbing to this point is easy.

1) 30 m, Climb an open chimney, then cross a slab on small holds in a rising traverse to the right to a good belay.
2) 45 m, Climb straight up on poor rock to easier ground.

THE WILD COLONIAL BOYS   295 m, 5.10c
S.DeMaio and C.Quinn, July 1987

The route climbs the steep face set at an angle to the main cliff at the far righthand end. It begins almost directly below the first subsidiary summit west of the Yamnuska col.

Scramble up for 20m to a large ledge.

1) 50 m, 5.9. Climb the lefthand of two 5 m corners to a ramp heading up and left. At the end of the ramp, climb up and right to a bolt. Continue up and right along a diagonal break and then go straight up to a belay below a corner.

2) 25 m, 5.8. Climb the corner until it is possible to step right onto a ledge.

3) 50 m, 5.10. Move back left into the corner and follow it for about 5 m to its end. Traverse left with difficulty across the wall for about 5 m and then move up to a ledge. Go back right to a large corner and climb this and a crack system above past an old piton belay to a ledge.

4) 50 m, 5.10. Pull over a small overhang directly above the belay and climb a corner to an old piton belay. Step left and climb another corner to a large ledge (2 bolt belay).

5) 40 m, 5.8. Move right across the ledge to a piton, downclimb a right-facing corner to its base, and then traverse right and up following the easiest line for 15 m to reach a corner. Climb the corner to a ledge.

6) 40 m, 5.10. Traverse right to below a right-trending seam. Follow the seam as it widens and eventually turns into a ledge system. Move up to belay in large cracks.

7) 40 m, 5.8. Climb up and then traverse left into a corner. Climb this past an overhang to the top.

YAMNUSKA

Yamnuska is the best-known cliff in the Canadian Rockies and is the subject of two previous guidebooks. A dozen or so new routes and aid eliminations have been made since the last guidebook was published in 1977 and the cliff seems far from worked out.

Yamnuska is situated about 70 km west of Calgary at the mountain front and its impressive south face extends along the whole side of the mountain reaching a height of 350 m. Because of its location and its southern aspect, the cliff has one of the longest climbing seasons of all those covered in the guidebook. Drainage is primarily down the back of the mountain and the face is very quick to dry. The moderate and difficult routes are typically steep and often follow corners, chimneys, and irregular cracks. Face climbing sections are characterized by well-defined, frequently horizontal incut holds. Significant danger from climber generated rockfall occurs on some easy routes, particularly Unnamed and Grillmair Chimneys.

Approach: See map on page 116. From Highway 1A, drive along a short gravel road to a parking area at the point where the road is blocked by a gate. Facilities here include an outhouse and a climbers' register box. Walk up the road through a quarry (spring water is available near the road at the bottom of the quarry) to a trail which heads directly up through trees from the top of the quarry near its left side. After numerous zigzags, the trail reaches the foot of the cliff near the start of Kahl Wall. Trails lead east and west from this point to each end of the cliff.

Descent: Easy descent routes lead down the east and west ridges and around the ends of the cliff. An obvious trail down scree slopes below Necromancer offers a fast alternative descent to the quarry.

† FALSE PROMISE   175 m, 5.7
A.Derbyshire and M.Toft, 1981

Halfway between Windy Slabs and the west end of the cliff is a big roof about 30 m above the trail. Start at a black, right-facing corner below the roof.

1) 25 m, 5.5. Climb the corner to a block.

2) 30 m, 5.7. Traverse left below the block on loose rock, moving around a rib to a small ledge. Climb the short, steep wall above to lower-angled slabs and continue up these to a good ledge with a deep crack at the back.

3) 40 m, 5.7. Climb a wide crack above the ledge to its top. Continue up a steep face below a second big roof, make a horizontal traverse left at the first opportunity, and then step down to reach a small pocket.

4) 50 m, 5.5. Traverse left to a well-defined rib, then move around the rib and step down to a small broken ledge. Continue up and left on easier ground to an obvious exit gully. Belay in the gully near the top.

5. Scramble to the top.

◊ *Al Pickel on CMC Wall, photo Brian Webster*

Yamnuska

WINDY SLABS *   200 m, 5.6.
J.Martin, M.Bowen and S.Slymon, October 1968

Begin at a small pillar about 35 m left of the ramp that marks the start of Unnamed.
1) Climb the pillar to its top, then move left through a small bay and climb a short corner to a large ledge.
2) Traverse left across slabs and descend slightly to a ledge with a small tree.
3) Climb the slabs above for about 15 m, then slant up left to a scree ledge.
4) From the top of the ledge, climb easily up and left to a belay below a sweeping slab.
5) Descend left to the slab and climb it slanting up and left past a small overhang. Traverse left to a corner and climb this to easy ground breaking out on the left wall after about 10 m.
6) Climb a short, vertical corner. (This pitch can be avoided).
7) Finish as for King's Chimney.

EASY STREET **   215 m, 5.5
J.Martin and S.Slymon, October 1968

1 & 2)   80 m, 5.5. Climb the first two pitches of King's Chimney.
3) 35 m, 5.5. Move left from the base of the chimney onto the wall and go up past an initial steep section to a good ledge just left of the chimney. The lower section can be avoided by climbing the chimney for 6-7 m and then moving left.
4) 30 m, 5.5. Traverse left to a groove and climb this and an easy gully above to a large ledge.
5) 30 m, 5.4. Climb past large blocks and follow a corner to the large platform at the end of the King's Chimney traverse.
6) 40 m, 5.5. Finish as for King's Chimney.

KING'S CHIMNEY **   225 m, 5.5
D.Vockeroth and B.King, June 1964

1 & 2)   Climb the first two pitches of Unnamed and continue further left on the ledge to the base of a prominent chimney.
3) 25 m, 5.4. Climb the chimney past a chockstone to a good belay.
4) 25 m, 5.5. Continue past two overhangs to a second belay in the chimney.
5) 30 m, 5.4. Climb to the top of the chimney and move left a few metres to a ledge.
6) 25 m, 5.5. Traverse left and down slightly (pitons) to a large platform on the west ridge.
7) 40 m, 5.5. Climb up to a ledge below a steep crack, move around left and continue up a slabby wall to the top.

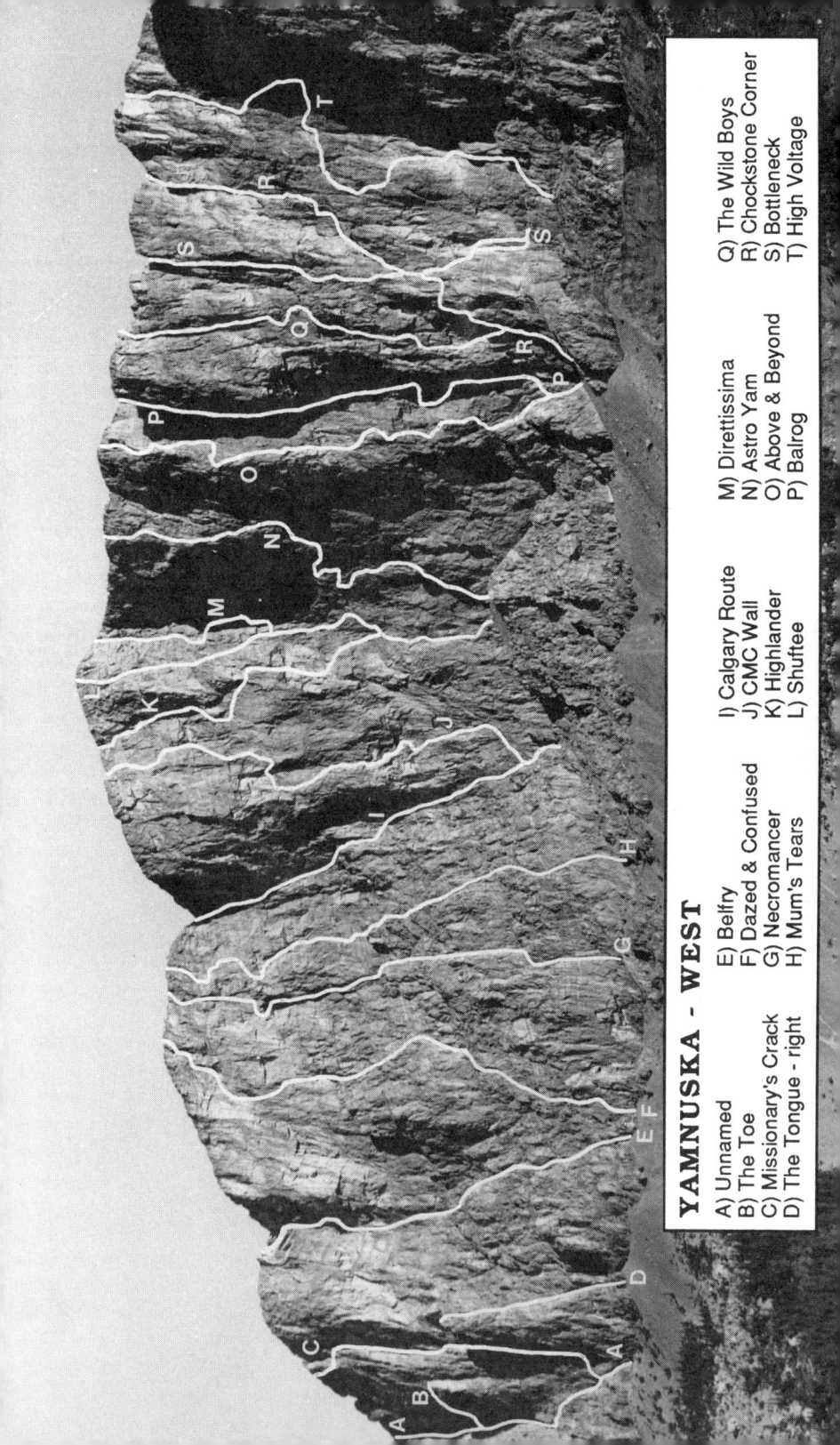

Yamnuska

UNNAMED   230 m, 5.6
B.Greenwood and J.Steen, 1961

This climbs the first large break at the east end of the cliff. It begins below and right of the break at a ramp leading up left. King's Chimney shares the same start.
Scramble up the ramp to the base of a chimney.
1) 35 m, 5.5. Climb about halfway up the chimney and either continue up or move left and go up the outside to the top. Move left and belay.
2) 25 m. Continue left along the ledge past a block to the base of a crack in the wall above.
3 & 4) 90 m, 5.5. Climb the crack and go up into the main gully belaying as high as possible. Continue up the gully moving left where it steepens near the top and continuing more easily on the left wall. Belay on the left edge of a scoop below a bottleneck where the gully narrows and becomes a steep chimney.
5) 50 m, 5.6. Start by climbing on the right and then move over to the left (piton). Climb straight up for 5 m and then move right or bridge the chimney on the right. Belay above on easier ground.
6) 30 m, 5.5. Climb the corner above to a steep wall a short distance below the top. Either move right and go up and left on good holds to finish or move left and climb a short ramp exiting on easier ground to the right.

GRAY GOOSE *   230 m, 5.6
J.Martin and L.Howard, 1978

1) Climb the first pitch of Windy Slabs.
2) Continuing by a groove above or by easy rock to the left, climb to the big ledge near the base of King's Chimney.
3) 20 m. Starting 6-7 m left of Unnamed (pitch 3), climb up and left to an obvious traverse line. Continue left, then go up to a good ledge below a groove.
4) 30 m. Climb the groove which slants left to a good belay overlooking the first stance on King's Chimney.
5) 45 m. Continue up and left by a discontinuous groove. When the line comes very close to King's Chimney, climb up and right on a steep wall to a ledge at the base of a slab.
6) Climb up and left on the slab to join the traverse on King's Chimney.
7 & 8) Finish as for King's Chimney.

THE TOE   160 m, 5.6
K.Hahn and party, 1963
The Toe is a large pinnacle on the wall right of Unnamed.
Start by climbing the first three pitches of Unnamed to the base of the gully.
1) 5.6. Move up and right and climb a steep wall, then make an awkward layback move into the chimney between the pinnacle and the main wall.
2) Walk along the bottom of the chimney to the base of the Toe.
3) Stem up to the ridge of the pinnacle and continue easily up this to a small, shattered summit.
Descend by downclimbing the last pitch and the chimney, and either rappel once to regain Unnamed or climb up for 8 m from the bottom of the chimney to gain an obvious traverse line which leads back left to Unnamed.

MISSIONARY'S CRACK *   260 m, 5.9
B.Greenwood and D.Vockeroth, 1964
Scramble up the ramp of Unnamed to the base of the chimney and belay at a traverse line leading right.
1) 45 m, 5.8. Traverse up and right to a piton and continue right to a second piton. Move up over a bulge and go across right to a large open-book corner. Climb the corner to a piton belay at ledges on the right.
2) 25 m, 5.8. Climb the steep broken wall on the left and continue over blocks to ledges further to the left.
3) 35 m, 5.6. Climb easy rock above, follow a gangway to the left, then continue up a corner and belay on a large chockstone at the back of the crack.
4) 30 m, 5.8. Traverse right into a shallow groove and climb this to a cave below a large jammed block. Climb over the block and continue up a short crack to a ledge.
5) Climb a chimney to another ledge.
6) 35 m, 5.8. Continue up a steep crack to an overhang. Pass the overhang on the right and continue up a steep slab to the top of a pillar. Belay on a chockstone.
7) 30 m, 5.9. Layback and jam the steep crack above and continue up a chimney to a ledge.
8) 20 m. Climb moderate rock to a belay.
9) Move down slightly and left to reach a gully which leads to the top.

THE TONGUE, LEFT SIDE   165 m, 5.9
B.Blanchard and A.Pickel, 1982
The Tongue is a large pinnacle to the right of Missionary's Crack. The climb starts at the base of Unnamed and goes up the righthand of two prominent V-corners, the left one being the second pitch of Missionary's Crack.
1) 40 m, 5.9. Climb a short distance up the ramp and then move up right and go up a shallow groove past a piton to a small overhang. Continue up and right to the base of the righthand V-corner.

2) 45 m, 5.8. Climb the corner for about 12 m and move out on the left wall under an overhang. Jam around the left side of the overhang, move back right to turn a second overhang, and continue for about 6 m over loose rock to a corner with a sweeping slab on the right. Make a semi-hanging belay a short distance up the corner.
3) 45 m, 5.7. Climb the corner past an overhang and continue up to the base of the wide crack that separates The Tongue from the main cliff.
4) 35 m, 5.8. Bridge up the outside of the crack until it becomes a wide chimney. About 10 m below the top of the pinnacle step on to the right wall and climb an off-width crack to the top.
Descend as for The Tongue, Right Side.

THE TONGUE, RIGHT SIDE   170 m, 5.4
J.Martin and M.Bowen, 1968

Start at a steep corner on the right side of The Tongue. Climb the corner and continue up a chimney to an area of loose blocks. Move right and climb an easy face and a cracked slab above to a large ledge. Walk left and descend into the gap between the pinnacle and the main wall, then climb to the top by a short crack on the left (east) side. To descend, downclimb as far as the base of the cracked slab and traverse east to easy rocks below Belfry.

BELFRY **   150 m, 5.8
B.Greenwood and R.Thomson, September 1957

This enjoyable route climbs an obvious break east of The Tongue. The lower section is 3rd class but the climbing in the upper corner is steep and sustained and on generally good rock.
Scramble up from the right to the base of the upper corner.
1) 45 m, 5.7. Climb a steep corner/crack on the right and angle back left on a ramp to a nut belay in the main corner.
2) 30 m, 5.8. Continue up the corner moving slightly left across a steep wall to a small belay below a large roof.
3) 25 m, 5.7. Move out right beneath the roof and climb a steep corner to a belay ledge on the left.
4) 50 m, 5.7. Climb the corner above and make an awkward move left to another corner. Continue up this and then follow a large slab up left to the top.

DAZED AND CONFUSED   440 m, 5.9.
B.Keller and J.Lauchlan, June 1976
F.F.A: G.Smith and M.Galbraith, May 1987

The climb is reportedly not as bad as its name implies.
Start just right of the most easterly corner/gully leading to the upper pitches of Belfry. Scramble up and right on easy ground for about 90 m.
1) 35 m, 5.7. Make a few awkward moves up a wall, then easier climbing up a break leads to a good ledge and belay.
2) 50 m, 5.6. Follow easy breaks first right, then back left, heading for an obvious break through the ridge above.
3) 45 m, 5.4. Continue up an easy crack line through the break to an indistinct ramp and gully system heading left.

4) 50 m, 5.5. Climb the ramp.
5) 15 m, 5.4. Continue to the top of the ramp and belay at a large block at the foot of a steep groove.
6) 30 m, 5.9. Climb the groove to an old piton high up on the left. Step right into the continuation groove and climb this to small, stepped overhang with a prominent blocky hold. Make a difficult move over the overhang and climb the ragged groove above to a good belay ledge.
7) 35 m, 5.7. Climb leftwards up the obvious break, traversing left where the crack steepens, until it is possible to climb back right up easy ledges and belay at the foot of a good corner.
8) 35 m, 5.8. Climb the corner for a few metres, then traverse right across the wall to a ramp leading around the skyline to a slab. Climb the slab to a faultline, go right and hand traverse under a large block. Belay at the base of a rotten corner which breaks through the wall above.
9) 25 m, 5.8. Climb the corner past a very loose overhang to a good belay at its top.
10) 30 m, 5.7. Move up and right across the wall above into a big corner. Traverse out of the corner below rotten overhangs and climb the right wall to the top.

NECROMANCER ** 370 m, 5.10a
G.Homer and J.Jones, 1971
F.F.A: J.Marshall and B.Blanchard, 1981

Necromancer climbs the prominent corner in the upper part of the wall left of Calgary Route. The lower section is contrived and broken but the upper pitches, where the corner ends, are sensationally exposed.
Scramble up a large ramp to a steep right-facing corner leading to a ledge with a second right-facing corner above.
1) 45 m, 5.7. Move left and climb the corner to its top.
2) 20 m. Go up and right over broken rock to a big ledge and walk right to a second corner-crack.
3) 45 m, 5.7. Climb the corner-crack to a belay on easier ground above.
4 & 5) 60 m. Continue easily to a large terrace and climb 4th class to the base of the main corner.
6) 30 m. Climb a chimney and belay under a loose wall.
7) 45 m, 5.8. Traverse right and climb a steep wall to a small ledge. Move up and left over loose blocks to reach the corner and climb this to a stance on a slab below a band of overhangs.
8) 30 m, 5.10a. Climb a steep wall just right of an obvious break to gain a steep slab below a second, larger band of overhangs. Follow a horizontal crack left across the slab past two pitons to a dubious pinnacle and a two bolt belay.
9) 30 m, 5.8. Move up and right to a small ledge (piton), traverse right and descend slightly to a slab under a roof, continue further right to a stance below a steep crack.
10) 20 m, 5.8. Climb the crack and belay under a short overhanging corner with a crack at the back.
11) 45 m, 5.8. Climb the corner, move left around a bulge and continue over steep, shattered rock to the top.

MUM'S TEARS 370 m, 5.8
C.Locke and D.Vockeroth, 1968

As on the two previous routes, the lower section of this climb is broken and easy and the real climbing does not start until halfway up the face. Climb 3rd and 4th class up broken rock between Necromancer and Calgary Route to big ledges about halfway up.
1) 30 m, 5.7. Climb a corner to a small roof and move left around a bulge to small ledges. Alternatively, climb the crack immediately left of the corner.
2) 35 m, 5.8. Traverse left for 3 m to a small ridge, cross this to easier climbing, and then go up a short wall. Continue for a short distance up a corner, traverse left with difficulty across the top of a slab to another corner and climb this to a good belay.
3) 30 m. Climb the steep crack above and follow a diagonal line up and left.
4) 40 m. Continue up and left past the level of a prominent roof and move back right to the start of an obvious traverse line leading rightwards.
5) 40 m, 5.7. Climb straight up a ragged crack (piton) and onto a block on the right. Traverse right into a groove and climb it for 10 m. Continue up a loose wall to a piton below a second groove. Climb the groove for 15 m to where it runs out and then move left across a slab to an exposed belay. Alternatively, follow the traverse line right from the belay, across a slab, and move up into the groove system mentioned above (original means of ascent).
6) 35 m, 5.7. Climb an open groove above the belay to a fault line. Hand traverse left around an edge to a shattered corner. Climb this and a ramp above moving back right to a piton. Climb up over loose blocks to the top. Two variation finishes, both of which end on Necromancer, have been done.
4.alt) Instead of moving back right, traverse left across a short slab and belay around the corner (top of Necromancer pitch 9).
5.alt) Climb up and then go diagonally up and left on a slab below a steep wall. When the slab ends, step around left into the corner of Necromancer (top of pitch 10).

CALGARY ROUTE 340 m, 5.5
F.Dopf and H.Gmoser, 1952

This route follows the first major break west of the summit. Much of the climbing is in chimneys which are polished and not well-protected. Care is necessary with loose rock on ledges.

Start in a wide, easy gully and continue up this as it steepens and narrows until an overhang appears to block the route. Climb the chimney behind blocks, then crawl out through a narrow hole and continue up a slab. Above the slab, climb a series of steep, narrow and strenuous chimneys to the top.

CMC WALL *** 270 m, 5.11a
U.Kallen and B.Davidson, June 1972
F.F.A: B.Stark and B.Wallace, 1984

This old aid route is currently considered one of the best hard climbs on Yamnuska. The climbing is steep and very exposed but the difficulties are short and well protected. Retreat is possible from high up on the climb despite its earier reputation.
Start up Calgary Route and then traverse out right for about 35 m on a ramp to a belay below and slightly left of a corner (the second of two) with a small overhang.
1) 45 m, 5.9. Climb a steep wall to gain the corner, go up the corner moving right round the overhang, and continue up and left to a ledge.
2) 50 m, 5.10b. Climb a corner, then move left and go up to a small roof. Move left round the roof and then step up and traverse right following a line of holds. Go up to a bolt and continue right to a bay below a large roof. Move left below the roof and climb a groove past a bolt and piton stance (old description) until a diagonal traverse left can be made below a second large roof to a belay at the base of the Great Corner.
3) 45 m, 5.11a. Climb the corner past bolts to a roof. Turn the roof on the right and continue up past bolts and a crack on the left wall to the second of two stances.
4) 30 m, 5.9. Move up and left across slabs through a loose band to a corner on the right side of a pinnacle. Climb the corner to a bolt belay.
5) 25 m, 5.10a. Make an ascending traverse right past bolts into the Great Corner. Descend the right wall to an exposed ledge on the right.
6) 20 m, 5.10c. Go up diagonally right and climb a crack which angles left to a hanging bolt belay. Alternatively climb the groove above the ledge past an overhang to a stance below and left of the hanging belay.
7) 25 m, 5.9. Go up and right across a slab following a line of bolts and rivets. Continue across to the base of a large corner. (Pitches 6 and 7 can be combined).
8) 45 m, 5.9. Climb the corner past an overhang and continue more easily to a second overhang. Traverse left and move up to a ledge.
9) 30 m, 5.8. Follow a line of bolts up and right across a slab and then move left to a chimney which leads to the top.

HIGHLANDER ** 340 m, 5.10d
S.DeMaio (solo), June 1986
F.F.A: S.DeMaio and S.Dougherty, August 1986

This worthwhile route moves left from partway up Direttissima and climbs a sensationally steep pitch to reach a prominent upper corner. A small selction of pitons is required for belays.
Follow Direttissima until partway up the third pitch and belay in a V-corner above slabs. The corner is the left of the "two cracks" noted in the description of that route.
1) 35 m, 5.9. Climb to the top of the V-corner and continue up the handcrack above. Move left and climb a V-slot. Continue right over loose blocks and then traverse back left to a large ledge.
2) 45 m, 5.10d. Climb a corner to a roof, undercling left and move up with difficulty into an overhanging groove. Climb the righthand of two cracks and contiue up and left on easier-angled rock to a ledge.

3) 45 m, 5.8. Step down left off the ledge and make a long traverse left below an overhanging arch, moving up and down as required, to reach a good ledge.
4) 50 m, 5.9. Climb up and right to the base of the upper corner and continue up this to a small belay.
5) 40 m, 5.9. Good climbing up the corner leads to a large ledge.
6) 20 m, 5.10a. From the left end of the ledge climb a corner to a bulge (piton). Move up and left with difficulty over this to the top.

SHUFTEE   340 m, 5.9
R.Lofthouse and R.Howe, 1971
F.F.A: R.Boiselle and friend, 1980

Shuftee moves left from Direttissima higher up than Highlander and climbs the upper wall between the two routes.
Climb the first four pitches of Direttissima to the belay in the V-corner. Continue up to the large roof, then traverse steeply left for about 5 m and step down to a block. Climb a short chimney and a slab above to a large ledge. Continue up slabs trending slightly left, then climb a crack on the left to another slab. Above this, go left and climb a corner over a bulge to the top (last 15 m very loose).

DIRETTISSIMA **   340 m, 5.8
H.Kahl, H.Gmoser and L.Grillmair, September 1957

This classic route follows a prominent corner system that leads directly to the summit of the mountain. Most of the climbing is relatively straightforward and overall the climb is easy for its grade.
Starting on the left, scramble up for about 100 m to a large scree ledge at the foot of the corner.
1) 50 m, 5.8. Start at a large boulder just left of the apex of the ledge and follow a rising traverse line up left to the corner. Climb the corner to a good ledge and piton belay on the right. The pitch may be split either by moving left a short distance up the corner to a ledge or by belaying at a small pinnacle a little higher.
2) 45 m, 5.7. Move up left across the corner and climb up to a large overhang. Pass the overhang on the right and climb a slanting crack to a second overhang. Step left, and continue up and right to a groove. Follow this for a short distance and then climb diagonally up left to a small ledge.
3) 50 m, 5.6. Make a rising traverse back right on steep easy rock and climb the righthand of two cracks. Go right and climb a groove system, moving left to belay.
4) 30 m, 5.6. Step left and climb a steep slab to a ledge below a large V-corner capped by roofs. The V-corner is located left of the main corner system and is followed for about 15 m until level with a faint traverse line leading horizontally right.
5) 30 m, 5.7. Follow the traverse line right past a piton to a rib (ignore a higher piton). Climb the right side of the rib to a roof, hand traverse right and move up to a left-facing slot. Belay at the top of the slot in a small cave.
6) 35 m, 5.6. Make a steep move right to easier ground and continue up to a belay in a corner about 15 m below a large roof.

◁ *Jeff Marshall on pitch 2 of Astro Yam, photo Brian Wallace*

7) 35 m, 5.6. Traverse horizontally left to a short corner. Continue up and left (pitons) to a ledge left of a rib. Climb steep rock above and angle right into a crack/chimney line.
8) 45 m, 5.7. Continue up to the final chimneys and belay below a large jammed block (register).
9) 20 m, 5.8. Either climb directly over the block by wide bridging or mantleshelf onto a small ledge slightly below the belay on the left wall and climb up and back right past a piton to the top of the block. Continue up the chimney to the top passing behind a large chockstone.
Variations:
3 & 4 alt) Climb directly to the V-corner from the lefthand of the "two cracks" (also climbed partly by Highlander).
4 - 6 alt) Instead of moving left to the V-corner and then back right, it is possible to follow the main corner system, which is fairly loose, directly to the large roof. Above pitch 3, gain an easy ledge that leads right to a big corner. Climb a wide crack in the corner and continue straight up until the ragular route is rejoined on the sixth pitch.
7 - 9 alt) The right side of the big roof above pitch 6 has been climbed (5.9, I.Heyes and C.Smith, 1971).

† ASTRO YAM   270 m, 5.11c
J.Marshall, B.Gross, B.Wallace and S.DeMaio, May 1986

This unlikely route takes a devious line up the steep wall to the right of Direttissima. The rock is excellent but the climbing is continuously difficult and frequently runout. It is currently considered the hardest climb on the cliff.
Start just right of Direttissima and climb to the top of an obvious pedestal (50 m, 5.6).
1) 40 m, 5.10b. From the top of the pedestal, climb a crack on the left for about 15 m to a bolt. Descend slightly and traverse left for a few metres to the bottom of a groove. Climb the groove and go left to a second bolt. Continue diagonally up right to a bolt belay.
2) 35 m, 5.11b. Move up to a bolt and traverse left and up slightly to a second bolt. Climb a small pillar on the left, traverse right to a third bolt, and continue up and right to a fourth bolt. Climb straight up past a piton to a bolt and piton belay. (Escape left onto Direttissima is possible at this point.)
3) 35 m, 5.10b. Go right up a ramp to a bolt, descend for about 3 m and make a long traverse right on small holds. Move up to the second of two bolts and climb diagonally up and right to a bolt belay.
4) 40 m, 5.11c. Traverse left for 3 m, move up and go back right to the top of a small pedestal. Move right and climb a break to a bolt. Continue to a small hole about 3 m above a second bolt, make a few moves left and then climb diagonally up and left to an outside edge (runout). Continue up the edge past a bolt to a bolt belay.
5) 30 m, 5.10a. Traverse left to a corner and go up this for 15 m to a small ledge. Move right for about 5 m and climb a crack that spilts a blank wall. Continue up more easily to a bolt belay.
6) 40 m, 5.9. Go up trending left to the top.

† ABOVE AND BEYOND 305 m, 5.11c, A0
J.Marshall, S.DeMaio and B.Gross, August 1986

Sustained climbing on good rock in an excellent position.
1) 50 m, 5.6. Climb to the top of a pedestal just left of Balrog.
2) 50 m, 5.11a. Climb a chimney to the top of a secondary pedestal. Step right and move up until it is possible to traverse right to a bolt. Move diagonally up right past a second bolt to a crack. Climb the crack and move left to a ledge with a bolt belay.
3) 45 m, 5.11c. From the left side of the ledge, climb up and then right to a bolt. Move up to a bolt, step left, and climb to the top of a right-facing corner (bolt). Either layback an edge to reach better holds or climb an easier line (5.10c) on the right. Move diagonally left and climb a break in the overhangs. Traverse right on a small ledge above the overhangs to a bolt at the base of a corner. Climb the corner and traverse right past a small roof at waist level to a right-facing corner. Follow this to a small, bolt belay. (A serious and runout pitch).
4) 45 m, 5.10c. Move up and left to below a prominent corner. Traverse left and climb a second corner past a bulge to a belay in a niche.
5) 45 m, 5.11c. Continue up the corner and move right to a bolt. Step left and move up with difficulty over a bulge. Move right to a bolt, and climb straight up until it is possible to traverse right into a short left-facing corner. Climb this to a hanging bolt belay on the left.
6) 45 m, 5.10a, A0. Move left and climb a corner, and then go right to a large ledge (bolt). Pendulum right from the bolt into a groove (ignore a bolt up and left of the ledge). Continue up the groove to a bolt belay.
7) 50 m, 5.10c. Continue up a right-facing corner on the left and then traverse left and climb a chimney to a ledge (bolt). Climb a short corner and then move left and continue up to a belay.
8) 20 m, 5.5. Easy climbing leads to the top.

BALROG * 345 m, 5.10b
B.Greenwood, J.Moss and R.Nicholas, 1969
F.F.A: D.Cheesmond and T.Friesen, 1982

"Balrog" climbs the first major break right of Direttissima. It was long considered the hardest climb on the cliff but is now overshadowed by its neighbours to the left. The climbing is strenuous and in places the rock is not good.
1) 35 m, 5.8. Climb a shallow corner on the left and traverse back right to a sloping ledge.
2) 15 m, 5.6. Climb up over loose blocks into the main corner and go up this to a belay on the left.
3) 35 m, 5.7. Step left and climb a break in a short wall. Move back right and climb the corner to a belay immediately below the first big overhang.
4) 20 m, 5.6. Undercling left and continue further left to a small ledge where the overhang eases.
5) 35 m, 5.8. Move up into the corner and climb a steep crack and a wide corner above to a piton below a steep wall. Descend to the right to a small pulpit of loose rock. Climb onto the slab above and step left over a bulge to easier ground.

6) 25 m, 5.7. Continue up the corner to where the wall steepens and then move left across a short slab to a belay at the bottom of a pinnacle.
7) 20 m, 5.8. Climb the left side of the pinnacle and traverse right across the wall to a belay below a bulge.
8) 40 m, 5.10b. Climb over the bulge and follow a steep corner/crack past three bolts on the left wall. From the top bolt, either continue up the corner moving left around the roof and up to a belay in the crack above, or make a few difficult moves left to reach a small foothold and then go up and left until a traverse back right can be made to the belay.
9) 35 m, 5.8. Climb the chimney above to a niche.
10) 15 m, 5.8. Climb the wall left of the chimney over a steep section to a belay.
11) 35 m, 5.7. Climb diagonally left across the wall and follow a break up and slightly right. Move back right to a belay below the final chimney.
12) 35 m, 5.7. Climb the chimney to the top.

† THE WILD BOYS   355 m, 5.10d
B.Gross, D.Cheesmond and C.Quinn, August 1985

This route climbs a prominent corner in the upper wall between Balrog and Bottleneck.
Start as for Chockstone Corner and climb up to the belay at the top of pitch 1 (40 m, 5.6.).
1) 45 m, 5.9. Go left across a slab and climb up to a small roof. Move over this on the left and continue up and left to a good ledge.
2) 25 m, 5.8. Climb steeply up and right to a small ledge at the base of a large, detached flake (probably dangerously loose).
3) 50 m, 5.9. Move right around an outside corner and climb up past a rotten roof to a belay.
4) 30 m, 5.8. Move right and climb a chimney to a large ledge. Go up and right along the ledge and belay below and slightly right of the upper corner.
5) 50 m, 5.10d. Climb the face and then move left with difficulty and go up to the top of a pinnacle. Move further left until it is possible to move up and right to easier ground. Continue up to a belay at the base of the upper corner.
6) 50 m, 5.10c. Climb the crack on good jams until forced onto the left wall for a few moves. Continue up to a belay ledge.
7 & 8) 65 m, 5.9. Climb the corner moving left below a roof and continue up to the top.

*Brian Gross on the first ascent of Above and ⇨
Beyond - pitch 5, photo Steve DeMaio*

Yamnuska

CHOCKSTONE CORNER *   290 m, 5.8
R.Lofthouse and H.Kahl, August 1963
A classic climb at the lower limit of its grade. Starting just right of Balrog, scramble right up broken slabs to a sloping stance below the righthand of two corners.
1) 40 m, 5.6. Climb to the base of the corner (belay) and continue up the corner to a belay on a small slab on the right.
2) 30 m, 5.6. Move across right to a larger slab and from near the top of this, climb a steep crack in the wall above. Move right around the corner to a large ledge.
3) 25 m, 5.5. Go right along the ledge, and then descend and walk right to a chimney on the left side of a pinnacle. Belay on a large jammed block at the top of the pinnacle.
4) 40 m, 5.8. Climb the crack in the steep wall above (2 pitons) and continue more easily following a crack up and slightly rightwards. Belay on a ledge just right of the crack.
5) 25 m. Continue to easy-angled slabs below a steep wall. Traverse right and belay below a steep V-groove (a bolt belay would be useful here).
6) 35 m, 5.8. Move right for 2 m and climb a shallow groove (piton) to a horizontal break. Traverse steeply right following the break around a rib to a ledge. Continue up a steep groove (pitons) into the main corner. Belay on the left at a large block where the corner steepens.
7) 25 m, 5.8. Climb up and right to a small ledge below a crack. Make a difficult move up the steep wall to the right and then continue using the crack into the start of the chimney system.
8) 25 m, 5.8. Climb the chimney past a difficult narrow section, move right slightly (piton), and continue up and left to a belay in the corner.
9) 45 m, 5.7. Climb the steep corner on the left and continue up the chimney following the righthand branch to the top.

BOTTLENECK **   225 m, 5.8.
The section above pitch three was first climbed from Chockstone Corner by A.Cole and R.Lofthouse whilst pitches 1-3 were added later by B.Greenwood and D.Vockeroth. The Lefthand Start was climbed by G.Homer and I.Heyes.
Scramble up to the large ledges at the start of Grillmair Chimneys. Climb an easy crack to a higher ledge and move left to a steep, right-facing corner.
1) 30 m, 5.8. Climb the corner to a prominent roof. Move out right and climb up to a small belay in the crack above.
2) 20 m, 5.8. Continue up the crack, and then move right and climb a steep, cracked wall to a ledge.
3) 35 m, 5.6. Move down and go left to gain the corner on the right side of a large pinnacle. Climb the corner to a belay at the top of the pinnacle (junction with pitch 3 of Chockstone Corner).
1-3 alt) Lefthand Start. 80 m, 5.9. Climb the wide crack immediately left of the corner to join the normal route partway up pitch 3.
4) 35 m, 5.7. Climb the steep wall on Chockstone Corner, and then move left and climb a short V-corner to a ledge. Move left and climb a second corner to a good ledge and piton belay.

5) 45 m, 5.8. Climb up and slightly right on an indistinct ramp to the base of a steep wall. This is climbed on the left via a shallow corner with a block at its top. From the top of the block, make a steep rising traverse to the right, past a piton at foot level, to easier ground.
6) 45 m, 5.7. Climb up trending right in a series of steep blocky corners to the base of the righthand chimney.
7) 45 m, 5.8. Climb the chimney for about 5 m past the Bottleneck, and then move right to a small ledge. Climb the steep corner above, move back left (belay), and follow chimneys to the top.

† HIGH VOLTAGE   380 m, 5.10a
C.Perry and M.White, September 1981

High Voltage climbs the prominent corner in the upper wall immediately right of Chockstone Corner. The corner is reached by a very wandering line which could probably be straightened out and improved. Follow the Lefthand Variation of Grillmair Chimneys for 2 pitches to the top of the first chimney (65 m, 5.5.)

1) 35 m, 5.8. Move up and traverse left on loose rock to the foot of a steep corner. Climb the corner moving right to an edge to bypass a steep section. Continue up the corner and at the top move up left onto a ledge. Climb the steep wall above to a small ledge with a piton belay.
2) 40 m, 5.10a. Continue up a steep groove (piton) and either climb it directly moving left and up to a ledge or step left and climb the arete (equally difficult). Traverse easily left, move up and then continue traversing left to a shallow groove. Climb the groove to a bolt and piton belay.
3) 30 m, 5.8. Climb a groove on the right and continue up right to a second, more difficult groove. Climb this to a narrow ledge (2 bolts) and go along this to a piton belay behind a large flake.
4) 20 m, 5.9. Traverse right across a steep undercut slab to an arete (piton). Move right around the arete and then climb down and right with difficulty to a sloping ledge below a bay.
5) 35 m, 5.9. Climb the steep wall above with difficulty, and continue up and right to a groove. Move right and make a long descending traverse right (poor protection - piton under small roof) to reach a large ramp and a two bolt belay.
6) 45 m, 5.6. Walk right along the ramp and move around an edge into a corner. Climb the corner trending back left to a pinnacle.
7) 30 m, 5.7. Climb up behind the pinnacle and move across left on ledges to the base of the upper corner.
8 & 9) 80 m, 5.8. Climb the corner, following a groove on the right near the top.
4-7 alt) It may be possible to improve the route by climbing directly to the upper corner from the arete on pitch 4.

Yamnuska

GRILLMAIR CHIMNEYS * 300 m, 5.5
L.Grillmair, H.Gmoser and I.Spreat, 1952

This popular easy climb follows a large slanting break in the right-centre of the face. Caution is necessary with loose rock when parties are above or below.
Scramble up from the left to a large ledge and move across right to a crack in a short wall. Climb the crack for 6 m, move right, and go up to a ledge. From here two almost completely separate lines may be followed: the Lefthand Variation, a series of chimneys and corners starting above the ledge and lying immediately right of the steep left wall, or the Righthand Variation, a series of gullies and broken chimneys reached by traversing right along the ledge. After 3 or 4 pitches the two lines come together beneath a steep wall about 100 m from the top. Climb the wall past pitons moving right to a niche and then up to easier ground. Belay at the base of the final chimney (not as hard as it looks). The chimney is best climbed first on the right, then by bridging up the outside (pitons), and finally by moving inside and exiting through a narrow hole (bolt belay at the top). The pitch can be split by belaying inside the chimney just below the top.

SPRING FEVER 335 m, 5.11a
A.Genereux and J.Jones, March 1987

This route basically climbs the arete to the right of Grillmair Chimneys. The first four pitches are good but above the rock deteriorates somewhat and the climbing is more broken.
Start about 45 m west of where the central path reaches the cliff below a left-facing corner with a prominent handcrack that leads to the right side of a large roof.
1) 45 m, 5.11a. Climb the corner to the roof. Traverse left below the roof to a V-slot (piton on left) and climb this with difficulty to a bolt. Continue up to a bolt belay. This pitch may be avoided by traversing right on the big scree ledge at the start of Grillmair Chimneys.
2) 35 m, 5.10a. From the big scree ledge, the route follows a long corner system for about 4 pitches. Climb the first corner past a difficult section to a belay in a bay.
3) 30 m, 5.9. Continue up the corner to a large, detached pillar and climb up behind this to a bolt belay at the top.
4) 50 m, 5.10c. Difficult face climbing above leads to a bolt. Move up and slightly right to a second bolt about 8 m higher and then go left to gain a shallow groove. Go up this and then back right to a third bolt. Move left with difficulty and go up to a prominent crack. This leads to the corner system which is followed to a small, sloping ledge.
5) 35 m. Move up to gain a large broken ledge system and go left along this for about 30 m to a prominent corner system.
6) 50 m, 5.8. Climb the corner to a bay.
7) 40 m, 5.8. Continue up the corner to ledges and follow these up and right to the base of an obvious handcrack.
8) 50 m, 5.10a. Climb the crack for about 20 m until it ends at a small ledge. Move left with difficulty to gain the lefthand of two shallow grooves. Climb the groove for about 12 m to below a roof and then move into the righthand groove to finish.

Yamnuska

THE HEAT IS ON *   355 m, 5.10a
B.Gross, D.Cheesmond and C.Quinn, June 1985

Starting where the central path reaches the cliff, climb a ramp up and left for about 30m to a small tree and belay below a crack 6m to the right.
1) 55 m, 5.8. Climb the crack and continue up a break to a large ledge.
2) 40 m, 5.8. Move up and right to a bottomless crack and climb it to a ledge. Move right and continue up to a ledge on the right.
3) 50 m, 5.8. Move back left and climb up to the base of a chimney. Follow the chimney to a ledge.
4) 45 m, 5.9. Climb easily to the top of a pinnacle. Continue up a steep crack, and where it arches left, move out right and up to a bolt. Go diagonally up right to a small ledge.
5) 50 m, 5.9. Climb a corner to a hand traverse leading left. Continue further left and up, and then go digonally left across a slab to a bolt belay below an overhang.
6) 35 m, 5.10a. Move down slightly and left from the belay and then climb a break to a roof. Go left under the roof and around, and then move up back right to a bolt. Continue straight up to easier ground and a stance on blocks on the right.
7) 40 m, 5.7. Traverse left to an obvious break and go up this to a belay.
8) 40 m, 5.7. Continue up and right and then climb over a blocky roof to the top.

KAHL WALL **   290 m, 5.10a
D.Vockeroth and T.Auger, July 1971
F.F.A: B.Blanchard and K.Dolye, 1981

A good climb with a sustained and well-positioned crux pitch. Start about 20 m right of where the central path reaches the cliff, below a small but prominent cave. Scramble up to a ledge, then climb the corner on the right to a higher ledge.
1) 35 m, 5.7. Climb the left wall of a corner for about 6m and then move out left and go up to a corner. Traverse left across a slab and continue up and across left to ledges. Belay in a corner at the left end of the ledges.
2) 45 m, 5.7. Follow the crack above to a higher ledge. Move right and climb a hidden chimney and crack system to a belay below a small, flaring chimney.
3) 30 m, 5.7. Climb the chimney and exit right onto ledges. Traverse easily right for 20-25 m to a piton belay.
4) 30 m, 5.8. Climb a shallow corner and move right on small holds to a groove. Climb this to easier ground, and then go across right and down to a small stance.
5) 45 m, 5.10a. Climb up left for about 6 m to the first bolt. Move up and right with difficulty to a shallow groove, and continue up the steep face above to a small ledge (bolts). Climb a corner until it is possible to traverse right onto the face. Continue up to a roof, traverse left into a corner, and go up this to a ledge.
6) 35 m, 5.9. Climb the corner above for about 6m until it steepens, and then move right and up to the base of a slabby wall. Climb the wall past two bolts to a good ledge.
7 & 8) 70 m, 5.8. Climb the upper corner to the top.

THE TRAP LINE   355 m, 5.11a, A1
W.Robinson and S.DeMaio, July 1987

The climb starts almost equidistant between Kahl Wall and Forbidden Corner. After some excellent climbing lower down, the route wanders about on easy ground following sections both the above mentioned routes. At present, there are no hangers on the bolts, only cap screws. Scramble up and left to a large ledge at the top of a short corner.

1) 45 m, 5.10c. Climb a blocky corner for 3 m to a ledge and then traverse right to a 45 m corner/groove system. Make a few moves up the groove and then go right onto the face. Climb up and back left into the groove and continue up to a bulge (bolt). Traverse left 3 m to a crack and go up this to a bolt belay.

2) 45 m, 5.9 A1. Traverse right for 2 m to a corner and go up this to a ledge. Step left and climb up and then back right into a short corner. Climb the corner to its end (3 m) and traverse left along a break to a short bolt ladder. Continue left from the end of the bolt ladder to a bolt belay at the base of a corner.

3) 45 m, 5.11a. Climb the corner for 10 m to a bolt and continue up with difficulty onto the wall above. Difficult climbing across left leads to easier ground. Continue up and left to a corner and belay on the second of two large ledges.

4) 75 m, 5.5. Climb a large left-facing flake/chimney to a ledge. Belay on the right end of a ledge at the top of pitch 6 of Forbidden Corner.

5) 35 m, 5.6. Follow pitch 7 of Forbidden Corner to a belay at the top of the short corner.

6) 40 m, 5.9. Continue up to where Forbidden Corner goes right, and then move up and left to a ledge system. Traverse left along a break past a bolt to the top of pitch 6 of Kahl Wall.

7 & 8) 70 m, 5.8. Continue up Kahl Wall to the top.

FORBIDDEN CORNER **   345 m, 5.8
D.Vockeroth and L.MacKay, October 1964

Forbidden Corner is generally considered the best of the classic 5.8's on Yamnuska. The climbing is varied and continuously interesting, and the exit pitches on the upper wall are superbly situated. The route follows a prominent right-facing corner which begins just above the base of the cliff and rises to about half height. Start at a large, flat-topped block about 200m left of Red Shirt and directly below the corner. Scramble up to the top of the block and continue up an easy crack to a higher ledge on the left.

1) 25 m, 5.8. Climb a shattered scoop in the steep wall directly above the ledge to a traverse line that leads up right to the base of the corner.

2) 20 m, 5.7. Follow the corner to a ledge on the right below a steep wall.

3) 40 m, 5.8. Climb the crack directly above the belay to easier ground. Follow the corner up leftwards, past a piton near the top, to a small ledge on the left (the second of two) located immediately below the steep upper corner.

Yamnuska

4) 30 m, 5.8. Climb over a bulge and continue up the corner (piton) for 2-3 m until a hand traverse line leads out right to a flake. Climb to the top of the flake, move right and climb a short corner to easier ground above. Belay in a bay where the corner steepens.
5) 35 m, 5.8. Climb the corner past a roof and then traverse up left past a small flake to the left arete (piton). Continue up the edge until a ledge system leads back right to the corner. Move up to a ledge at the top of the main corner.
6) 40 m. Climb up left on easy rock, past a pinnacle, to a good ledge just to the right of a left-facing chimney.
7) 30 m, 5.6. Follow the chimney to a traverse line leading left below a yellow, overhanging wall to a sloping stance at the foot of a short corner. Alternatively, climb more or less diagonally left and then up across steep slabs to the base of the corner. (A belay can be taken higher up at the top of the corner).
8) 35 m, 5.8. Climb the corner to a ledge and continue up a second corner for about 5 m to an overhang (piton). Traverse right onto the face and climb the blocky wall (piton) until small ledges lead right to an exposed stance with a bolt and piton belay.
9) 30 m, 5.8. Move across right with difficulty to a pinnacle and climb this to the top (piton). Descend the other side for a short distance and then traverse right below a bulge to a small foot ledge. Climb the wall above (difficult at first) and follow a rising break up right to a ledge.
10) 35 m. Traverse horizontally left for about 25 m and move up left to a ledge below a slanting corner.
11) 25 m, 5.7. Climb to corner to the top.

† BROWN TROUSERS   300 m, 5.10c A0
D.Cheesmond, B.Gross and C.Quinn, June 1985

The route climbs a steep corner system left of Red Shirt. Start about 35 m right of Forbidden Corner, directly below a bottomless pillar about 30m up the cliff.
1) 50 m, 5.9. Go up to a crack on the left side of a rotten wall. Climb the crack and continue up to a ledge on the right. Climb to the top of a pinnacle on the right and then go up left and back right to the base of a wide, flaring crack. Move diagonally left and up to a bolt belay.
2) 30 m, 5.10a. Drop down and traverse right, then climb up on small holds to a roof. Go over this on the right and continue up to bolt. Climb diagonally right, move around a corner and continue up a short crack to a ledge. Belay on a higher ledge.
3) 50 m, 5.10a. Make a difficult move off the ledge and continue to easier ground on the right. Climb the main corner for about 30 m to an overhang and then exit left to a good ledge.
4) 30 m, 5.10c, A0. Drop down and tension across to a jam crack in the righthand wall. (This section was seconded free on the first ascent - placement of a bolt runner is recommended to allow a free lead). Climb the crack for about 25 m to to belay in an alcove.
5) 45 m, 5.9. Climb over the roof and continue until about 6m below an second, larger roof. Move left around this and go up to a belay or climb the roof on its righthand side (5.10c).

6) 45 m, 5.8. Go up and left for about 25 m and continue up and back left slightly to a piton belay. Red Shirt is now about 10 m to the right.
7) 50 m, 5.8. Continue up and left below overhangs and climb a short crack to the top.

RED SHIRT ROUTE ** 270 m, 5.7
B.Greenwood, H.Kahl and R.Lofthouse, June 1962

This justifiably popular climb takes an intricate and exposed line up a steep section of the face. It is mainly 5.6 in difficulty with only a few moves of 5.7. Start at a short corner behind two large spruce trees growing a short distance from the face. The V-shaped chimney of the second pitch is prominent above.

1) 40 m, 5.6. Start in the corner but traverse left at the first opportunity to a small pillar. Climb this on its right side and continue past a ledge over a blocky ramp to a good belay below a prominent chimney.
2) 35 m, 5.6. Climb the chimney for about 15 m until it is possible to break out onto the left edge. Climb the edge trending slightly left and belay at a good ledge.
3) 35 m, 5.6. Step down and right and climb a steep little wall to gain a crack line. Continue up this and the wall above to a belay (pitons) partway up a short chimney.
4) 15 m, 5.5. Step up and then move left around an outside corner onto an exposed slab. From a piton, climb down and left across the slab to a small and very exposed ledge (bolt and nut belay). **Note:** Common mistakes are to climb too far up the chimney or even up the difficult corner above.
5) 30 m, 5.6 A0, or 5.7. Step left and climb a steep corner past fixed pitons (5.7 free). At the first small ledge (piton), traverse left for about 15 m, making a short descent along the way, and then climb up to a belay. Alternatively, traverse left for about 3 m for the small ledge, climb over a small overhang, continue up a steep wall, and then go easily left to the belay.
6) 40 m, 5.6. Climb to a small bay and continue up a short chimney on the left. Follow the corner above to a good belay.
7) 45 m, 5.6. Step onto the short wall above the belay, cross it to the left, and go around the corner. Climb straight up, working right after around 25 m to a yellow bulge. Climb a short wall to the right of this and continue up to ledges, moving right to belay.
8) 30 m, 5.6. Climb up a short distance and traverse right across the bottom of a steep slab. Continue traversing right past a broken pillar and around an exposed outside corner (pitons), and either climb steeply up and right to the top or continue traversing to an easier exit ramp.

Yamnuska

THE BOWL   165 m, 5.9.
L.MacKay and D.Vockeroth, May 1965
F.F.A: A.Burgess, J.Lauchlan and P.Thexton, 1973

Begin by some large pinnacles left of Yellow Edge and climb to the top of a 4th class ramp and corner system that slants up left for about 100m. Belay as far left as possible below a short corner capped by a roof.

1) 35 m, 5.7. Start up the corner and then step right and climb a crack to the roof. Traverse right for about 15 m to a right-facing corner and belay where this steepens, about 10 m below a large overhang.

1 alt) On the first ascent, the right-facing corner described above was reached directly from the ramp using aid to surmount a small overhang. This has been seconded free at 5.10d.

2) 35 m, 5.9. Climb the corner to the overhang, undercling right and follow the steep crack above to ledges on the left.

3) 45 m, 5.7. Climb the corner system above for about 35 m until it steepens and becomes difficult. Traverse steeply left on good holds and continue up to a belay on small ledges.

4) 30 m, 5.9. Move up right and climb a thin, overhanging crack which is the only weakness in the bulging wall above. Continue with difficulty past a second overhang to a small ledge. Step down a traverse left to a bolt belay.

5) 20 m, 5.8. Traverse left around a rib and climb an easy corner to the top.

† EAST END BOYS   255 m, 5.11a
S.DeMaio and B.Betts, June 1986

This route takes a direct line above the first pitch of Yellow Edge to reach a prominent upper corner. It is probably the steepest route on Yamnuska and may well go free in the near future.

1) 30 m, 5.9. Climb the first pitch of Yellow Edge to the top of the pinnacle.

2) 35 m, 5.11a, A1. Climb up a few metres to a ledge, step left and follow a layback crack to a bolt below a small roof. Climb over the roof (one point of aid), and continue to a fixed hanging belay.

3) 40 m, 5.10c , A2. Use two bolts and two nuts for aid and continue free up and left to a niche under a small roof. Step right over the roof and climb a flared corner to a large ledge.

4) 35 m, 5.11a, A1. Climb a steep hand crack past a small roof (2 points of aid) to a hanging bolt belay below a large roof.

5) 45 m, 5.7, A3. Climb over the roof using aid and continue more easily to a ledge in the upper corner.

6) 30 m, 5.10a, A1. Climb the corner using a few points of aid to a ledge on the left.

7) 40 m, 5.9. Continue up the corner, move left and climb a corner/chimney system to the top.

YELLOW EDGE **   225 m, 5.11b
B. Davidson and U.Kallen, May 1974
F.F.A: P.Croft and C.Zacharias, January 1986
This excellent climb was originally a major aid route. It is comparable in difficulty and quality to CMC Wall although more continuous and serious. Start in an overhanging V-corner directly below the "edge", a very prominent feature in this part of the face.
1) 30 m, 5.9. Climb the overhanging corner moving slightly right past a small roof (old bolts) to a belay on top of a pinnacle.
2) 20 m, 5.10d. Climb a loose, bulging wall to a crack that arches up and right. Follow the crack past a difficult and strenuous roof to a bolt belay below a small roof.
3) 40 m, 5.10c. Layback the edge of a left-facing corner and then go up and left to a steep wall (bolts). Climb the wall and follow a break up and slightly right to a line of old rivets. Ignore the rivets and continue up a shallow corner/crack until it is possible to face climb right to a stance below a large right-facing corner. Alternatively, move across to the line of rivets lower down, follow them until a traverse right around an arete can be made and then go straight up to the ledge.
4) 45 m, 5.11a. Climb the corner which narrows to a thin finger crack (5.11a) and move up to the first bolt of a bolt ladder that diagonals up right to a ledge. Make an awkward step down and traverse right on finger flakes to reach a corner below the ledge. Move up to the ledge and belay. (Protection for the second can be improved by clipping the last bolt of the ladder).
5) 40 m, 5.11b. Traverse horizontally right across a grey slab and climb a short left-facing flake to below a steep wall. Difficult and strenuous climbing up and right past fixed protection and a short, overhanging crack leads to a good ledge below a bolt ladder.
6) 50 m, 5.10c. Clip the first six bolts on good holds and then go right and up to an obvious grey dihedral (stance). Climb this until an exit right can be made and then continue up to the top.

† MARRIAGE RITES   250 m, 5.10b A1
A.Sole and D.Morgan, 1981
This route climbs the steep corner system immediately right of Yellow Edge.
1 & 2) 75 m, 5.7. Climb the first two pitches of Corkscrew.
3) 45 m, 5.8. Move right and up as for Corkscrew but instead of continuing right, go up and left following a series of corners to the foot of the main, steep corner leading to a large roof.
4) 35 m, 5.10b. Climb the corner with difficult moves to begin and finish and belay on the slab above.
5) 20 m, 5.9. A1. Free climb to the roof and use aid (approximately 8 nuts-all sizes) to gain the lip. Continue free to a small ledge.
6) 35 m, 5.8. Continue up the corner for 15-20 m, and then make a poorly protected traverse horizontally rightwards following a faint ledge system. After about 15 m, a difficult move leads to a bolt belay.
7) 40 m, 5.9. Make an awkward move right past a bolt, and continue right and up with poor protection to the top.

Yamnuska

CORKSCREW ** 235 m, 5.8 A1
D.Vockeroth, H.Fuhrer and B.Greenwood, 1967

An interesting climb with a bit of everything. It was originally begun as an attempt on the corner of Marriage Rites but deviated well to the right. Starting just right of the buttress below Yellow Edge, scramble up to a ledge system and belay on the right.
1) 35 m, 5.4. Follow the ledge rightwards to its end and climb a wall to a belay below a big corner.
2) 40 m, 5.7. Climb the crack on the left wall of the corner past bulges to a belay in a wide crack.
3) 30 m, 5.7. Traverse right on good holds and go up to a piton. Go right again, climb a short bulge and then traverse right to an outside corner and a small ledge with a piton. Make an awkward move right to a good belay.
4) 20 m, 5.7. Climb two short corners to a bolt belay below a steep wall.
5) 35 m, 5.8. Climb a bolt ladder and make a dificult move up right into a short corner. Tension down right to reach a narrow ledge (5.9 free), move across right and climb a short steep wall. Continue more easily up to a belay.
6) 30 m, 5.7. Move up and right and climb a left-leaning corner to a belay on the right.
7) 45 m, 5.8. Traverse right for about 12 m and climb a steep wall until it is possible to move up and right around an outside corner. Continue up a ramp to the top.

FREAK OUT 210 m, 5.9
B.Davidson and J.Horne, July 1971

This loose and strenuous climb has had only a few ascents. Start just left of some large boulders at a prominent regular crack in an area of yellow-orange rock.
1) 30 m, 5.9. Climb the crack to a small ledge.
2) 40 m, 5.9. Continue over the overhang, make an awkward move left, and then go up to the second and larger of two ledges.
3) 40 m, 5.9. Move right a short distance and climb a wall. Step left and continue to a ledge.
4) 40 m, 5.9. Follow a ramp up and right to the second of two steep corners. Climb the corner, move right and continue until a step left can be made onto a belay ledge.
5) 15 m, 5.8. Step down and make a short traverse right to a flake. Climb the flake onto a slab and move right to belay.
6) 45 m, 5.9. Start up a small crack and continue up and right on face holds to a corner. Climb over a small roof and then step right onto a ledge. Continue up the steep crack above to the top.

PANGOLIN ** 160 m, 5.9
B.Greenwood, R.Lofthouse and D.Vockeroth, 1965
F.F.A: J.Horne and I.Heyes, 1970

This excellent climb follows a discontinuous series of very steep cracks, trending leftward toward an obvious exit chimney. Start by scrambling up and left for about 15 m to the top of a roughly triangular buttress that lies in low relief against the face.
1) 20 m, 5.9. Move left and climb steep rock past fixed pitons into a short corner. Continue up the corner until it closes, then swing left to a bolt belay on a small ledge.
2) 20 m, 5.9. Either move left and climb a short crack to a ledge or continue up the steep crack on the right, passing a small roof and moving back left to the belay ledge (more difficult).
3) 45 m, 5.9. Follow the crack above over an impressive roof, and continue up to a ledge system that leads across left to an alcove below the final chimney.
4) 30 m, 5.8. Climb up via a steep wall to the base of the chimney.
5) 45 m, 5.7. Climb the chimney (no protection at first) and either move slightly right at the top to finish or go left past a nest and then up (5.9).

SMEAGOL ** 120 m, 5.9
B.Greenwood and U.Kallen, May 1970

About 50 m right of Pangolin is a prominent left-facing corner system, above which are three exit cracks in an overhung yellow wall. Smeagol follows the left of these cracks, cutting directly through three overhangs and giving one of the best steep pitches on Yamnuska.
1) 40 m, 5.7. Climb easily up the corner for about 15 m, then continue up steeper rock passing a bulge. After about 30 m, traverse left to a small stance at the base of a right-facing corner.
2) 40 m, 5.8. Climb the corner and, near the top, move left under a bulge and go up to a small ledge. Climb up and slightly right over a bulge, then continue more easily to a good ledge below the exit crack.
3) 40 m, 5.9. Climb up on top of a big block, then squeeze through the first overhang. Climb a short slab, make a long reach to surmount the second overhang (5.9), then continue more easily to the top, passing the last overhang on big holds.

DICKS' ROUTE * 120 m, 5.8
R.Howe and R.Lofthouse, 1970

Dicks' Route takes the central of the three cracks mentioned under Smeagol. Start as for Smeagol and Gollum Grooves.
1) 35 m, 5.7. Climb the main groove for about 35 m to a small ledge.
2) 40 m, 5.8. Climb the corner-crack system above to an overhang where it doglegs right. Continue straight up a short, steep corner, then step left onto a small ledge with a bolt belay.
3) 45 m, 5.8. Step left, then go diagonally right into the obvious crack above. Follow this to a roof, move right into another crack, and climb this for about 6 m to an overhang. Traverse right for about 3 m across a steep wall, then climb easily to the top.

Yamnuska

GOLLUM GROOVES * 115 m, 5.7
B.Greenwood and R.Lofthouse, 1962
Starting as do Smeagol and Dicks' Route, Gollum Grooves follows the right exit crack.
1) 35 m, 5.6. Climb the main groove for about 15 m, then move up and right for a short distance to a corner-crack with a slab on the left. Climb the crack to a ledge (piton belay).
2) 40 m, 5.7. Climb a slab and go left up a chimney system to a ledge. Continue up a crack to another ledge, move right, and climb up left to a good stance behind a large block.
3) 40 m, 5.7. Follow the chimney above for about 6 m to a ring piton and then traverse right for about 6 m. Climb slabs to the exit chimney and continue up this to the top.

DICKEL 125 m, 5.7
D.Lofthouse and D.Howe, 1970
The main pitch of this climb follows an obvious open book corner right of Gollum Grooves.
1) Starting at the base of Gollum Groove, move up and right under a bulge, then climb a corner to a belay below an overhang. The corner can also be reached directly from below, starting down and right from Gollum Grooves.
2) Move left, climb up, then traverse right to the foot of a crack at the back of the open book corner.
3) Climb the crack to an overhang, then step right to another crack and follow this to belay on easier ground.
4) Climb easy rock to the top.

A ROUTE 125 m, 5.6
B.Greenwood and G.Crocker, 1963
Start immediately left of a smooth wall capped by a small overhang.
1) Climb broken rock to a short steep wall and go up this to a ledge.
2) Work right to an obvious broken groove line, follow this up, and then move right to a comfortable ledge.
3) Climb the broken groove line above, then trend left up a sharp, rickety pinnacle. Step left from the top of the pinnacle into a gully and continue up, then right over scattered rock to the top.

A CRACK * 40 m, 5.8.
W.Lee and J.Martin, 1983
This is a steep, well-protected crack climb which ends on A Route after one pitch. It follows a hand-sized crack left of a prominent roof.

B ROUTE 120 m, 5.6
B.Greenwood and D.Lofthouse, 1965
Start at a chimney/groove in an outside corner.
1) Climb the chimney to good ledges.
2) Continue to the right past a short wall to easy ledges.
3) Move left below a steep section, make a few thin moves up, and then continue easily to the top.

C PLUS   110 m, 5.7
C.Perry and J.Martin, 1980

To the right of B Route is a dark slot. Climb easy rock to a belay below the yellow wall immediately right of this slot.
1)   Climb a short, overhanging corner at the right edge of the yellow wall, then continue up the groove above to a ledge.
2)   Traverse left about 5m to a groove and follow it to a ledge below a layback crack.
3)   Climb the layback crack, then move past a bulge and continue to the top.

C ROUTE   110 m, 5.7
B.Greenwood and W.Schrauth, 1964

C Route takes the wall to the right of C Plus.
1)   Climb an easy slab and continue up a short corner to a belay.
2)   Move left to a steep corner and follow this to a belay below a small overhang.
3)   Move right to a slab and climb out above this.

To the right of C Route several short climbs have been done, none of which are of much interest.

MOUNT DOOM

On the north side of Yamnuska, a broad ridge, surrounded by cliffs, extends out into CMC Valley. The ridge forms a subsidiary summit called Mount Doom which is separated from the main summit by a deep notch (Windy Gap).

EAST FACE ROUTE   5.4
A.McKeith, September 1971

This is the easiest route to the summit and is mainly 3rd and 4th class. Break through the first rock tier well left of the gully on the east side of Windy Gap. Cross terraces up and right to join the gully which is followed by several easy chimney pitches on good rock to a broad tree-lined ledge. Cross the ledge and an exposed depression in the east face by narrow, sloping ledges (cairns). Climb a short gully, descend a ledge, and go up a second gully. Take the first easy break in the final tier (2 cairns) to reach scree slopes and the summit ridge. Descend the same route or rappel to Windy Gap.

WINDGROOVE   45 m, 5.4
A.McKeith, 1971

Approach as for the first part of East Face Route and continue up the gully to Windy Gap. Alternatively, ascend scree slopes on the west side of the gap. Climb straight up from the gap for 10 m and then move round left to join a steep V-groove. Exit right from this onto easier ground which leads to the top. Good rock. Downclimb the route or rappel to the gap.

BACKSEAT DRIVER   140 m, 5.9 A1
C.Perry and B.Keller, 1974

Farther north, a left-facing chimney and gully system splits the east face and starts above a steep lower tier. Backseat Driver climbs the lower tier to the base of the chimney and then exits left on ledges.
Starting directly below the chimney, climb easy rock to the base of a steep, shallow crack. Climb the crack with difficulty (5.9) to a ledge and then move up and left to a belay below a large overhang. Bypass the overhang on the left using a few points of aid (5.9 A1) and belay a short distance above. Continue to the base of the chimney and then traverse off left on ledges.

CMC VALLEY

This quiet and secluded valley lies immediately north of Yamnuska and contains a number of south-facing cliffs smaller in size than Yamnuska and frequently more sheltered (see map page 116). Access up the valley from the east is blocked by Indian land and this, coupled with its remote location, gives the valley a quiet charm all of its own. It was popular as an early and late season climbing area in the early seventies but emphasis later shifted to the development of the more accessible areas of Grotto Canyon and Heart Creek. With the rise in climbing standards and the acceptance of bolt protection, the area appears to be due for a revival. Certainly, a number of impressive lines remain to be climbed, principally in the area of Hidden Gully.

Although good camping sites abound, most climbers stay at the Simpson Hut particularly in the Spring and Fall when it serves as a warm, sociable meeting place. It is owned and maintained by the CMC and is named after Archie Simpson who was largely responsible for its renovation from an old logging building. Although fairly spartan accommodation, there is no charge for its use and the hut is open to non-members. The CMC asks only that it be kept clean, garbage is carried out, and that the outhouse by the stream is used. Normally the hut is equiped with wood and gas stoves, cooking and eating utensils, foam mattresses, and an axe and saw. Water is available year-round from the nearby creek.

Approach: The best approach to the Simpson Hut begins at the Yamnuska parking area and crosses the long ridge to the east of Yamnuska. It takes about an hour and a quarter.

Follow the trail for Yamnuska and fork right instead of left just above the quarry. The right fork gradually narrows and contours the wooded hillside above the lower sandstone cliffs. After about a kilometre, a dry stream bed is crossed and the trail heads directly up the hillside following the east edge of the stream bank. About halfway to the ridge, the trail contours to the east and then ascends diagonally through a poplar forest. When an open slope is reached, follow the left fork which climbs steeply up to the ridge and then turns westward towards Yamnuska. Stay on the trail just south of the ridge and after a steep section to regain the crest, turn right and cross a barbed-wire fence. Move across to the north side of the ridge and pick up a smaller trail heading northwest and over–looking CMC Valley. The trail contours the hillside for a while and then descends an open ridge to trees. The next section is overgrown but relatively easy to follow. The trail descends and then turns east entering a stand of mature trees. After another overgrown section, the end of an old road coming in from the east is reached. Bear round to the left and follow a rocky track straight down to the valley floor. The hut is located on the right where the track levels out and becomes marshy.

◁ *Andy Genereux on pitch 3 of The Maker, photo Jon Jones*

WAKONDA BUTTRESS

Wakonda buttress is a large cliff of steep yellow rock at the west end of the band of cliffs on the north side of the valley. It is bounded on the left by a small wing ,The West Wing, and on the right by a long section of relatively featureless rock which extends eastwards to Hidden Gully.
Descent: is to the west down easy scree slopes.

West Wing

S. MIT R.   60 m, 5.5
J.Kuenzel and party, 1971

This climbs the loose corner at the left end of the cliff.

CREAME OF AFTERBIRTH   85 m, 5.7
J. Lauchlan and R. Amann, April 1973

At the right end of The West Wing is a prominent corner at the junction of the cliff and the main face. About 20 m left of the corner is a chimney system which is undercut and choked by blocks in its lower section. The route starts to the right of this below a cracked yellow corner which begins about 10 m above the base of the cliff.
1) 40 m, 5.7. Climb up to the corner and pass the first roof on the left. Continue to a second roof which again is passed on the left, and then climb up to ledges.
2) 45 m, Walk left to the base of the final chimney and climb this to the top.

MAYFLOWER *   100 m, 5.7
G. Homer, J. Jones and P. Morrow, April 1971

This climbs the corner at the junction of the The West Wing and the main face. At the top, one of three exits can be taken.
1) 40 m, Climb easy rock left of the corner to a belay below a groove.
2) 30 m, Continue up and right to the middle crack.
3) 30 m, 5.7. Climb the crack to the top.
3a) 5.7. Exit up the wider, more difficult crack on the right.
2,3 alt)   From part way up pitch 2, move up and left to the left-hand crack and follow this (5.7) to the top.

CMC Valley

Main Buttress

IRON SUSPENDER   250 m, 5.7, A4
W.Davidson and G.Homer, 1971

This climbs directly up the steepest part of Wakonda Buttress and is typical of Billy Davidson's quest for big wall routes in the Canadian Rockies. Extensive amounts of aid are used but the route is reported to be a worthwhile outing.

The usual method is to fix the first two pitches and then complete the route in a day. Some of the bolts or rivets may be in poor condition and carrying a bolt kit is advisable.

Equipment: 5 knifeblades, 10 small leepers and angles, and assorted skyhooks. Start "where a drop of water falls from the summit" at a pile of big blocks below a shallow, overhanging groove.

1) 35 m, A4. Climb the shallow groove and continue up the wall mainly on bolts to a small ledge.

2) 40 m, A3. Follow the bolts up right until skyhook moves allow a small ramp to be reached. Continue up this (pitons) to a ledge.

3) 10 m, 5.7. Use rivets to gain a groove which leads to a ramp and bolt belay.

4) 35 m, 5.7. Free climb up right to a large detached flake "The Lug" and continue up the right side of this to a belay on top (bivvy site).

5) 40 m, Climb up to a bolt ladder and follow this up and right across a steep wall. Continue up with the odd free move to a hanging belay below roofs.

6) 40 m, Follow the corner on the right (mixed free and aid, or 5.10a free) to a large ledge.

7) 50 m, Easy free climbing leads to the top.

POST-ORGASMIC DISGUST **   285 m, 5.10c A1
D.Cheesmond, S.Dougherty and B.Gross, July 1985

This route is, in essence, a free climb but is forced left onto Iron Suspender at about half height. It uses a bolt ladder on that route and then continues free to the summit. It is extremely steep and difficult in the lower section, and is comparable to the free versions of The Yellow Edge and CMC Wall on Yamnuska. Start as for Waracrasquechimsla.

1) 40 m, 5.10b. Move up easily to a steep, left-facing corner and climb this to a ledge at the top of the flake (bolt protection and belay).

2) 30 m, 5.10b. Continue up over bulges (three points of aid - piton and wire fixed) to gain a crack line which trends up rightwards. Belay on a ledge (bolts).

3) 40 m, 5.10c. Climb the corner above to easier ground and belay on the highest ledge.

4) 45 m, 5.9. Traverse up and left to a small ledge with a fixed piton and carabiner, and then lower or downclimb a few metres to a large ledge. Traverse easily left around a steep rib and climb the right side of The Lug to the belay on Iron Suspender.

5-7) Use the bolt ladder on pitch 5 of Iron Suspender and free climb the remainder of that route to the top.

† WARACRASQUECHIMSLA 300 m, 5.8
M. Galbraith and B. McKeith, September 1971

The route follows the prominent ramp and chimney system on the right side of Wakonda Buttress and continues up the edge of the buttress to the top. Start below the lower, left end of the ramp.
1) 5.6. Climb a shattered wall to reach the start of the ramp.
2) Follow the ramp to a corner crack below the upper chimney.
3-6) 5.6-5.8. Climb the crack and chimney above to the base of the upper scree bowl.
7-11) Follow the crack on the edge of the buttress to the top (mainly easy 5th class climbing).

WAKONDA BUTTRESS TO HIDDEN GULLY

Between Wakonda Buttress and Hidden Gully the cliffs are steep and relatively featureless, and few natural lines are evident. Ripple Wall is a buttress of good grey rock immediately left of Hidden Gully. Left again, on the front of a buttress is Isengard, a partially detached pinnacle which rises to about three-quarters height.

ROBBIE'S ROUTE
First ascent unknown

Just to the right of Waracrasquechimsla is a large square-cut boulder at the base of the cliff. A short, practice aid climb consisting primarily of a bolt ladder is located on its west side. The climb may go free and could be CMC Valley's answer to Grotto Canyon!

ISENGARD 120 m, 5.10a
J.Firth, C.Perry and T.Jones, 1975

Only the crack on the left side of the pinnacle has been climbed since the chimney on the right is choked by loose blocks. Start a few metres left of a subsidiary buttress below the left side of the pinnacle.
1) 35 m, 5.8. Climb the wall behind the right-hand tree for about 5 m, then traverse left at an obvious line to a ledge below a left-facing groove. Follow the groove and then move up right across a wall to a small bolt belay below a roof.
2) 25 m, 5.10a. Climb the thin crack to the right of the roof (crux) and continue more easily to the base of the chimney.
3,4) 60 m, Follow the chimney to the top of the pinnacle.
To descend, downclimb the short top pitch and then rappel the route.

RIPPLE WALL
A) The Maker
B) Gangbang (incomplete)

FOURTH OF FIRTH *   170 m, 5.9, A1
J. Firth and B. McKeith, May 1973

This route follows the prominent open book between Isengard and the water chute on the left side of Ripple Wall. Aid is presently required to reach the upper corner but this may be eliminated as the loose rock in this section is removed. The climbing is mainly good and the line is excellent. Start 5 m left of a tree and about 25 m left of the water chute below a broken groove of grey rock.

1) 45 m, 5.7. Climb the groove and continue trending right to a large ledge below the upper corner.
1a) 5.8. The ledge may be reached by climbing a shallow corner which slants up left from near the water chute.
2) 45 m, 5.7. Follow the wide crack to a bolt belay beneath the roof.
3) 20 m, 5.8, A1. Climb the wall on the right side of the roof to a bolt belay below the open book.
4) 30 m, 5.9. Follow the corner with difficulty to a ledge.
5) 30 m, 5.7. Continue up a wide crack and then easier ground to the top.

Traverse across right and descend Hidden Gully.

THE MAKER ***   215 m, 5.10b
B. Keller and J. Lauchlan, October 1977

This route takes a direct line near the centre of Ripple Wall. Excellent rock combined with sustained climbing make this an outstanding route. Technically, the climb is only just 5.10 but the run-out nature of some of the pitches requires steady climbing at this level. Protection is mainly by bolts.
Start left of centre by a shattered block lying against the face.

1) 25 m, 5.9. The loose pitch. From the top of the block, make a hard move up left to easier ground. Step back right into a shallow groove and continue to a block belay in a small cave.
2) 35 m, 5.9. A taste of things to come. From the right end of the ledge make steep moves up onto a slab. Traverse left along the lip of the cave until it is possible to step up into a slanting groove. Climb the groove past a bolt to an overhang. Belay on the ledge above (bolt and piton).
3) 30 m, 5.9. From the left end of the ledge, climb up onto a ramp which is followed until it is possible to traverse rightward (bolt) into a short corner. Follow this to a stance.
4) 40 m, 5.10b. Step down slightly from the belay and make an unprotected, committing rightward traverse until the base of a groove can be reached. Continue more easily up this with many possibilities for protection to a two bolt belay.
5) 40 m, 5.10a. Traverse right along a shallow break and then step up to a small ledge (bolt). Continue up and left, and then move steeply back right, past a small flake, to a large ledge with a bolt. Having recovered, move right into a large, loose corner and climb it for 5 m. Traverse across the right wall of the corner onto the front face and continue up and right to a large ledge and belay.

6) 45 m, 5.9. The easy pitch! Climb the groove above to a higher ledge and traverse right for 10 m to below a prominent groove. Continue traversing the ledge system until it is possible to climb diagonally up and right to the top.
6a) 45 m, 5.10c. Climb the prominent groove on pitch 6 moving right and then back left to reach the top. This is the original finish but is unrepeated to date due to its reputation for difficulty and seriousness.
To descend, traverse right into Hidden Gully.

Note: An incomplete aid route called Gangbang climbs part way up the steep face on the right side of Ripple Wall. It begins about 35 m right of The Maker and climbs up to a band of overhangs that arches up and right to an undercut corner in the upper wall. The first pitch follows a line of small, right-facing overhangs and then moves right and up into a bay. A short, fixed rope marks the high point on the second pitch which begins the traverse across to the upper corner. (A3, small pitons and skyhooks required).

HIDDEN GULLY TO KILN BUTTRESS

Hidden Gully is a deep, narrow gully separating the Wakonda area from Frodo Buttress.
Descent: From the section of cliff described here, descent can be made either down Hidden Gully or by traversing east across the hillside to the descent gully between Frodo and Bilbo Buttresses.

HIDDEN GULLY   200 m, 4th class
P. Davis, G. Homer, J. Jones and C. Smith, November 1970
Climb the short wall at the base of the gully (rappel bolt in place) and continue easily over a number of rock steps, bearing left at a steep 15 m wall.

PULMONATA *   100 m, 5.8
J.Jones and C.Perry, October 1977
To the right of Hidden Gully is a small buttress separated from the main face by the deep chimney of Inner Limits. Start by a large block in the scree about 5 m left of Inner Limits.
1) 25 m, 5.7. Climb the wall to a small ledge, then traverse up left to a shallow groove. Continue up the groove to a ledge below a V-corner.
2) 40 m, 5.8. Traverse left across the wall and climb a series of shallow corners which diagonal slightly left across the face to a more prominent groove above. Belay on a small ledge on the left at top of groove (bolt).
3) 35 m, 5.6. Move left to a groove and climb this to easier ground and the top of the buttress.
4,5) Join Inner Limits and continue as for that route.
Descent: As an alternative to the descent routes described above, it may be possible to fix a rappel route down the left side of the buttress into Hidden Gully. This would serve as a convenient descent route for Pulmonata and the lower section of inner Limits.

CMC Valley

INNER LIMITS   200 m, 5.7
R. Amann and J. Frey, October 1973

The climbing in the lower chimney is quite interesting and leads to an easy-angled section at about half height. The continuation chimney is loose and fairly easy.

FALSE MODESTY **   200 m, 5.9
W.Davidson, G.Homer and J.Jones, June 1973.

Approximately halfway between Inner Limits and the large bay of Parasite is a thin crack in the front of the buttress leading to a bowl. The climb starts here and angles up left to the ridge. It offers good crack and face climbing and is highly recommended.
1)   40 m, 5.9. Climb the crack to a belay in the bowl.
2)   30 m, 5.8. Climb the wide crack on the left side of the bowl and continue to the top of a pinnacle.
3)   40 m, 5.9. Move left from the pinnacle and climb a steep slab (piton) past a shattered block on the left to a corner and a second piton runner. Move up and make a difficult traverse left to easier ground. Continue up a groove to the ridge.
4-6)   Easy 5th class climbing up the ridge leads to the top of the buttress.

THE SPIKE *   55 m, 5.10b
D.Guthrie and J.Buszowski, May 1985

This short route starts about 10 m right of False Modesty and climbs a crack which starts about 30 m up the cliff and ends at ledges. Descent is then made by rappel.
1)   30 m, 5.10b. Climb a shallow corner with a piton at the top, then move right and climb a steep wall. Continue up and right to a chimney and follow this to a belay.
2)   25 m, 5.10b. Traverse left and climb the crack. At the top, move up right to a bolt belay. One rappel reaches the ground.

POPULAR MISCONCEPTION   180 m, 5.9
J. Lauchlan and S. Sutton, August 1973

On the left side of the bay of Parasite, just in from the edge of the buttress, is a wide crack which leads up to steep yellow rock. The line continues as a series of broken corners to the edge of the ridge. The climbing is difficult and the rock on pitch 2 is poor.
1)   30 m, Climb the crack to a pedestal belay on the right.
2)   40 m, Continue mainly to the left of the corner line to a belay at some large blocks.
3)   45 m, Move right to the steep corner system and climb this (crux) to easier ground leading up to the ridge.
4,5)   75 m, Continue up the ridge as for False Modesty.

PARASITE   190 m, 5.8
D. Jones and B. Haggerstone, May 1972

This climb follows the crack system on the right at the back of the bay and is reported to be quite loose.

1)   15 m, Scramble over broken rock and ledges to where the gully steepens. Belay below a crack to the right of the main chimney.
2)   35 m, 5.6. Move left and climb the chimney. Continue up and right to a belay below a loose overhang.
3)   30 m, 5.7. Pass the overhang on the right and follow a groove to a second overhang. Step left and climb up to a large ledge.
4)   25 m, 5.6. Climb the left side of a double crack system to a ledge on the right.
5)   35 m, 5.8. Move up and diagonally right on loose blocks. Continue right round the corner and climb a steep crack.
6)   40 m, Move up and left to an obvious crack. Climb this and continue up and right to a belay.
7)   10 m, Easy climbing leads to the top.

KILN BUTTRESS   200 m, 5.6
J. Jones, B.Greenwood and G.Homer, 1971

This is a long and fairly easy climb up the buttress to the right of Parasite. The first two pitches are the most difficult. Start just to the left of a short yellow slot on the front of the buttress.

1)   15 m, 5.6. Climb diagonally right across the wall to ledges above the slot. Continue right round the edge of the buttress and climb up to a belay ledge below a short corner.
2)   40 m, 5.6. Climb the steep wall left of the belay to an easy-angled section.

Continue more easily to the summit, staying near the edge of the buttress.

SOUTH FACE OF FRODO BUTTRESS

This area extends east from Kiln Buttress to the gully at the right end of the crag which separates it from the first of the Rune buttresses. Existing routes are confined to the right side of the face which is shown in the photograph. The two most prominent features are the large, slanting corner systems of The Iliad and Luminous Pigeon.

Descent is normally made down the narrow gully at the right end of the cliff adjacent to the First Rune (2 short rappels), but for climbs going to the top of the buttress the main descent gully between the Runes and Bilbo Buttress is probably easier.

S-CRACK   35 m, 5.8
B. Keller and C. Perry, April 1977

This short, one-pitch route climbs a shallow corner just left of The Iliad and finishes at about one-quarter height.
Start about 40 m left of The Iliad below a shallow, curving crack. Scramble up to a ledge with a small tree about 10 m above the ground. Follow the crack, moving left to a rib at a difficult section. Continue to a fixed belay in a groove. Descent is by rappel; although the route could be extended as a variation start to The Iliad.

THE ILIAD *   170 m, 5.8
G. Homer and R. Wood, November 1970

In its lower section, the climb follows a prominent slanting chimney and then moves left to climb a corner and crack system in the upper wall.
1) 40 m, Follow the chimney until it steepens.
2) 50 m, Either climb the clean corner directly above the belay (5.9), or move left and climb up more easily. Continue via a steep crack to an overhang (possible belay) and then follow cracks up and left to a large ledge.
3) 40 m, 5.8. Walk left along the ledge, then move up and slightly left to a large right-facing corner. Climb the corner past a difficult wide section to a small ledge.
4) 40 m, 5.8. Follow layback flakes up to a good hand-crack and climb this directly to the top. Alternatively, climb partway up the crack and then move left to a sloping, exposed ledge. Traverse left for 5 m to a fixed piton and climb a short wall to the top.

CMC Valley

LUMINOUS PIGEON *   145 m, 5.7
J. Jones and R. Schneider, October 1970

This climbs the righthand of the two corner systems staying left in the lower section to avoid a narrow, overhanging chimney. Start slightly to the right at a corner below the overhanging chimney.
1) 30 m, Climb the crack until it steepens and then move left and up to a ledge. From the left side of the ledge climb up a short distance to a belay in the corner.
2) 45 m, Move left to a thin crack in the slabs and climb this to a corner. Continue up the corner (crux) and then move easily up right to the upper chimney.
2a) 5.7. Move up right and climb the overhanging chimney. This involves a tight squeeze past a constriction followed by more pleasant climbing above on the outside of the chimney.
3,4) 70 m, Follow the chimney to the top.

WORMTONGUE   40 m, 5.8
C.Perry and P.Dickson, October 1977

This one pitch route climbs a corner about 30 m right of Luminous Pigeon to large, sloping ledges.
Climb a short groove on the left and then traverse right into the corner. Follow this to a bolt belay at the ledges. Descent is made by rappel.

KAZAK   30 m, 5.7
S.Jennings and C.Perry, February 1973

Start about 45 m right of Luminous Pigeon behind a small pinnacle.
1) 30 m, 5.6. Follow a system of grooves which slants up to the right to a piton belay.
2) 30 m, 5.7. Move right and climb a corner at the side of a loose stack. Move back left to a groove and follow this to a ledge on the right (piton belay).
3) 30 m, 5.7. Move up right over a pinnacle, then drop down and traverse delicately right to the base of a chimney. Climb this to a belay on the left.
4) 40 m, 5.6. Continue up the chimney to ledges on the right. Move up and left to reach a large exit gully.

At the east end of Frodo Buttress, near the first Rune, is a large flake with a crack on its left side (Flake Crack). Just left of this, a series of ledges leading up steeply to the left forms a ramp which terminates in a corner capped by a roof (Decision). Near the start of the ramp a corner system leads up slightly rightwards to a chimney (Indecision).

DECISION 135 m, 5.7
J. Firth and J. Jones, March 1973

Start at the base of the ramp, about 10 m left of Flake Crack.
1) 55 m, Climb up left following a series of ledges and belay as high as possible near the base of a corner capped by a square-cut overhang.
2) 40 m, Climb the corner until a traverse left below the overhang can be made. Move up with difficulty to a crack. Climb the crack to a ledge, and then move right to belay.
3) 40 m, Climb up and then right to a prominent crack and follow this to the top.

INDECISION 80 m, 5.8
J. Jones and C. Smith, November 1970

Start at the ramp as for Decision.
1) Climb up to below a triangular overhang at the base of the corner leading to the upper chimney. Pass the overhang on the right and continue up the corner for 15 - 20 m until a ledge about 5 m to the right can be reached. Belay below a good crack.
2) Make an awkward move left across the steep wall and climb up to a good ledge. Move left into the chimney and belay.
3) Climb the chimney, passing two overhangs (piton at first).

FLAKE CRACK 70 m, 5.8
P. Morrow, C. Perry and S. Jennings, March 1974

1) 45 m, Climb the obvious crack and chimney to the top of the flake.
2) 15 m, Move left and then climb up to a crack (crux) which leads up to a ledge with a small tree.
3) 15 m, Move left and climb the wall to a large ledge.

THE RUNES

The Runes are three relatively small buttresses separated by deep gullies and situated between Frodo and Bilbo Buttresses. They are numbered from west to east. Climbs on the Third Rune are particularly good since the rock is well-weathered and generally gives solid, technical climbing.

First Rune

EULOGY 80 m, 5.9, A?
R.Amann and party, 1982

Eulogy climbs a steep crack in the left wall of the gully between the First and Second Runes. If loose rock is removed it may be possible to free climb the crack making it an impressive pitch.
1) 30 m, Climb easy grey rock to a belay below the corner.
2) 50 m, Climb the corner (mixed free and aid).

CMC Valley

THIRD RUNE
A) Shirtlifter
B) Snakecharmer
C) Weed
D) Chingle
E) Hurricane Holocaust
F) Route 3

Second Rune

DOUBLE DIRECT *   110 m, 5.7
J. Martin and J. White, May 1971
(Alt. D.Guthrie and J.Buszowski, May 1985)

This climbs the obvious corner/chimney which splits the upper half of the buttress. The first pitch is surprisingly sustained but can be adequately protected by pitons. Start directly below the upper corner.
1)   35 m, 5.7. Climb the wall trending slightly right to a small ledge. Move up and left to a short corner which is climbed to a small ledge at the base of the upper corner.
1a)   35 m, 5.9. Climb a short, overhanging corner just around the left edge of the buttress in the gully. Continue up easier ground to a belay, and then move right to join the normal route.
2)   30 m, 5.6. Climb the corner to a steep wall, move right and climb up to a belay in the chimney.
3)   30 m, 5.4. Climb the chimney to large ledges.
Scramble up to a level portion of the buttress, traverse off right and descend the gully.

BROWN OAF   90 m, 5.7
B. Greenwood and J. Jones, April 1973

Start by a single, forked tree about 15 m right of Double Direct.
1)   45 m, 5.7. Climb up and then diagonally left across the steep face to a short V-groove. Climb this and the easier face above to a belay on the slabs below a break in the roofs.
2)   45 m, Either climb directly through the roofs (5.9) or cross them at a smaller break on the right (5.7). Continue more easily to the arete and follow this to a level section.
Traverse off right and descend the gully.

Third Rune

On the left side of the buttress, a prominent water groove separates a lower cliff from the main face. Weed climbs the water groove while Shirtlifter and Snakecharmer are located on the smaller cliff to the left. All three are good, short routes.

SHIRTLIFTER   60 m, 5.7
J. Jones and S. Slymon, March 1973

Start below a corner about 10 m left of Weed.
1)   30 m, 5.7. Climb the corner past a bulge and continue to a large ledge on the left.
2)   30 m, 5.7. Move right and climb the steep face via an obvious break to large ledges.
Descend as for Weed.

CMC Valley

SNAKECHARMER ** 60 m, 5.8
J. Horne, J. Jones and R. Amann, March 1973

Following a sinuous line between Shirtlifter and Weed, the climb starts at a thin crack a few metres left of the latter.
1) 30 m, 5.8. Climb the crack to a corner below a bulge, place a runner as high as possible and move right up a steep slab to a shallow groove just to the left of Weed. Continue up the face trending slightly left to a belay in a groove below overhangs.
2) 30 m, 5.7. Climb the groove and move right to the edge overlooking Weed. Continue up the steep corner above to large ledges.
Descend as for Weed.

WEED *** 60 m, 5.6
J. Jones and S. Slymon, March 1971

An excellent climb which follows the prominent water groove. The rock is good and the climbing is continuously interesting.
1) 30 m, 5.6. Climb the groove and belay below the upper bulge.
2) 30 m, 5.6. Continue past the bulge (crux) to large ledges on the left side of the buttress.
To descend, climb down a short distance to a small scree bowl on the left (west) side of the buttress. Descend the scree to the edge of the gully and rappel from 2 bolts (one 45 m rope is sufficient).

LOOSEY GOOSEY 5.6
J. Elzinga and J. Martin, 1978

This route follows a short crack in the gully wall just left of the descent route.

CHINGLE ** 100 m, 5.8
B. Greenwood and J. Jones, October 1971

A good face climb with only one hard section which follows the edge of the main buttress to the right of Weed. Start about 7 m right of Weed at a steep corner.
1) 45 m, 5.8. Climb the corner to a ledge and continue up a crack on the right to a block. From the top of the block (piton), move left and climb the wall (crux) to small ledges. Continue up and right to a ledge at the base of a hidden corner.
2) 10 m, Climb the corner to a flat ledge below the upper wall.
3) 45 m, Climb out left over a bulge and continue up good grey rock to a groove near the top. Climb the groove to a large ledge.
Descent: Either continue easily to the top of the buttress or traverse left on good ledges to scree slopes above Weed and descend as for that route. From the top of the buttress, the main descent gully between The Runes and Bilbo Buttress can be reached by scrambling down the east side and crossing a smaller gully above Grumbit.

HURRICANE HOLOCAUST ** 125 m, 5.9
J. Lauchlan and B. Keller, 1975

A excellent route giving steep face climbing in airy positions. Start below the highest point of the buttress at a dead tree about 30 m right of Weed.
1) 35 m, 5.9. Climb a shallow groove to an overhang (piton) and move up left with difficulty to a short corner. Climb this and the wall above to another corner (piton), then traverse right to a small slab beneath an overhang. Cross the slab to easier ground on the right and move up to a bolt belay.
2) 30 m, 5.8. Move back down to the left and traverse left to the foot of a prominent corner (piton). Climb the corner (piton) to a ledge and belay on the right below a crack.
3) 30 m, 5.9. Climb a short distance up the crack then traverse left onto the face. Move diagonally left to easier ground and continue directly up the face past a fixed piton to a small ledge with two bolts below and left of the final groove.
3a) 30 m, 5.9. Climb further up the crack to a small overhang (fixed piton). Now traverse left across steep rock to a V- groove. Move down and traverse left to join the original pitch.
4) 30 m, 5.9. Move right and then up into the groove. Climb this with difficulty (poor protection), moving left near the top to a ledge. Alternatively traverse left from the base of the groove for a few metres to a flake line that diagonals rightward up the steep wall. Follow this (Friend placement) to the large ledge.
Descend as for Chingle.

ROUTE 3   125 m, 5.9
J. Firth and J. Jones, April 1973

On the right side of the buttress is a small grassy slab a short distance above the ground. The route traverses across the slab and climbs a shallow corner to the right edge of the buttress which is then followed to the top. Start below the lower, left corner of the slab.
1) 40 m, 5.8. Move up onto the slab and cross it low down to its right side. Climb a short wall to a groove and continue up this to a small ledge on the left.
2) 25 m, 5.9. Traverse right to a blind crack which leads up with difficulty to ledges on the arete.
3,4) Continue more easily up the edge of the buttress.
Descend to the east as for Chingle.

GRUMBIT   45 m, 5.7
R. Amann, J. Lauchlan and G. Jennings, March 1974

This short face climb is situated just to the left of the main descent gully between the Runes and Bilbo Buttress. It begins at a small pillar and angles up left to a chimney.
1) 20 m, 5.7. Climb to the top of the pillar and continue up left to a scoop which leads to the base of the chimney.
2) 25 m, Continue easily up the chimney.
Descend by rappel or by moving east into the main descent gully.

CMC Valley

COLD WAR   45 m, 5.7
S. Jennings and C. Perry, March 1974

This route starts at the same point as Grumbit and climbs the edge of the buttress between that route and the descent gully.
1)   45 m, 5.7. Climb to the top of the pillar and move up right to a thin crack near the edge. Climb over an overlap to a left-facing crack and continue to the top of the pinnacle overlooking the descent gully. Move right and follow a ramp to the top. Alternatively, go left from above the left-facing crack and climb the front face via a break in the bulges.

Descent Gully Area

The following climbs are located on the left (west) side of the main descent gully.

WHORE'S HEART   40 m, 5.7
J.Lauchlan and J.Martin, April 1974

A short distance above the small cliff at the base of the descent gully are two shallow corners in the left wall. Whore's Heart climbs the left-hand of these.

SOMETHING SOMEWHERE   15 m, 5.7
J.Lauchlan, P.Merkley, M.Sawyer, J.Sterner and D.Wightt, 1974

Farther up the Descent Gully where it starts to widen out is a small pinnacle. To the right of which is a short wall. The route climbs the corner on the left side of the wall adjacent to the pinnacle.

LOST RUNE 150 m, 5.6
J.Martin, G.Mathew and J.Tanner, 1974

Up and to the right of the previous route is a long pillar with a broad, clean wall at its base. The route climbs the wall (5.6) and continues up a series of easier pitches on the crest of the pillar.

BILBO BUTTRESS

Bilbo Buttress is the prominent crag directly across the valley from the Simpson Hut. The routes lie on two sections: a short, west-facing wall adjacent to The Runes (The Runewall), and a longer south-facing cliff with several prominent ribs and gullies which lies directly across the valley from the hut.

Descent from all the routes is the same. Follow scree and easy slabs into the main descent gully between The Runes and Bilbo Buttress.

The Runewall

GROUNDFALL WALL *   25 m, 5.10b
J. Lauchlan, B.Keller and M.Keller, 1975

This short test-piece climbs the wall immediately right of the descent gully. Adequate protection is difficult to arrange.
Start about 10 m right of the descent gully at good holds below and left of a fixed pin. Climb up a short distance, then traverse right to below the fixed pin. Continue more or less directly up the wall past a second fixed pin to finish on the edge of the buttress.
Either go left into the main descent gully or traverse to the belay on Edna's Armpit and rappel.

EDNA'S ARMPIT *   50 m, 5.7
J. Lauchlan and R. Amann, April 1973

On the right edge of Groundfall Wall is a shallow corner and right again is a chimney. Edna's Armpit follows the corner and gives one pitch of good technical climbing.
1) 30 m, 5.7. Climb the corner to a small ledge in a scoop (fixed belay).
2) 20 m, Either rappel or scramble up loose easy rock to the top.

THE SKOOPE   60 m, 5.7
J. Lauchlan and R. Lefurgey, August 1971

This route follows the chimney just right of Edna's Armpit.
1) 20 m, Climb the chimney and belay a few metres above a chockstone.
2) 40 m, Continue up into a scoop and either climb a smooth ramp on the left (5.7) or exit right up a chimney which leads to the ridge.

SKOOPE BUTTRESS   75 m, 5.6
J. Lauchlan and J. Sterner, April 1974

A small buttress forms the right side of the chimney and higher up turns into an easy ridge. The climb starts in a corner near the edge of the buttress.
1) 35 m, Climb the corner, move left and continue up the buttress to an easier angled section.
2) 40 m, Continue up the ridge to the top.

THE MORNING AFTER 75 m, 5.6
J. Lauchlan and J. Sterner, April 1974

This route climbs a corner just to the right of the previous route and joins it at about half height.

CLAUSTROPHOBIA 70 m, 5.5
J. Sterner, D. Zaychuk, J. Martin and J. Tanner, April 1974

To the right again is a large, sloping ledge at about one-third height. Start below the lower, left end of the ledge.
1) 20 m. Scramble up to the ledge and move right a short distance to belay.
2) 30 m. Move back left and climb the corner which becomes a tight squeeze at the top.
3) 20 m. Continue as for Skoope Buttress

ANTICLIMACTIC CORNER 65 m, 5.7
J. Lauchlan and J. Sterner, April 1974

This climbs a corner at the right end of the ledge of Claustrophobia.
1) 30 m. Scramble up to the right end of the ledge and belay at the foot of the corner.
2) 40 m. Climb the corner, staying on the right at first.

MONA BONA * 70 m, 5.6
C. Perry and P. Merkley, April 1974

About 20 m to the right of the previous two routes is a small corner with a thin crack in the wall above.
1) 40 m, 5.6. Climb the corner to an easier-angled section. Move up and traverse right below a steep yellow wall to reach a smooth, sloping ledge (bolt belay)
2) 15 m, 5.6. Traverse right onto the steep wall overlooking Crappy Corner, move up with difficulty and continue up left to a stance.
3) 15 m. Scramble up to the top.

RUBBLE ROUSER 60 m, 5.9, A1
J. Lauchlan and J. Firth, April 1974

This is a direct finish to Mona Bona
1) 30 m. Climb the first part of Mona Bona to a belay below the continuation crack in the steep yellow wall.
2) 30 m. Climb the crack on its left side using mixed free and aid. Where the crack peters out, hand traverse right and climb up to a small ledge. Follow the steep wall and jamcrack to the top.

MONA BONA ERECT 35 m, 5.7
P. Merkley, M. Sawyer and D. Wightt, April 1974

This climbs the steep, gray corner which leads directly to the belay at the top of pitch 1 of Mona Bona.

CRAPPY CORNER 60 m, 5.7
G. Homer and J. Jones, April 1971

Immediately right of Mona Bona Erect is a prominent open book which is Crappy Corner.
1) 35 m, 5.7. Climb the corner to shattered ledges.
2) Exit to the left or the right.

WATCHMAN'S CRACK 60 m, 5.5
J. Kuenzel and F. Williamson, May 1971

Start at the top of a large scree cone at the base of the gully right of Crappy Corner. Follow the gully for two pitches, exiting up the right-hand chimney.

DIRTY DAGO ** 95 m, 5.9 (5.8 alt)
G. Homer and J. Jones, April 1971
(Pitch 3 alt. C. Perry and J. Martin, July 1982)

To the right of Watchman's Crack, before the edge of the buttress, is a steep, open corner. This is climbed by Dirty Dago - one of the best technical climbs in the valley.
1) 20 m, 5.8. Climb a few metres up the groove and traverse right onto the face at an obvious break. Continue diagonally up right to bypass a steep section, then go up and back left to a ledge in the main groove. (The ledge can be reached directly at 5.10a as on the first ascent).
2) 35 m, 5.8. Climb a cracked wall on the left to ledges. Step right into the main groove and climb it to a fixed pin. Traverse diagonally right to below a steep section and continue immediately below this round an arete. Climb up to a large ledge.
There are three lines of weakness above the ledge: the main groove on the left, a shallow groove above the belay, and a crack near the right arete.
3) 40 m, 5.9. Climb the shallow groove to a ramp which slants up left. At the top of the ramp above a fixed pin either make a difficult mantle right onto a ledge in the groove or move left and up to another fixed pin, step right onto the ledge. Continue easily to a ledge near the top.
3a) 45 m, 5.8. Traverse right and climb the crack near the arete.

South Face of Bilbo Buttress

On the front of the buttress, just east of Dirty Dago, is a wall of good grey rock bounded on the right by a pillar. Two routes climb the wall, both of which start from ledges left of the top of a short chimney.

DOG'S BISCUIT ** 70 m, 5.7
C.Perry and S.Jennings, March 1973

This is the easier of the two routes and is highly recommended. Scramble up the chimney and continue left on ledges to a bolt belay.
1) 35 m, 5.7. Climb up easily for about 15 m and move right to a bolt. Move up and left, then step right and continue directly up the wall. Traverse left to the foot of a groove and belay a few metres up this in a niche.
2) 35 m, 5.7. Climb the groove to a bulge, move out left and continue more easily to the top.

CMC Valley

EL CID * 85 m, 5.7 (5.8)
J.Firth and C.Perry, April 1973
Alt. N.Helliwell and C.Perry, February 1977

Start near the top of the chimney below a shallow groove.
1) 40 m, 5.7. Climb the groove and continue up the wall, trending right. Move left and belay on a small ledge.
2) 45 m, 5.7. Follow a ramp and corner system on the left to the top.
2a) 20 m, 5.8. Traverse right and down slightly to the top of a groove. (An unclimbed line reaches this point directly from below). Continue right with difficulty to a ledge below a right-facing corner.
3) 30 m, Climb the corner to a ledge on the left.
4) 25 m, Continue to the top.

DOGLEG CORNER   130 m, 5.9
R.Breeze and J.Horne, 1972

This route climbs the steep, yellow corner at the right end of the wall left of the pillar.
1) Climb the left side of the pillar past a prominent yellow corner until just right of a groove near the apex of the pillar.
2) 5.9. Move left with difficulty to gain the groove and continue up this until it steepens. Traverse left and climb a short overhanging wall, then move back left into the prominent corner.
1,2 alt) On the original ascent a traverse left into the groove may have been made earlier.
3) 5.6. Continue up the corner to the top.

LACQUERED CROW   110 m, 5.6
J.Jones, B.Schneider and C.Smith, October 1970

Lacquered Crow climbs the large corner system on the east side of the pillar. Scramble up the gully for about 45 m and belay below a bottleneck.
1) 30 m, Climb the bottleneck (crux) and continue up cracks to a ledge.
2) 30 m, Climb the gully above, following the left-hand break to a large ledge.
3) 30 m, Climb up above the ledge to a belay.
4) 20 m, Trend up and right over easy, broken rock to the top.

CROWLEY'S CORNER   130 m, 5.8
J.White and P.Zvengrowski, May 1971

The climb follows the well-defined rib to the right of Lacquered Crow and immediately left of a deep gully. The bottom section can be climbed either directly up the corner or via the wall on the left.
1) 10 m, Climb up to a protruding ledge left of the main corner.
2) 5.8. Traverse up left on easy ground for 5-10 m, then move right and up with difficulty to a belay at the top of the main corner.
1a) 5.8. Climb directly up the corner.
3) 5.6. Move right and climb up to a double dihedral. Follow this on good holds to a belay on the left.
4) 5.6. Climb the face above, first to the left, then moving right almost to a corner. Layback up to a belay.
5,6) Follow the crest of the rib easily to the top.

PEANUT POINT   90 m, 5.5
J.Martin and G.Pilkington, April 1971

To the right of Crowley's Corner is a buttress that reaches about halfway up the cliff. This is Peanut Point. The route, which follows the rib on the right side of the buttress, begins just right of the rib at a ledge with some small trees.
1)   25 m, Climb a groove to a small ledge.
2)   25 m, Continue easily up left and climb a short, loose wall. Move left and up slightly to a tree belay.
3)   40 m, 5.5. Climb the obvious crack above, then traverse right a short distance below an overhang to a groove. Climb this and the crack above to the top.

An easy route to the top of the cliff leads up left from the small col behind Peanut Point. Two other routes, Devil's Dessert and Devil's Banquet, climb the two prominent corner systems in the steep wall above. Alternatively, there is an easy descent in the gully to the right (east) which can also be used as an approach to the upper climbs.

DEVIL'S DESSERT   60 m, 5.7
R.Breeze and J.Horne, May 1972

This route climbs the left of the two corner systems mentioned above.

DEVIL'S BANQUET   80 m, 5.6
G.Pilkington and S.Slymon, April 1971

Devil's Banquet climbs the corner on the right above Peanut Point.
1)   Move up right into the main corner.
2)   45 m, Continue up the corner to a belay on the left.
3)   Climb the loose wall above to the top.

KNACKERED CAT   150 m, 5.6
B.Greenwood, J.Kuenzel and F.Williamson, April 1971

Immediately right of Peanut Point is a buttress with a protruding rib on its right side at the bottom. Knackered Cat begins below a shallow corner immediately left of the rib and right of a crack. Easy climbing leads almost to the base of the corner.
1)   Move left and then back right to gain the corner. Continue up to a small stance on a slab.
2)   Climb diagonally left across the slab, over a bulge and up to a small stance below a corner.
3)   Climb the corner. From a pinnacle on the left side of the buttress, climb diagonally left across a wall and then climb easy rock up and right to a big ledge on the crest of the buttress.
4)   Follow the crest of the buttress to the top.

CAT KNACKERER   150 m, 5.9
B.Greenwood and S.Slymon, May 1971

This route climbs the protruding rib.
1) Scramble up the rib to the base of a steep slab.
2) Climb the slab to an overhang. Bypass this on the right and then climb straight up until the wall steepens. Traverse left and move up to a ledge.
3) Climb slabs above to a steep wall. Climb this (5.9, fixed pitons) and gain a chimney which is followed to a good belay (top of pitch 3 of Knackered Cat).
4) Follow the crest of the buttress as for Knackered Cat.

THE SOAL *   90 m, 5.8
J.Firth and J.Horne, June 1973

On the wall to the right of the Cat Knackerer buttress are two corner systems. The Soal which follows the right-hand system, starts below and right of the corner 5-10 m left of a rib.
1) 40 m, Move up left on a ramp and then climb up over a bulge into a groove. Continue up this and climb a second bulge to a tree. Move left and up to a belay below the crack.
2) 50 m, Climb the crack, which is very steep, to a small ledge, then continue up a chimney to the top.
The route ends on the crest of a rib (Blackened Rat). An easy descent leads down the gully to the right (east).

BLACKENED RAT   160 m, 5.5
J.Martin, S.Slymon and S.Stahl, April 1971

This route follows the rib to the right of Cat Knackerer. Scramble up to a steep section.
1) 30 m, Climb a short distance up slabs; then traverse left to a corner and follow it to a treed ledge.
2) 35 m, Traverse up and right to a corner on the right edge of the rib. Climb this (loose blocks) and then traverse up and left on slabs to a belay at the left edge of the rib.
3) 30 m, Traverse right on slabs to a steep groove. Climb this (5.5) until the angle eases and continue easily to a large ledge (top of The Soal).
4,5) 65 m, Follow the crest of the rib easily to the top.

VEGETABLE   170 m, 5.6 A1
J.Martin, P.Zvengrowski and D.Knaak, May 1972

Vegetable follows a broken rib a short distance right of Blackened Rat. Scramble up to a short steep wall on the rib.
1) Climb the steep wall and the rib above to a large tree.
2) Continue easily up a ridge to a belay above a short wall.
3) Climb the wall on the right side and continue to a tree ledge.
4) Walk and traverse easily left past a small dead tree. Climb a short, steep wall (2 or 3 aid moves) and pull up left into a corner. Follow the corner to a belay behind a pinnacle.
5) Climb the corner/gully on the left to the top.

CMC Valley

BISHOP'S DAUGHTER   180 m, 5.7
T.Mould and M.Toft, May 1973

Scramble up the gully right of Vegetable to a prominent crack.
1)   40 m, Climb the crack and belay on large ledges on the left.
2)   30 m, Climb straight up a steep wall and continue over a bulge to a ledge with a small tree.
3)   20 m, Go up and right over blocks, then drop down and traverse further right to an inside corner. Climb the corner (5.7) to a ledge.
4)   45 m, Climb an obvious chimney, then go slightly left and up to a loose bulge. Climb this and continue to a good ledge.
5)   45 m, Aim for the final exit groove and follow this past some steep layback moves to the top.

ELECTRIC APPLES *   165 m, 5.7
J.Martin and J.White, June 1971

This route starts in the gully right of Vegetable and finishes in a prominent exit gully near the high point of the crag. Start as for Bishop's Daughter. The routes diverge after one pitch.
2)   35 m, Descend a few feet to the right, then continue right to a steep corner/crack. Climb (5.7) to the top of the corner and belay above loose blocks.
3)   30 m, Climb the wall to the right and continue up a slabby groove. Climb the chimney above and when it ends at an overhanging wall, traverse right across steep slabs to a large ledge at the base of the exit gully.
4)   20 m, Climb a short chimney, then continue more easily to a belay on the left below a steep section.
5)   40 m, Climb the steep wall on the left and continue without difficulty to the top.

MAGNETIC FLOSS   160 m, 5.7
J.Martin and J.White, October 1971

This route follows a scrappy rib right of Electric Apples. (The line marked on the photograph is approximate).
Climb up the first gully right of Electric Apples and traverse left onto the rib where it steepens.
1)   Climb easily to a short overhanging wall. After a few awkward moves, traverse left to a steep corner/crack and follow this to a tree ledge.
2)   Traverse left around a rib into a corner which overhangs at the top. Climb nearly to the top of the corner; then step right and climb a short face to ledges.
3)   Traverse left and climb an easy chimney. Belay down right at a tree.
4)   From the top of a tottery block, step across to a steep wall. Move up and right, then climb a slab to a large ledge.
5)   Climb the steep rib above on its right side to the top.

CMC Valley

EPHEL DUATH

Ephel Duath is a large cliff at the head of a side valley west of Wakonda Buttress. It consists of a series of impressive buttresses and extends across the side of Wendell Mountain. There are relatively few natural lines however, and generally the rock is mediocre.

Approach & Descent: All climbs require an early start since the approach takes 1.5 to 2 hours from the Simpson Hut and descent via the east ridge is exposed and time-consuming. An alternative descent down easy scree slopes on the west side of the mountain takes considerably longer, particularly if return to the base of the cliff is necessary.

The following two climbs are situated on a smaller triangular buttress at the east side of the cliffs directly above the side valley.

HITCHCOCK RAILWAY   375 m, 5.8
J.Jones and J.Horne, May 1971

This climb follows the east ridge of the triangular buttress and is mainly 5.5. Start below a shallow groove immediately left of a large gully.
1) 40 m, Climb the groove to a large ledge on the left.
2) 20 m, Move up and then traverse left to the top of a short crack. Continue left and belay on a small pinnacle.
3) 40 m, 5.6. Climb up and left towards trees. Belay by a small tree.
4) 20 m, Climb the crack above, then traverse left to a large ledge with cracks above.
5) 35 m, After climbing the left-hand crack for about 10 m, follow an easy break right until level with a base of a chimney.
6) 40 m, Climb the chimney and continue up to the second large fir tree.
7) 35 m, 5.6. Climb a steep wall to the right and then diagonal right following a ramp. Move round the corner to easier climbing which leads to a ledge on the ridge.
8) 40 m, Follow the ridge to an awkward stance in a groove.
9) 35 m, Move up a short distance, and then step round left and climb a small corner. Follow the groove above and continue over loose rock to a large ledge situated to the left of a yellow overhang (visible from the stance).
10) 40 m, 5.8. Climb up and right on steep rock until easier climbing is reached on the ridge. Follow the ridge to a stance below loose rock.
11) 30 m, Climb rotten rock to the top of the buttress.

BORKUM RIFF   350 m, 5.8
G.Homer and J.Jones, 1972

This route climbs the west edge of the buttress and is mainly 5.6 - 5.7 with only one pitch of 5.8. White Slabs, a route climbed in 1978 by U.Kallen, basically follows the same line.
Scramble up from the right to a ledge with a small tree just right of a snowpatch. Follow a slanting groove up right until a traverse left can be made (2 pitches). Continue up and then go up and left towards a large gully. Follow the first possible groove up to a band of overhangs, traverse beneath them, and climb a smooth wall (5.8) to the edge of the buttress. Stay on slabs left of the edge for three long pitches until a tree at the base of a ramp is reached. One more pitch leads to easy ground and the top of the buttress.

SOUTH PILLAR   600 m, 5.8
U.Kallen and G. Spohr, May 1978

This is the right-hand of the three main pillars on Ephel Duath. Start beneath a groove on the left side of a small, pear-shaped buttress below the pillar.
1) 45 m, 5.8. Climb the wall and make a difficult move to gain the base of the groove. Continue up the groove to a bolt belay.
2) 25 m, 5.6. Climb over a bulge and follow the right-hand groove. Move up left past a big loose block to a scoop.
3) 45 m, 5.8. Continue up slabby rock, over a bulge, and up to a ridge at the top of the small buttress.
4,5) 90 m, Scramble up left and follow an easy water runnel to a belay below a left-slanting groove.
6) 45 m, 5.6. Climb the groove and follow a crack back right to a belay in a scoop.
7,8) 70 m, Continue up easy ground to big ledges with a tree.
9,10) 85 m, 5.6. Walk right to the end of the ledges and climb up and right on sloping holds to gain an easy runnel. Go up this to a large scoop.
11) 40 m, 5.8. Climb the left side of the scoop and follow a steep pillar to a small niche.
12) 45 m, 5.7. Traverse right over exposed rock and follow grooves to the top of a small pillar. Belay 5-10 m higher.
13) 45 m, 5.8. Climb back left over slabby rock to a runnel which is climbed past a bulge to easier ground.
14) 45 m, 5.7. Continue up to a notch on the ridge. Follow the ridge past a bulge, drop down the other side and climb partway up a groove.
15) Continue up the groove to the summit ridge.

Index

INDEX of CLIMBS and CRAGS

7-Up 38	C Plus 184	Dickel 183
A Crack 183	C Route 184	Die Young, Stay Pretty 59
A Route 183	Calgary Route 162	Direttissima 165
A Touch Soft 27	California Dreaming 62	Dirty Dago 211
Ablutor 84	Callisto 13	Dirty Work 11
Above and Beyond 167	Canary in a Coalmine 85	Divers from Anaerobic Zone . 129
Across the River and Into the	CANMORE WALL 48	Docter Watson 99
Trees 83	Cat Knackerer 214	Dog's Biscuit 211
Afternoon Delight 110	Catsenjammer 91	Dogleg Corner 212
Aggressive Treatment 91	Cavebird 9	Double Direct 203
Alien 110	Caveling 9	Dr. Tongue's 3D House
All Spruced Up 106	Central Groove 79	of Beef 113
ALLEY, THE 95	Central Park 110	Dream of Electric Sheep 144
Anticlimatic Corner 209	Cerebral Goretex 83	Dream Weaver 115
Arch Slab 23	Chainsaw Wall 106	Drifter 128
ARMADILLO BUTTRESS ... 107	Chance It 90	Dropout 71
Artful Dodger 90	Cheap Thrills 119	Dynamic Dumpling 9
Astro Yam 166	CHINAMAN'S PEAK 49	E. Face, First Sister 46
Asylum 107	Chingle 204	East End Boys 178
B Route 183	Choc-a-Bloc 7	EAST END OF RUNDLE 63
Back to Zero 9	Chockstone Corner 170	East Face Route 185
Backseat Driver 185	Chocolate Frog 139	Easy Street 156
Bad Habits 27	Claustrophobia 209	Edge of Night 121
Baker Street 99	Clean Living 95	Edna's Armpit 208
BALCONY, THE 95	CMC VALLEY 187	EEOR 63
Balrog 167	CMC Wall 163	Eeyore's Tail 67
Balzac 69	Coarse and Juggy 125	El Cid 212
Barchetta 96	Codgers' Crack 103	Electric Apples 215
BATHTUB CRAGS 113	Coire Dubh 141	End Game 96
Bedtime Story 133	Cold War 206	EPHEL DUATH 216
Belfry 160	Conifer Crack 106	Eulogy 201
Bermuda Triangle 113	Connoisseur's Crack 103	Evening Star 134
BILBO BUTTRESS 208	Corkscrew 180	Excitable Boy 104
Bishop's Daughter 215	Coroner's Inqust 94	EXSHAW SLAB 115
Bitch 11	Coup-Jack 142	Facelift 105
Black Slab 28	Cousin Schlomo's Revenge 60	Fall Thing 109
Blackened Rat 214	CRAG X 76	Falling form Heaven 88
Blackheart 16	Crappy Corner 211	False Modesty 196
Blik 97	Crapuleuse 131	False Promise 155
Blue Bubble Connection 121	Creame of Afterbirth 188	Farewell to Arms 86
Blue Movie 131	Crossroad 96	Fat City 104
Blue Threads 139	Crowley's Corner 212	Fear of Flying 29
Bluebell Way 28	Cruisin' for Burgers 110	Feeding Frenzy 128
Bogus 97	Cruising 127	Feel on Baby 9
Bomb Bay Groove 78	Dandelions 11	FIFTH BUTTRESS 74
Borbaronomy 103	Dark Chocolate 13	Finishing Touch 56
Borkum Riff 217	Darkest Africa 32	FIRST ROCK 7
Bottleneck 170	Dawntreader 125	FIRST SISTER, THE 46
Bozoids from Planet X 114	Daylight Sailing 122	Flake Crack 201
Breakaway 94	Dazed and Confused 160	Flake Line 88
Breakdown 129	Dead Flowers 11	Flipside 90
Breezin 85	Deadhead 114	Footloose 88
Breezy 119	Deception 136	For Whom the Bell Tolls 83
Brontes 13	Decision 201	For Your Eyes Only 15
Brown Oaf 203	DELUSION ROCK 102	Forbidden Corner 175
Brown Sugar 11	Devient Behavior 84	FOURTH BUTTRESS 74
Brown Trousers 176	Devil's Banquet 213	Fourth of Firth 193
Brownian Motion 145	Devil's Dessert 213	Freak Out 180
Buddha Ridge 73	Diamond Cross Face 34	Fred 18
Burnt Weenie Sandwich 102	Dick's Route 181	Friendly Persuasion 115

218

Index

Fumbles	63
Gangplank	103
GARDEN ROCK	106
Gardners Question Time	57
George of the Jungle	100
Geriatric	63
Glenfiddich	105
Goat Buttress	147
GOAT MOUNTAIN	117
GOAT SLABS	141
GOAT WALL	147
Goffer Gulch	93
Gollum's Groove	183
Gollywog	35
Grace Under Pressure	96
Grand Delusion	102
Grand Illusion	99
Grand Larceny	86
GRASSI LAKES	57
Grassi Route	46
Grassman Route	144
Gray Goose	158
Gray Waves	122
Great White Hope	135
Grey Matter	86
Grillmair Chimneys	172
GROTTO CANYON	81
GROTTO CORNER	75
Grotto Crack	75
GROTTO FALLS	96
GROTTO MOUNTAIN	75
GROTTO SLAB	109
Groundfall Wall	208
Grovel	18
Grumbit	205
Guides Route	68
Half Life	125
Happy Hour	33
Harder than it Looks	99
Hazy Daze	123
HEADWALL, THE	93
Heart and Sole	12
HEART AND SOLE	12
Heart Crack	16
HEART CREEK	7
Heart of Darkness	15
Heart of Gold	15
Heart of the Patriot	21
HEART SLAB	21
Heartbeat	19
Heartburn	12
Heartland	19
Heartline	7
HEMMINGWAY WALL	86
Here and There	79
Hesitation	136
Hiatus	39
Hidden Gully	194
High Octane	89
High Voltage	171
Highlander	163
Highlight	124
Hitchcock Railway	216
Hollow Victory	95
Honkey Tonk Woman	9
Hurricane Holocaust	205
Ill Wind	85
ILLUSION ROCK	99
Imagination	37
Impending Impact	100
Indecision	201
Inner Limits	196
Into the Night	133
Iron Suspender	190
Isengard	191
Jackomer	100
Jughead Wall	75
JUPITER ROCK	12
K.P. Special	90
Kahl Crack	39
Kahl Wall	174
Kaka Corner	114
KANGA CRAG	62
Kazak	200
Keelhaul Wall	123
KID GOAT	117
Kidding Around	130
Kiln Buttress	197
King's Chimney	156
Knackered Cat	213
Knight Moves	95
Lacquered Crow	212
Left Side Story	79
Leftover Grooves	119
Leftover Slab	109
Lemon Pie	93
Less Than Zero	7
Lies and Whispers	124
Lip Service	84
Little Canadian Corner	88
Live Now, Pay Later	59
Lively-up Yourself	88
Livingstone Falls	32
Loose Lips Sink Ships	84
Loosey Goosey	204
Lost Rune	206
Lost World	99
LOWER HEART CRAG	16
LOWER NARROWS	97
Luminous Pigeon	200
Lunatic Madness	91
MacKay Route	71
Magnetic Floss	215
Maiden Century	95
Mandala	104
Manitou	150
Marriage Rites	179
Max Headroom	127
Mayflower	188
MCCONNELL RIDGE	34
MCGILLIVRAY SLABS	35
Midnight Rambler	9
Mighty Mite	97
Misguided Variation	69
Missionary's Crack	159
Mix-up	21
Moist and Easy	114
Mona Bona	209
Mona Bona Erect	209
Monkey in a Rage	99
Moonabago	97
Moriarty	99
MOUNT DOOM	185
MOUNT RUNDLE	57
Mountaineer's Route	145
Mr. Olympia	89
Mr. Percival	12
Mud Gets in Your Eyes	57
Mum's Tears	162
N. Buttress, Windtower	44
N. Face Route, Chinaman's	51
N. Ridge, Fifth Buttress	74
N. Ridge, Rundle	72
N. Ridge, Second Buttress	73
N. Ridge, Second Sister	47
N.E. Face, Chinaman's	49
N.E. Face, Windtower	43
N.E. Ridge, Windtower	41
NANNY GOAT	131
Neandocrawl	115
Necromancer	161
Nerve Gas	32
New Hope for the Dead	128
Night Sensation	133
Night Shift	119
Nightcap	134
Nightland	133
No Place for a Friend	107
North Corner	109
North Gully, Goat Slab	145
North Ridge	15
North Slab	23
NUMBERED BUTTRESSES	73
Nymphet	88
Octopoids from the Deep	114
Oh No Not Another	88
One Night Stand	135
Oreamnos	149
Original Route	59
Original Sin	27
Overhang Route	39
Overly Hung	18
Overnight Sensation	133
Pangolin	181
Parasite	197
Passing Slab	29
Patriot's Groove	19
Patty's Climb	110
Peanut Point	213
PEANUT, THE	90
Pensioner's Outing	103
Peter Pan	90
PIGEON MOUNTAIN	40
Pigeon N.E. Buttress	40
Pining Away	106
Pinko	44
Pitrun	93
Pitter Patter	38
Pixie	37

219

Index

Plimsoll Line	27
Poopy Corner	113
Popular Misconception	196
Post-Orgasmic Disgust	190
Potentilla Pillar	7
Power Play	84
Predator	131
Prelude	109
Premature Ejaculation	54
Pulmonata	194
Pumpkin Smasher	113
Puppet on a Chain	15
Purple Haze	33
Pushing Forty	58
Pythagoras	37
Quasar	66
Quick Release	55
Quicksilver	29
Quiet Terror	79
Raindust	85
Rat Patrol	104
Rat Trap	60
Recess Corner	91
Red Menace	58
Red Shirt Route	177
Red Slab	28
Reflex Action	83
Remembrance Wall	54
Reprobate	65
Rescue Route	78
RIGHT WING, THE	91
RIMWALL	44
Riparian	13
Ripoff	117
Rising Damp	89
Robbie's Route	191
ROSE AND CROWN CRAG	33
Rough Mix	24
Route 3	205
Rubble Rouser	209
Rubble Without a Cause	38
RUNDLE, MOUNT	57
RUNES, THE	201
Runnel Route	109
S-Crack	198
S. FACE FRODO	198
S. Mit R	188
S.U.M.C. Buttress	12
Sailaway	122
Scarface	84
Sea of Dreams	93
Search Pattern	104
SECOND BUTTRESS	73
SECOND SISTER, THE	47
Shakedown	129
Ship's Prow	47
SHIP'S PROW	47
Shirtlifter	203
Short and Curly	89
Shuftee	165
Sideline	76
Skid Row	24
Skoope Buttress	208
Skylight	123
Skylight Direct	123
Skywalk	138
Slanting Slab	23
Slingsby's Overhangs Direct	119
Slingsby's Overhangs Indirect	121
Slipkid	117
Slow Hand	129
Smeagol	181
Smoking Mirror	127
Snakecharmer	204
Soft Touch	27
Sole Food	12
Something Else	206
Sou'wester	141
South Corner	59
South Pillar, CMC Valley	217
Space Cadet	110
Spacewalk	110
Splashdance	110
Spring Clean	84
Spring Feaver	172
Spring Thing	109
Squirrel Breath	105
Staircase	93
STEVE CANYON	113
Sticky Fingers	11
Sticky Fingers	129
Stormy Weather	97
Strictly for Bolten	115
Student's Route	39
Student's Route	60
Styx	16
Submission	96
Supplication	91
Tabemaquered	102
Take Five	115
Takedown	128
Talk Dirty to Me	128
Temptress	88
The Alley	100
The Bowl	178
The Devil Drives	114
The Gambler	44
The Grander Illusion	100
The Heat is On	174
The Hook	24
The Hump	114
The Illiad	198
The Importance of Being Ernest	86
The Maker	193
The Midden	97
The Morning After	209
The Ramp	152
The Scoop	28
The Skoope	208
The Soal	214
The Spike	196
The Stand	110
The Sting	83
The Swell	125
The Toe	159
The Tongue, Left Side	159
The Tongue, Right Side	160
The Trap Line	175
The Verdict	94
The Wild Boys	168
The Wild Colonial Boys	153
Things are Roof All Over	60
THIRD BUTTRESS	73
Third Degree	138
THREE SISTERS	46
THREE TIER BUTTRESS	89
Tickicide	113
Tiny Tim	100
Tip-Off	119
Tony's Route	38
Too Low for Zero	89
Touch and Go	32
Tower of Pisa	91
Trading Places	102
Traverse of the Mods	93
Trident	23
Trivial Pursuit	110
Tropicana	86
True Stories	124
TV Buttress	40
Twilight	124
Twilight Zone	121
Twinkletoe	146
Unnamed	158
UPPER HEART CRAG	29
UPPER NARROWS	102
UPPER TIER, THE	104
Vegetable	214
Venus	13
Verflixt	143
Wages of Thin	139
WAKONDA BUTTRESS	188
Walk on the Wilde Side	86
Waracrasquechimsla	191
Warm Heart	32
Watchman's Crack	211
WATER WALL	83
Wave Goodby	127
Wearing Thin	110
Weed	204
Wendigo	152
West Coast Idea	97
Where's the Beef	113
WHISKEY WALL	105
White Imperialist	58
White Line Special	27
White Slab	28
WHITEMAN CRAG	58
Whore's Heart	206
Wild Horses	12
WIND VALLEY	41
Windbreaker	32
Windgroove	185
Windy Slabs	156
Wormtongue	200
Worst Route in the Rockies	141
YAMNUSKA	155
Yellow Edge	179
Yellow Wedge	93